# THE FATHERS
# OF THE CHURCH

A NEW TRANSLATION

VOLUME 125

# THE FATHERS
# OF THE CHURCH

A NEW TRANSLATION

# ST. HILARY OF POITIERS

## COMMENTARY ON MATTHEW

*Translated by*

D. H. WILLIAMS

THE CATHOLIC UNIVERSITY OF AMERICA PRESS
Washington, D.C.

Copyright @ 2012
THE CATHOLIC UNIVERSITY OF AMERICA PRESS
All rights reserved
Printed in the United States of America

The paper used in this publication meets the minimum requirements
of the American National Standards for Information Science—
Permanence of Paper for Printed Library Materials, ANSI Z39.48-1984.

∞

English biblical quotations in footnotes and introduction are drawn
from the first edition of the Revised Standard Version of the Bible,
copyright 1952 [2nd edition, 1971] by the Division of Christian
Education of the National Council of the Churches of Christ in the
United States of America. Used by permission. All rights reserved.

LIBRARY OF CONGRESS CATALOGING-IN-PUBLICATION DATA
Hilary, Saint, Bishop of Poitiers, d. 367?
[In Matthaeum. English]
Commentary on Matthew / St. Hilary of Poitiers ;
translated by D H. Williams.
p. cm. — (The fathers of the church ; v. 125)
Includes bibliographical references and indexes.
ISBN 978-0-8132-0125-2 (cloth : alk. paper)
1. Bible. N.T. Matthew—Commentaries—Early works to 1800.
I. Williams, Daniel H.  II. Title.
BS2575.53.H5513 2013
226.207—dc23
2012012493

# CONTENTS

# CONTENTS

## APPENDICES AND INDICES

# ACKNOWLEDGMENTS

I had much help in the gradual unfolding of this project. In 2000, a University Teacher's Fellowship from The National Endowment for the Humanities University enabled me to begin the task of collating and producing an initial translation. Four years later I received a Research Grant, Baylor University (Summer–Fall, 2004), allowing me another semester to work on this translation relatively unhindered.

I am also grateful for the number of graduate students over the years who aided with much of the English editing. Among these Jesse Hoover has been most helpful in making final corrections lest the project take any longer. Special thanks must also go to my editor, Carole Monica C. Burnett, who contributed several substantive suggestions.

It would be inexcusable not to acknowledge the breadth of scholarship that Jean Doignon has presented in his critical edition of Hilary's commentary, which served as the basis for this translation. Anyone who has done serious work in Hilary's writings has benefited from Doignon's legacy, especially the way in which he brought classical and Christian Latin sources to bear on interpreting Christian texts in the fourth century.

DHW

# ABBREVIATIONS

ANF    Ante-Nicene Fathers. 1890. Reprint. Grand
       Rapids: Eerdmans, 1994.

CAP    *Collectanea Antiariana Parisina (fragmenta historica)*, CSEL 65.

CCSL   Corpus Christianorum, series latina. Turnholt, 1954–.

CSEL   Corpus Scriptorum Ecclesiasticorum Latinorum. Vienna,
       1866–.

Kinnavey   Raymond James Kinnavey, *The Vocabulary of St. Hilary of Poitiers.*

Itala   *Itala: Das Neue Testament*, Vol. 1, ed. A. Jülicher with
        W. Matzkow and K. Aland, 1938.

LXX    Septuagint.

PL     Patrologiae cursus completus, series latina. Paris, 1844–1864;
       second edition, 1878–1890.

PLRE   *The Prosopography of the Later Roman Empire*, A. H. M. Jones,
       J. R. Martindale, J. Morris. Cambridge University Press, 1971–.

RB     *Revue Bénédictine*. Maredsous.

SC     Sources Chrétiennes. Paris: Cerf, 1941–.

Sur Matt.   *Sur Matthieu* I–II, ed. J. Doignon, SC 254 and 258.

VC     *Vigiliae Christianae.*

Vg.    Vulgate.

# SELECT BIBLIOGRAPHY

*Texts*

Hilary of Poitiers. *Collectanea Antiariana Parisina (fragmenta historica)*. Edited by A. Feder. CSEL 65. Vienna, 1916.
———. *Sur Matthieu* I-II. Edited by Jean Doignon. SC 254 and 258. Paris: Cerf, 1978.
*Itala: Das Neue Testament in Altlateinischer Uberlieferung*. Vol. 1: *Matthäus Evangelium*. Edited by Adolf Jülicher with Walter Matzkow and Kurt Aland. Berlin: Walter De Gruyter, 1972.

*Literature*

Borchardt, C. F. A. *Hilary of Poitiers' Role in the Arian Struggle*. The Hague: Martinus Nijhoff, 1966.
Brennecke, Hans Christof. *Hilarius von Poitiers und die Bischofsopposition gegen Konstantius II*. Berlin and New York: W. de Gruyter, 1984.
Burns, Paul C. *The Christology in Hilary of Poitiers' Commentary on Matthew*. Studia ephemeridis Augustinianum 16. Rome: Institutum Patristicum Augustinianum, 1981.
———. "Hilary of Poitiers' Road to Béziers: Politics or Religion?" *Journal of Early Christian Studies* 2 (1994): 273–89.
———. "Hilary's Use of Communally Sanctioned Texts to Construct His Autobiography." *Zeitschrift für antikes Christentum* 2.1 (Jan. 1, 1998): 65–83.
Doignon, Jean. *Hilaire de Poitiers: Disciple et témoin de la vérité (356–367)*. Collection des Études Augustiniennes, Série Antiquité 175. Paris: Institut d'Études Augustiniennes, 2005.
———. "Les premiers commentateurs latins de l'Ecriture et l'oeuvre exégétique d'Hilaire de Poitiers." *Le monde latin antique et la Bible*. Paris: Beauchesne, 1985.
———. "La Comparaison de Matth. 23, 27, *Sicut Gallina ... sub alas suas*, dans l'exégèse d'Hilaire de Poitiers: une mise au point à propos de la *sollicitudo* du Christ." *Laval théologique et philosophique* 39.1 (février 1983): 21–26.
———. "L'*Argumentatio* d'Hilaire de Poitiers dans l'*exemplum* de la tentation de Jésus (*In Matthaeum* 3, 1–5)." *Vigiliae Christianae* 29 (1975): 296–308.
———. "Le sens d'une formule relative à Jean-Baptiste dans l'*In Mat-*

*thaeum* d'Hilaire de Poitiers." *Vetera Christianorum* 21 (1984): 27–32.

———. "De l'absence ou la présence d'Origène dans l'exégèse d'Hilaire de Poitiers: deux cas typiques." In *Origeniana Sexta,* 693–99. Edited by Gilles Dorival and Alain le Boulluec. Leuven: Peeters, 1995.

———. "La scène évangélique du baptême de Jésus commentée par Lactance et Hilaire de Poitiers." In *Epektasis,* 63–73. Paris: Editions Beauchesne, 1972.

———. *Hilaire de Poitiers avant l'exil.* Paris: Etudes Augustiniennes, 1971.

Duval, Y. M. "Vrais et Faux Problèmes concernants le Retour d'Exil d'Hilaire de Poitiers et Son Action en Italie en 360–363." *Athenaeum* 48 (1970): 251–75.

Jacobs, J. W. "The Western Roots of the Christology of St Hilary of Poitiers." *Studia Patristica* 13.2 (1975): 198–203.

Kinnavey, Raymond James. *The Vocabulary of St. Hilary of Poitiers as contained in* Commentarius in Matthaeum, Liber I ad Constantium *and* De Trinitate: A Morphological and Semasiological Study. Washington, DC: The Catholic University of America Press, 1935.

Lemaire, Jean-Louis. "Histoire et exégèse dans l'*In Matthaeum* d'Hilaire de Poitiers." In *Penser La Foi: Recherches en théologie aujourd'hui: mélanges offerts à Joseph Moingt,* 437–48. Edited by Joseph Doré and Christoph Theobald. Paris: Cerf, 1993.

McDermott, John M. "Hilary of Poitiers: The Infinite Nature of God." *Vigiliae Christianae* 27 (1973): 172–202.

Meslin, Michel. "Hilaire et la crise arienne." In *Hilaire et son temps: Actes du Colloque de Poitiers 29 septembre–3 octobre 1968 à l'occasion du XVIe centenaire de la mort de saint Hilaire,* 19–42. Paris: Etudes Augustiniennes, 1969.

Perrin, M. "Comptes Rendus." *Mélanges de science religieuse* 38.3 (1981): 144–46.

Simonetti, Manlio. "Note sul commento a Matteo di Ilario di Poitiers." *Vetera Christianorum* 1 (1969): 35–64.

Smulders, P. *Hilary of Poitiers' Preface to His "Opus Historicum."* Leiden and New York: E. J. Brill, 1995.

Williams, D. H. "A Reassessment of the Early Career and Exile of Hilary of Poitiers." *Journal of Ecclesiastical History* 42 (1991): 212–17.

———. "The Anti-Arian Campaigns of Hilary of Poitiers and the 'Liber Contra Auxentium.'" *Church History* 61 (1992): 7–22.

———. "Defining Orthodoxy in Hilary of Poitiers' *Commentarium in Matthaeum,*" *Journal of Early Christian Studies* 9 (2001): 151–71.

# INTRODUCTION

# INTRODUCTION

*St. Hilary, bishop of Poitiers.... With God's aid he reverently brings up the deep abysses of Divine Scripture to make the obscurity of parables visible to the enlightened mind.* (Cassiodorus, *Institutes* 1.18)*

The first half of the fourth century yielded few texts produced by Latin writers. All of the surviving remnants from this period come from the genre of biblical exposition: an abbreviated commentary on the Apocalypse by Victorinus of Poetovio (martyred in 304);[1] a fragmented commentary or scholia on the Gospels by Fortunatianus of Aquileia,[2] a handful of sermonettes on three of the Gospels by Arnobius of Sicca,[3] and two of the pseudo-Cyprianic sermons that are thought to come from the fourth century.[4] Hilary's commentary on the Gospel of Matthew provides the only nearly complete text,[5] also making it the first full Latin commentary on the Gospel to be preserved[6] and

---

*Trans. James W. and Barbara Halporn, http://www9.georgetown.edu/faculty/jod/inst-trans.html, accessed Aug. 20, 2012.

1. In the preface to his translation of Origen's homilies on Luke (c. 388), Jerome writes that he had in his possession a commentary on Matthew by Victorinus along with Hilary's; see SC 87.97. Victorinus's commentary is now lost. See *De viris illust.* 74 for the list of other commentaries that Victorinus was known to have published.

2. CCSL 9.367–70. Jerome mentions only that Fortunatianus wrote "short and rustic" commentaries on the Gospels, of which three small portions (two on Matthew's Gospel) survive (*De viris illust.* 97). In his own commentary on St. Matthew, Jerome offers a list of sources, mainly Greek, which he has used, including a commentary of Hippolytus "the martyr," of which only a small, single fragment is extant (GCS 1, 2 [1897], 211), but also *Latinorum Hilarii, Victorini, Fortunatiani opuscula* (SC 242.68).

3. Arnobius of Sicca, *Expositiunculae in Evangelium Iohannis Evangelistae Matthei et Lucae,* CCSL 25A. The brief remarks on Matthew are the most extensive of the three (pp. 276–94).

4. These are *De centesima, sexagesima, tricesima,* and *De montibus Sion et Sinai* (*Clavis Patrum Latinorum,* 3d ed. [Brepols: Editores Pontificii, 1995], 19), although Daniélou has argued for a late second-century date.

5. Both the preface and treatment of the last seven verses of the Gospel are missing. See below in Introduction.

6. Because of the commentary's historical isolation it is problematic to

---

3

therefore of value in reconstructing the exegetical and intellectual history of the west during the 350s. Written in classical style, the commentary found favor with succeeding generations of readers who were as pleased with its grammatical technique as they were with its content. No small praise is offered by Jerome, who, in the preface to his translation of Origen's homilies on Luke, declared Hilary to be "that master of eloquence."[7] Hilarius[8] was born in Gaul (probably between 310 and 320), where he was also educated. There is only scant biographical information apart from Hilary's own comments in the beginning of his *De trinitate* (1.1–14).[9] It has been rightly observed that Hilary's comments are less purely autobiographical and more of a stylized account, based on the rhetorical model of "confessions,"[10] a pattern Augustine would also later follow. While we cannot be absolutely certain that Hilary came from a pagan family, there is no doubt that he had a standard classical education as evidenced by his frequent, though not ostentatious, use of ancient Latin authors.[11]

It appears that Hilary was the first bishop of Poitiers since there are no records of a bishop from that see attending any one of the many councils that convened from 325–355.[12] How long

distinguish features of its own unique style from those that were considered the norm.

7. PL 26:220A.

8. A common Roman name. *PLRE* 1.433–35.

9. Critical editions are Smulders, ed., CCSL 62–62A, and Figura et al., eds., SC 443.

10. *Hilaire de Poitiers: La Trinité,* ed. M. Figura et al., SC 443 (Paris: Les Éditions du Cerf, 1999), 13; P. Burns, "Hilary's Use of Communally Sanctioned Texts to Construct His Autobiography," *Zeitschrift für antikes Christentum* 2 (1998): 65–83. Such a rhetorical model lay behind Augustine's more famous *Confessions*. While Augustine's quest for truth is articulated in conventional philosophical terms, his reorientation of philosophical studies in the wake of reading Scripture have strong parallels in Hilary. It is generally assumed that Augustine read Hilary perhaps as early as 387 or the year of his baptism. J. J. O'Donnell, *Augustine: Confessions, Introduction and Text,* vol. 1 (Oxford, 1992), xlvii n.85.

11. As Doignon has painstakingly demonstrated; *Hilaire de Poitiers: Disciple et témoin de la vérité (356–367),* Collection des Études Augustiniennes, Série Antiquité 175 (Paris: Institut d'Études Augustiniennes, 2005), 83–89.

12. We would expect the church of Poitiers to have sent a bishop, if there had been one, to the Council of Arles in 314. See *Concilia Galliae A. 314–A. 506,* C. Munier, ed., CCSL 148.14–24, for the evidence of the subscriptions at Arles (314).

he had been bishop before 356 is unknown. Whatever the time-frame of Hilary's episcopacy, four or five were spent in the Greek east because of his forced exile in Asia Minor (356–360).[13] In the year 356, at a council of Gallic bishops located in the coastal town of Béziers (Baeterrae), Hilary was removed from his see[14] and exiled to the east by imperial order. The reasons for his condemnation by this council are not clear[15]—neither the content nor the charges. Since the councils of Arles (353) and Milan (355), western bishops were being forced to ratify a relatively new creed, quite possibly the anti-Photinian formula of Sirmium (351)[16] or one similar to it.[17] But Hilary later says that the primary issue had to do with his excommunication of Saturninus, the bishop of Arles. He and other (unknown) Gallic bishops separated themselves from communion with Saturninus in 356.[18] Again, the events behind Hilary's action are never stated,[19] but its repercussions resulted in Hilary's deposition from Poitiers.

The bishop wasted no time in exile. A year after Béziers, a new formula of faith was issued by a small group of bishops at

13. On the dates of his exile and return to the west, see D. H. Williams, *Ambrose of Milan and the End of the Nicene-Arian Conflicts* (Oxford: Oxford University Press, 1995), 38–49.

14. It seems that no bishop was installed in his place, which usually was not the case. The preface of *De synodis* indicates that even after his exile Hilary still shared communion with bishops of most the provinces in Gaul. Years after his return to Gaul, Hilary declared in his *Contra Auxentium* that he was never deposed by a council. It is possible to dismiss these remarks as the bishop's refusal to accept his situation, according to T. D. Barnes, "Hilary of Poitiers on His Exile," *VC* 46 (1992): 136, but this assumes an unnecessary amount of suspicion.

15. Especially complicated by Hilary's assertion four years later: "I am in exile not for a crime but on account of schism and false reports submitted to you, pious emperor"; *Ad Const.* 2.2.1–2 (CSEL 65.198).

16. *De synodis* 38–61 (PL 10:509B–522A). It is the only credal formula in *De syn.* where Hilary appends an explanatory gloss to each of the anathemas.

17. If Hilary had indeed been compelled to subscribe to the Sirmium (351) formula, it is difficult to explain why he cites the same Sirmium formula only a year or two after his exile with approbation as an orthodox formula; see n.15, above. It is too far a stretch to think Hilary was exiled for not accepting a creed only to expound on it at length with favor a short while later.

18. *De syn.* 2 (PL 10:481A).

19. I now think that whatever the reasons for Hilary's condemnation, they must have had some religious or doctrinal purpose, though it need not have been linked to anti-"Arianism." Paul Burns, "Hilary of Poitiers' Road to Béziers: Politics or Religion?" *JECS* 2 (1994): 289.

Sirmium, which limited description of the relation of the Father and the Son to mere "likeness" (*homoios* or *similis*), rejecting any mention of terms that contained "substance" or "nature." In response, Hilary called this statement "the *blasphemia*" and composed a treatise in the form of a letter to his fellow-bishops in Gaul, known as *De synodis*.[20] Herein he displays his new acquaintance with the "creeds of the east," including the Nicene, so that the Gallic bishops could understand that the issues now affecting the west were but the tip of the iceberg. He likewise identifies the modalist interpretation of Nicaea's *homoousios* that had so galvanized eastern bishops in their eagerness to adopt an alternative creed.

Hilary was allowed an unusual amount of mobility during his banishment in Asia Minor.[21] He was in attendance at the council of Seleucia (359), and immediately after, is found in Constantinople, probably having accompanied the delegates who were commissioned by the council at Seleucia to represent its decisions. In Constantinople Hilary sought an audience with the emperor in order to block the official ratification (January 360) of the Homoian creed promulgated at Ariminum and Seleucia,[22] but to no avail.

Hilary's pleas went unheard. The Homoian formula from Ariminum was formally endorsed by the synod, and on 15 February 360, by Constantius. Sometime during the first half of 360, Hilary quietly slipped away from Constantinople and returned to Poitiers without imperial authorization. In the wake of his defiant departure, Hilary wrote a scathing and provocative manifesto in which he attacked the emperor (Constantius II) as an enemy of the true faith and a persecutor of Christians.[23] Whereas the emperor's actions were excused in Hilary's

20. The only critical edition of this work is found in PL 10:471–546. A text found in the lines of some manuscripts of *De syn.*, known as *Apologetica ad reprehensores libri de synodis responsa* (PL 10:545–48) may be a later gloss on *De syn.*, though some scholars have argued that the excised passages are Hilary's own response to those that criticized *De syn.*

21. *De syn.* 63 (PL 10:522C).

22. His plea to the emperor is found in the document erroneously called *Liber II ad Constantium* (CSEL 65.193–205). The so-called "Liber I" is really part of the western synodical letter from Serdica (343); hence Liber II is rightfully named *Liber ad Constantium*.

23. Namely, *In Constantium* (also known as *Contra Constantium*).

previous letter because of his heretical counselors and therefore Constantius was being "deceived" by false reports, now
Constantius is no longer regarded as a legitimate emperor, but
an "antichrist" and an "enemy to divine religion." There is no
reason why Hilary should be constrained by the laws of such a
ruler, including the terms of his banishment. The bishop was
undoubtedly taking a certain amount of risk in his actions,
though the rise of Julian's power as the new Augustus of the
west had the effect of creating a haven for Gallic bishops who
were exiled by Constantius in the 350s.[24]

As a result of his forced exile in 356, including his opposition to the emperor, Hilary would become ever after recognized as a confessor of the Church.[25] Confessorship by the latter half of the fourth century had as much to do with defense
of orthodoxy as it had with being martyred or exiled. Repeatedly Hilary expressed his desire to stand boldly as a "confessor"
before Constantius just as if he were before Nero or Decius.
Such stalwart words did not go unnoticed. The reasons for Hilary's exile are made absolutely clear by Gregory of Tours: "Hilary, blessed defender of the undivided Trinity and for its sake
driven into exile, was both restored to his own country and entered Paradise."[26]

Now back in the west,[27] Hilary easily reassumed his see since
a new bishop had never been installed in his place. He completed the so-called *De trinitate* in twelve books, which Jerome more
accurately described as "adversus arrianos libri."[28] Thereafter,

24. Julian, who was proclaimed Augustus early in 360 by his troops (Ammianus Marcellinus, *Res gestae* 20.4.4–20), was content to allow, even encour-
age, resentment among western bishops in hopes of unsettling Constantius's
position in particular and weakening the catholic Church in general.

25. Jerome is the first to call him a "confessor" (*Ep.* 70.5), followed thereafter by Rufinus (*HE* 2.30–31), John Cassian (*Contra Nestorium* 7.24), and Venan-
tius Fortunatus, *Vita Sancti Hilarii Episcopi Pictaviensis* (PL 88:439–54).

26. *Historia Francorum* 3, prol. (PL 71:241).

27. For a detailed account of Hilary's stop at Rome on the way west and the
likelihood of a meeting with the Roman bishop, Liberius, see *Ambrose of Milan
and the End of the Nicene-Arian Conflicts,* 45.

28. Critical editions in P. Smulders, ed., CCSL 62–63 and *La Trinité,* SC
443, 448, 462. Whether Hilary completed this treatise just before or after his
return to Gaul matters little since it was issued in Latin and therefore in the
west.

two other polemical works were written before 366. The first was a dossier of credal and epistolary documents, now in fragmentary form, which served to implicate two leading Homoian bishops, Valens (of Mursa) and Ursacius (of Singidunum), with doctrinal duplicity and heretical intentions. Hilary's years among the Greeks introduced him to the present and past of theological conflicts, completely altering his perspective on the west's role in the controversies. While he was still in exile, Hilary began collecting conciliar and confessional texts (beginning with the council[s] of Serdica, 343), accompanied by a brief narration of and sporadic comments on the reasons for which they were originally written.[29] The extant documents are all that remains of a collection made in three stages over the course of nine years or so. Exactly how the assorted texts and glosses should be arranged and why they were chosen remain a mystery.[30]

The second polemical document was a fierce diatribe accusing Auxentius, the Homoian bishop of Milan (355–74), of "Arianism." The impetus for this work was Hilary's visit to Milan and lack of success in convincing a panel of bishops of Auxentius's guilt.[31] This was the one major setback in what sounds like a string of successes by Hilary and Eusebius of Vercelli as they sought to redeem western sees from the debacle of Ariminum and introduce a neo-Nicene Trinitarianism. As a result of their efforts, councils were convened in Gaul and Italy that condemned "Arianism" (for example, the Homoian confession). Among these councils Hilary alone preserves the record of one held in Paris (361). Besides its affirmation of pro-Nicenism, it

29. Edited in CSEL 65 by Alfred Feder, who gives it the title (in English): *Excerpts from Saint Hilary's Lost Historical Work, Seemingly in Three Books, Against Valens and Ursacius.* Hilary never mentions the title, though it is later called *Adversus Valentem et Ursacium.* Valens and Ursacius had been the primary architects of the Homoian confession and the perceived villains at the major western council of Ariminum (359).

30. For an explanation of the three-part arrangement, see L. Wickham, *Hilary of Poitiers: Conflicts of Conscience and Law in the Fourth-Century Church* (Liverpool: Liverpool University Press, 1997); D. H. Williams, "A Reassessment of the Early Career and Exile of Hilary of Poitiers," *Journal of Ecclesiastical History* 42 (1991): 202–17.

31. For the events, D. H. Williams, "The Anti-Arian Campaigns of Hilary of Poitiers and the *Liber Contra Auxentium,*" *Church History* 61 (1992): 7–22.

is of importance that the synod's affirmation of *homoousios* was associated with a studied rejection of neo-Sabellianism, thus confirming their distance from Photinian (and Marcellan) theology. Besides condemning the temporal generation of the Son, the similitude between Father and Son is accepted, but in the sense of true God from true God, "so that not a singularity of divinity (*unio divinitatis*) but a unity (*unitas*) of divinity is understood."[32] Throughout his career, Hilary was aware of and warned western bishops against this way of describing the relation of the Father and the Son.

As a result of his substantial literary activity, most of which was widely circulated soon after his death,[33] Hilary of Poitiers became one of the west's most celebrated theologians and anti-"Arian" figures of the fourth century. We should not be surprised at the historical eminence ascribed to him by a fellow countryman, Sulpicius Severus, who, in chronicling the aftermath of the infamous council of Constantinople (360), mentions Hilary alone as one who set the west free from the stain of heresy.[34]

While the latter has been rightfully celebrated since the fifth century as a defender of the orthodox faith[35] and confessor, this bishop of Poitiers in southern Gaul was pre-eminently a pastor and expositor of the Bible. Just as the conventional accounts of Augustine, which sketch his career according to his role within various controversies, are incomplete when one sees the totality of his writing, so the same can be said for Hilary. After his return to Poitiers, Hilary picked up the task of producing expositions of biblical books. Besides the Matthew commentary, the only other surviving text of substance was the *tractatus* on the Psalms.[36] Also attributed to Hilary are small fragments,

---

32. *CAP* A.I.2 (CSEL 65.44).

33. Charles Kannengiesser, "L'héritage d'Hilaire de Poitiers," *Recherches de Science Religieuse* 56 (1968): 435–56, for a survey of fourth- to eighth-century cognizance of Hilary's writings.

34. *Chronicon* 2.45.7.

35. His feast day is on January 13th, the presumed date of his death in 367, as recognized by all church calendars.

36. Jerome tells us that Hilary wrote commentaries on Psalms 1, 2, 51–62, 118–150 (*De viris illust.* 100), but commentary has survived also for Psalms 9, 13, 14, 63–69, and 91. Internal references suggest that the work was original-

preserved from later writers, that come from *Tractatus in Iob*,[37] and a commentary on 1 Timothy.[38] Jerome also associates with Hilary "a short treatise against Dioscorus the physician," about which nothing more is known.[39] Among Hilary's later works is his *Tractatus mysteriorum*,[40] where one finds his treatment of persons and events in the Old Testament set out most pointedly in figurative exegesis. Besides these, four hymns[41] are ascribed to the bishop's handiwork, though there is no definitive evidence that they are authentic.

According to Sulpicius Severus, Hilary died in his native land in the sixth year of his return from exile, which puts the date at 366.[42] At some prior point, Hilary had completed another installment of *Adv. Val. et Urs.* Since we do not hear from Hilary after this, it is reasonable to place his death after 367.

## EXEGETICAL PURPOSES IN *IN MATTHAEUM*

There is very little in the commentary that helps us pinpoint the occasion for its writing. Nor is it certain whether the content of the commentary was first delivered as a series in the course of Hilary's preaching. It appears that many of the earliest commentaries we possess, such as those of Origen, Chrysostom, and Ambrose, were composed, or rather compiled and edited, after their oral presentation. But there is no conclusive proof that Hilary's commentary was first presented orally. There are no

---

ly even more extensive than this, as does a seventh-century manuscript that, if authentic, contains three more commentaries, namely, on Psalms 15, 31, and 41 (PL 9:891–908). Critical editions on two Psalms have been published by Doignon, *Tractatus super Psalmos: Commentaires sur les Psaumes 1–14*, SC 515 and 19bis; *Commentaires sur le Psaume 118 (1–8)*, SC 244; and *Commentaires sur le Psaume 118 (9–22)*, SC 347.

37. CSEL 65.229–31.

38. CSEL 65.233. Jerome declared that both of these works were mere translations of Origen (*Ep.* 61.2).

39. *De viris illust.* 100; *Ep.* 70. 5.

40. Not discovered until 1887. Critical editions are available in A. Feder, CSEL 65.1–38, and in J. P. Brisson, SC 19bis.

41. *CPL* 462–63.

42. *Chronicon* 2.45. Gregory of Tours (*The History of the Franks* 1.39) claims that Hilary went up to heaven in the fourth year of the joint reign of the emperors Valentinian and Valens, that is, 367 CE.

traces of doxologies or remarks to the hearers, nor are there allusions in earlier comments as found in his *Tractatus in Psalmos*.[43] Hilary addresses the reader at one point (*In Matt.* 19.2), and there is the occasional stylistic use of repeating clauses, apparent in the Latin: for example, *Ex his enim iam credentes, ex his iam apostoli, ex his iam regnum caelorum* (11.7). These and several other passages lend themselves to placing the commentary, or some parts of it, in an original homiletical or didactic context, though this is hardly decisive.

With greater confidence it can be observed that the way in which the commentary presents sequential explanations of (most of) the Gospel betokens a format of *lectio continua*.[44] A biblical book or a series of books was read through consecutively, usually in some liturgical context,[45] taking up on each occasion where it had concluded previously. In a homiletical setting, it was common that the sermon would follow the day's reading of Scripture, resulting in a series of expositions on a given book.[46] By means of *lectio continua,* the listener heard not only most of the Scriptures read over time, but was able to grasp sequences of events and the logic of arguments.[47] Any reader of the commentary cannot fail to notice how very important it was to Hilary to make such connections.

This latter remark, however, should not be taken to mean that Hilary covered every verse of Matthew. Given the exigencies of Hilary's original purposes, some pericopes are passed over. A good example is in 13.1, where Mt 13.3–9, 13–15, 18–30, and 36–43 are not explained for unknown reasons. But Hila-

43. Doignon, *Sur Matt.* 1.20.

44. P. Smulders, "Hilarius van Poitiers als Exegeet van Mattheüs" ("Hilary of Poitiers as an Exegete of Matthew"), *Bijdragen* 44 (1983): 62.

45. Such as reading in congregational worship or for clerical instruction.

46. For example, Augustine begins a sermon (*Sermon* 83) on Mt 18.21–22 with the words, "Yesterday, the holy Gospel ... [cites 18.15–17]. Today the passage that follows this, which we heard when it was read just now, deals with the same point." Cf. Peter Chrysologus, *Sermon* 80.1.

47. Harry Gamble, *Books and Readers in the Early Church: A History of Early Christian Texts* (Yale University Press, 1995), 217. As the concept of the "ecclesiastical year" developed in the liturgical life of churches, consecutive reading of Scripture was interrupted at important seasonal festivals, such as Easter, Pentecost, and Epiphany, when certain texts were selected as appropriate for the occasion.

ry states his reason when he does not remark about the Lord's Prayer (Mt 5): because earlier writers, namely, Tertullian and Cyprian, had already provided sufficient guidance (*In Matt.* 5.1). The implication here is that the reader should consult them for an explanation of this part of Matthew. Presumably, then, Hilary's readers knew or had access to these texts—a circumstance that suggests the intended readership was sufficiently literate and had other books at its disposal. Jean Doignon has proposed that the commentary was originally intended for Hilary's fellow clerics in Poitiers, on the basis of Jerome's remark that the work "is hardly a reading for the more simple brothers."[48] But this seems implausible. Assuming that Hilary is the first bishop of Poitiers, it is doubtful there was a body of clergy sufficiently large to warrant such a composition. The hint of educated readers, however, indicates that the commentary was prepared for other bishops in western and central Gaul.[49]

THE INTERPRETIVE TASK

In keeping with the practice of previous ancient commentators, Hilary perceives the Gospel text as a literary whole, and its message as a doctrinal unity. If the Gospel is allowed to speak for itself, the inquirer will be able to find in any given pericope a general coherence. The reader does not bring his or her own interpretation to the text. Whether obvious or hidden, the meaning of the text is already within the text. Hilary also operates on the principle that Scripture should interpret Scripture. Throughout the Commentary, references to what has already been said in the text are common, and Hilary is content to let certain parts of Matthew interpret other parts. If followed faithfully, there may still be conflicting views about the proper interpretation, but these are unnecessary.[50]

Hilary tries to be consistent in applying certain exegetical principles: first, "The Lord instructs through things as well as

---

48. Jerome, *Ep.* 58.10.
49. Viz., Tours is only sixty-one miles from Poitiers.
50. "Even if there are conflicting interpretations and differences in the account about how we should treat these matters, the process of heavenly realities gives assurance…" (*In Matt.* 21.3).

through words," an oft-repeated concept throughout his commentary. A crucial component to unlocking a text's meaning can always be found in Christ's own *dicta* (words) and *facta* (actions). These alternating successions of the Lord's words and deeds should not be regarded as mere indications of the Gospel's narrative style. Instead, they provide the very tissue of the Gospel's rationality. It should be axiomatic for the reader to understand that "the Lord teaches us that deeds and words, speech and action, in equal proportion guide us in the faith of our hope."[51] Most importantly, the divine identity is revealed in this double means of communication. When Hilary describes Peter's confession and Jesus' response in Mt 16, we are told that in the course of his words and works, he presented to his disciples a certain pattern and reason for how he should be understood as God.[52]

In the light of a sequential reading of the text (verse by verse), Hilary very often adjures the reader to see the significance of the *ordo*, or patterned flow of events, which the Gospel recounts. The point of discovering the *ordo* in Scripture was internal to the text itself and, if not immediately apparent through a plain reading, it was detectable through allegorical exegesis. In other words, every passage of Scripture houses an inner logic meant for the believer to understand.

Examples of the above can be found in the commentary on the parable of the man who had two sons (Mt 21.28–32), where Hilary states, "There are many important facts which can confound our understanding unless we observe an order (*ordo*) of what comes first and that which follows."[53] Identifying the text's *ordo* is what provides the links between ideas and events expressed such that a sense of the whole will result. In each account in the Gospel, no detail about the facts presented should be bypassed as insignificant: "so we teach that the events themselves contain the development of the facts in their order (*consequentium*). For nothing is omitted from the truth, since the truth is what we follow in imitation" (7.1).[54] Even in seemingly

---

51. *In Matt.* 17.1.                        52. *In Matt.* 16.4.
53. *In Matt.* 21.11.
54. Cf. 12.11: "At that time, they brought to him a man possessing a demon

contradictory circumstances, such as that of Herod, who feared to kill John the Baptist yet promised to bring his head on a platter, "there is a pattern in the facts" (*ordo rerum*) in which things present correspond to reasons as set forth.[55]

At the heart of the *ordo intelligentiae* or *ratio* is that which is inherent to God's revelation in Christ, a process of unfolding the truth, whether for the present good of believers or, just as often, for the future. This same exegetical principle is at work years later in the preface of Hilary's *Tractatus mysteriorum*, where all of Scripture is said to pertain to the advent of our Lord Jesus Christ, "announced by the words and revealed by its facts" (1.1). Thus, in *In Matt.* 3.16–17, the divine *ordo* is that which is revealed by the triple manifestation of the Trinity at Christ's baptism: "the *ordo* of the heavenly mystery is portrayed in him."[56] The *ordo mysterii* is also found in Jesus' raising the paralytic.[57] The crowd is said to have feared the power of the Lord's words and deeds so that the truth of present circumstances might be joined to an image of things to come.[58]

It is particularly important to discover the *ratio* or *ordo* of a passage when the events as narrated seem self-contradictory or nonsensical. When a disciple sought to be given time in order to bury his father (Mt 8.20), his request was refused by Jesus; such a response was not in the usual course of "human piety and service." In defense of Jesus' action, Hilary states,

We should clarify two things here: the reason for such important and diverse events contained in the text, as well as the profound causes of its truth so that an understanding of interior significance may be explained.[59]

Jesus' refusal is found, not in the basic narrative, but by ascertaining the salvific pattern of God's working in the world.

---

who was blind and mute, etc." There follows a healing suited to the blind and mute demoniac. It is not without reason, after he had spoken of healing to all the crowd in common, that the blind and deaf demoniac is then brought in from outside, in order that the same pattern of intelligibility follows without any ambiguity.

55. *In Matt.* 14.8.                    56. *In Matt.* 2.6.
57. *In Matt.* 7.8.
58. I.e., when the Lord comes in judgment.
59. *In Matt.* 7.8.

As Hilary explains it, only those who are "dead" to God will be concerned with burying the dead, nor should we mix the unbelieving dead with remembrances of the saints.

## LAW AND GOSPEL

The God of the Law is the God of the Gospel. The Law is from God, and Christ's birth and work are set forth in the Law. Therefore, it was to Israel a "way of knowledge." Hilary is probably taking the Pauline instruction that the Law was the Gospel's pedagogue as an implicit hermeneutical rule. The Law in the commentary, as Smulders notes, was "the shadow of what is to come" or that "shadow of the truth" of what is to follow after the Law.[60] There is no doubt for Hilary that the purpose of the Law is christologically oriented. It is entirely focused on and thus understood by the revelation of Christ. Several times does Hilary refer to Christ as the *meditatio legis*—a term found in his Latin predecessors, Tertullian, Commodianus, and Victorinus of Poetovio. Within this unity God's mode of acting in history will change, as the revelation of himself grows, with each new era. With the coming of the Gospel, divine revelation has ascended to its highest point because Christ is the means by which the Law is ultimately understood and applied. Indeed, the Law is not complete without Christ, meaning that the Law must be read in terms of the Gospel. The Law has now fulfilled its task and consequently no longer fulfills its original task except in a retrospective way that Jesus and the apostles use. "With the coming of Christ, reliance upon the Law was useless because Christ is not sanctified by the Law, but the Law by Christ."[61] To the point of redundancy, Hilary's exegesis never strays far from interpreting the Gospel as primarily revealing the tension and continuity with the Old Testament, which makes sense given Matthew's heavy reliance on Old Testament precedents.

This being said, we should note that Hilary at no point presents an exposition of a particular Old Testament text. Whereas the *In Matt.* makes scores of allusions to Old Testament events

60. "Hilarius van Poitiers als Exegeet van Mattheüs," 72–73.
61. *In Matt.* 24.6.

or people, it has very little interest in opening specific passages. It may well be that Hilary deemed this as unnecessary, given his theological understanding, which regarded the Gospel and apostolic message as completely supplanting the provisions of the Old Covenant. Whatever the reason, Hilary is clearly not as interested in looking back into the history of the Gospel as he is in looking forward. This may explain why he rarely utilizes the other three Gospels[62] but often draws upon passages from the Pauline letters and Acts since they best articulate the fulfillment and purposes of the Gospel. As such, the apostolic message for Hilary most often comes from a Pauline perspective.

Typical of ancient writers, unfortunately, is the anti-Judaism which characterizes nearly every chapter in this work. Hilary seems the most belligerent when he discusses the history of Israel's disobedience of the Law, which created a "lineage" of unbelief, and which explains the Jews' rejection of Jesus as the Christ.[63] In 18.3 he says that "the Jewish people are designated as the author of this stumbling." Because of their denial of Christ in his Passion, "all the world is jeopardized." While the anti-Judaism is certainly problematic, Hilary's opinion is not motivated by anti-Semitism. His argument is not about race. Rather, he seems preoccupied with the relation of the Jews to Christ and the Christian Gospel. Hilary claims that God had given Jews the first "honor" (15.4) of salvation because of divine affection for them, and that they were instrumental in the revelation of the Law (18.2). In several places he makes this emphasis very plain.[64] Nonetheless, the faith of the pagans or Gentiles in the prophets and in Christ acts as a witness against Jewish unbelief because the former has received the gift of grace that the latter refused.

But the dominating motif of Hilary's "deeper" interpretation of many passages in Matthew has to do with the way in which the Gospel succeeded the Law. The Law had been established for the redemption of body and soul for all of Israel,[65] and is

---

62. Two in one bed; prayer at the feeding of the five thousand; the order of the cup and bread of the Last Supper; the salvation of the good murderer.

63. E.g., 15.8.

64. Cf. *In Matt.* 11.10; also, 12.18: "they understand that the works of Christ are beyond human power."

65. *In Matt.* 17.10.

figured in the venerable person of John the Baptist, the young man of Mt 19, the ninety-nine sheep, the vineyard of Mt 20, even the disciples themselves before the Resurrection, whereas the promise of the Gospel is broad and envelops all the nations of the world, which Hilary refers to as "the pagans." Christ's Transfiguration offers the most transparent example of the way in which the "brightness" of salvation exceeded that of Moses and Elijah. Here is a prefiguration about the way in which the pagans would believe in God.[66]

## SIMPLE MEANING

Since the Lord teaches through words, deeds, persons, and events, it stands to reason that the method of understanding should be open to the understanding of all. This is invariably labeled by Hilary as the "simple" meaning rather than "literal" or "historical." Even when he limits himself to a short summary of the Gospel events, the content of the text is carefully formulated according to a descriptive format. Nearly every passage has the capacity to speak simply. Interpreting Jesus' instructions to the disciples in Mt 10.11 about searching for worthy households to enter, Hilary supposes that the purpose of giving directions for their entering, dwelling, and leaving was apparent: "This simple understanding agrees with the modesty of the saints, that hospitality may be offered to one who is worthy."[67]

Hilary comes closest to offering an exegetical principle when discussing how "the Word of God is rich," and can and should be read on different levels, with the interpreter providing "every kind of proof for various meanings. It exhibits from itself an abundance of examples."[68] Hilary declares that whether it is understood in a simple fashion or studied for the inner meaning, both steps play a necessary role for interpreting the text.

66. *In Matt.* 17.3.                    67. *In Matt.* 10.6.
68. *In Matt.* 12.12.

## TYPOLOGICAL EXEGESIS

With respect to Hilary's use of symbolic and allegorical exegesis, or what he calls "typological," precedents for his approach were already established within Latin Christian literature. In the middle of the third century, Novatian had argued in *On Jewish Foods* that the source of the Jews' error was their literal, rather than spiritual, interpretation of the Law. The brief homilies of pseudo-Cyprian (*De centesima* and *De montibus Sina et Sion*) develop scriptural themes in a moralist fashion, while Victorinus of Poetovio in the *Commentary on the Apocalypse*[69] and Fortunatianus of Aquileia's scholia on the Gospel[70] were well known to Hilary. Fortunatianus uses almost entirely a symbolic and typological exegesis: for example, the three groups of gems arranged on Aaron's ephod declare the Trinity (frag. I); and the donkey that the disciples found tied, in accordance with Jesus' instructions (Mt 21.2), is interpreted as the synagogue established under the bonds of the Law (frag. II).[71]

Like the above western writers, Hilary had not been exposed to the kind of allegorical exegesis that one finds in Origen. Such eastern influence was not necessary given the widespread use of allegory in the west, very apparent in the Matthew Commentary. For Hilary, however, there is nearly always a reason for triggering the move to a figurative explanation. Concerning Mt 8.18, "When Jesus saw the great crowd gathered around him, he gave orders for his disciples to go across to the other side of the sea," Hilary acknowledges that a simple interpretation of the text is presented by the words. Jesus, however, gives the impression of having acted callously toward the needy crowds when he abruptly sent the disciples away. Since such an insinuation is contradictory to the Lord's nature and intentions

69. If Jerome is correct, Victorinus also published commentaries on Genesis, Exodus, Leviticus, Isaiah, Ezekiel, Habakkuk, Ecclesiastes, and Song of Songs (*De viris illust.* 74). None of these survive.

70. Jerome knew of and describes the work among others as a "commentary" (*De viris illust.* 97), but the acknowledged brevity of the exercise seems more aptly described as a select series of comments on various passages.

71. It is most evident that Hilary uses literal and figurative meanings as a way to contrast Jewish versus Christian appropriation of the Law.

for humanity, Hilary sees a warrant for a spiritual explanation. Certainly the reader must not force an understanding on the narrative, seeing that the narrative should be allowed to establish its own understanding. Given the lack of logical coherence or theological continuity with what we know about Christ from other parts of the Gospel, the passage permits a less obvious interpretation.

Many things happened that invite an ordinary interpretation. We do not contrive an understanding since the events themselves produce the understanding for us. Nor does the reality of events accommodate itself to our understanding, but understanding is accommodated to the reality. The crowd is large, and the Lord instructs the disciples to go across the sea to the other side. I do not think that it was a lapse in the Savior's goodness that he wanted to leave those who were around him and to choose a secret place for the imparting of salvation. (7.8)

Spiritual reasoning was necessary for resolving those exegetical problems that the straightforward narrative could not. The same logic is applied to the scene of Jesus walking across the sea to the disciples and Peter's attempt and failure to do likewise (Mt 14.31). This presents a problem for Hilary. Why did the Lord not grant to Peter, in his fear, the power of reaching out to him, but extended his hand, caught him, and held him up (Mt 14.31)? A typological pattern (*typicus ordo*) was a major part of the answer: it was necessary to show how Peter was in need of the Lord, who alone was going to suffer for all, because only he forgives the sins of all.[72] Whatever is granted to the whole world is granted by the one who admits no associate in the obtaining of salvation.

While Hilary never uses the word "allegory," he has a battery of terms that seem to function more or less synonymously: *typica significantia* ("figurative meaning"), *typica ratio* ("figurative reason"), *interior significantia* or *interior causa* ("deeper meaning" or "deeper purpose"), *forma* ("image"), *meditatio* ("preparation"), and, rarely, *species* ("image"), *praeceptum caeleste* or *intelligentia caelestis* ("heavenly teaching" or "heavenly un-

72. 14.16.
73. The most common is *typicus*: 7. 9; 8.8; 12.24; 14.10; 17.8; 19.1, 3; 20.11; 33.3, where Hilary uses a Latin transliteration of the Greek τύπος. Paul allows for the term's inherent flexibility: Adam is a type of the One to come

derstanding").[73] Figurative reasoning becomes necessary when one needs to find a deeper (hidden) meaning in the text. In every chapter, Hilary makes a statement at some point such as in 12.12: "Let us pass over those things that are commonly understood, and focus on interior causes." By "interior" he means the use of typology or figurative exegesis. Whether the "type" is found in the Old Testament and revealed in the New, or whether it is a person or event in the Gospel that unveils a spiritual truth for the apostolic age, the "figurative meaning" (*typica significantia*) holds the clue for rendering the true meaning of a passage. Of course Hilary does not see his action as importing an interpretation not otherwise present. He has no doubt that Jesus uttered the recorded words of the text knowing full well its prophetic and deeper significance.

While purely historical events that are recounted should be taken literally, again, there are very often events or words spoken that are incongruent or contradictory, or violate common sense. In these instances the reader should look for "the underlying cause [that] is prefigured"[74] since these events or characters are meant to prompt the search for a deeper or spiritual meaning. In other words, the actions or personalities in the verse are representative of a future work of God. Not surprisingly, Hilary's use of "type" is most similar to the way Paul uses the word. That is, there exists a past event in salvation history that corresponds to a later one—a correspondence that itself becomes the means for clarifying both. Examples of this exegesis abound. The Canaanite woman who confesses Christ as Lord and Son of David is not herself in need of healing but is pleading for help for her daughter, that is, for the people of the pagans; the daughter of the Canaanite woman is said to contain a figure (*typus*) of the Church.[75] The point of prohibiting the little children was another fulfillment of a type. The Lord

---

(Rom 5.14), whereas Rom 6.17 uses the word as a model or form in the sense of a norm. Acts 7.44 resembles Paul's usage, referring to the earthly tabernacle that Moses constructed according to its heavenly archetype or heavenly pattern. Hilary, however, wants to keep the meaning of *typicus* limited to the mode of a one-to-one correspondence.

74. *In Matt.* 14.3.
75. *In Matt.* 15.4.

said that they should not be prohibited because for such is the Kingdom of heaven, which was expressed by the Holy Spirit and bestowed on the pagans through the laying-on of hands and prayer (Acts 8.14–17).[76] Then there is the instance of the two blind men who were healed, receiving not only physical eyesight, but "vision of the knowledge of God." This happened "in order that a figure (*typus*) of the pagans called to believe find fulfillment."[77] In these three cases, the corresponding *typi* are not only connections between the Old and New Testaments. Hilary makes use of the latter, as is more familiar, although he is equally intent to show how the events and people in the Gospel account prefigured things to come in the age of the Church.[78]

## ADVERSARIES IN THE COMMENTARY

This use of typology raises the question of when Hilary actually encountered doctrinal formulations that are commonly regarded as "Arian." Since the persuasive theses of P. Smulders,[79] modern scholarship in this century has generally favored the idea that the bishop had some familiarity with "Arian" antagonists, ranging from an actual knowledge of Arius's writings[80] to a vague acquaintance with contemporary subordinationist issues.[81] This has meant that the dating of the commentary has been placed in the mid-350s, immediately before his exile to Asia Minor.

76. *In Matt.* 19.3.
77. *In Matt.* 20.13.
78. Hilary tends to equate "apostolic writings" with those of the Church, since the era of the Church is also his own era.

79. *La doctrine trinitaire d'Hilaire de Poitiers* (Rome: Aedes Universitatis Gregorianae, 1944).
80. M. Simonetti, "Note sul commento a Mateo di Ilario di Poitiers," *Vetera Christianorum* 1 (1969): 55–56; C. Kannengiesser, "L'exégèse d'Hilaire," in *Hilaire et son temps, actes du colloque de Poitiers, 29 septembre–3 octobre*, Études augustiniennes (Paris, 1969), 132.
81. So M. Simonetti, *La crisi ariana nel IV secolo* (Rome: Institutum Patristicum Augustinianum, 1975), 298; Paul Burns, *Christology in Hilary of Poitiers' Commentary on Matthew*, Studia ephemeridis "Augustinianum" (Rome: Institutum Patristicum Augustinianum, 1981), 22, 33, et passim; R. P. C. Hanson, *The Search for the Christian Doctrine of God* (Edinburgh: T & T Clark, 1988), 473.

The problem here is that there exists no unequivocal evidence that Hilary was familiar with the events that transpired prior to and during the western council held at Arles (353) until the time of his own exile.[82] Three years after Arles, Hilary states that he became aware of the ecclesiastical-political issues that dominated the proceedings there[83] and, later, in the council of Milan (355). It is at this time when Hilary also first learned of the Nicene creed: "Though I was regenerated long ago and for some time have been a bishop, I never heard the Nicene creed (*fidem*) until I was about to be exiled."[84] Whether he means by this statement that he had never heard the Nicene creed actually recited or that he simply had never before learned of it, the difference is not a large one. The upshot is that this western bishop had had no reason to use the creed, much less integrate it into his theological understanding. This was not unusual for western bishops at this time.[85] By 356 Hilary himself was condemned at Béziers and his remark about having just learned of the Nicene creed is probably a reference to the events that had transpired the year before at the council of Milan.[86]

But none of this awareness, either of identifiable "Arian" arguments or of pro-Nicene refutations, is evidenced in the kinds of concerns raised in the Matthean commentary.[87] Despite re-

---

82. Since the council of Sirmium (351), Constantius II was eager to have a more uniform understanding of the faith inculcated among the western bishops. There was much vacillation on all sides over which confession was the best expression of the catholic faith, but it seemed to Constantius that the Nicene creed was too schismatic. As an unfortunate tribute to the emperor's zeal, the councils of Arles and Milan (355) were scenes where dissenting bishops were banished: Paulinus at Arles (353), and Dionysius of Milan, Eusebius of Vercelli, Lucifer of Cagliari at Milan (355). It is certain that a formula of faith was submitted at these councils for signatures, though it is difficult to be certain about its exact content.

83. *CAP* B.I.6 (CSEL 65.102).

84. *De synodis* 91: *Regeneratus pridem et in episcopatu aliquantisper manens fidem Nicaenam nunquam nisi exsulaturus audivi.*

85. J. Ulrich, "Nicaea and the West," *VC* 51 (1997): 10–24.

86. When Eusebius of Vercelli presented the Nicene creed for signatures at the synod of Milan, an emotional outburst from Valens of Mursa, a long-time opponent of Athanasius, scuttled the attempt, and the synod concluded with a majority of western bishops endorsing the decisions made at Arles. See *Liber I ad Constantium* 8 (CSEL 65.186–87).

87. As I argued in "Defining Orthodoxy in Hilary of Poitiers' *Commentarium in Matthaeum*," *JECS* 9 (2001): 151–71.

cent attempts to "hear" echoes of the theological controversies that Hilary would encounter after his exile, there is a manifest lack of such evidence in the commentary. It is most feasible, therefore, to place its composition before 353. Since the conciliar document that emerged from Arles was sent around to western bishops for signatures,[88] as were the decisions of Milan (355), it seems the most likely venue in which Hilary and many other western bishops were shocked out of their relative ignorance by the doctrinal issues that had been afflicting the east for so long.[89] Undoubtedly, this was the context as a result of which Hilary says he heard for the first time the Nicene creed before his exile.[90]

What is clear about the character of this commentary is that it was not written with a polemical agenda.[91] To be sure, several kinds of detractors from the catholic faith are mentioned: Hilary briefly discusses or simply alludes to opponents with nebulous-sounding phrases such as "many irreligious people" (1.3) and "very depraved men" who claim that Mary could not have borne Christ as a virgin, or "the view of heretics" (5.8) with regard to what kind of body the believer will possess at the resurrection, or those who "have boiled over into various heretical allegiances" "by divesting the Lord of the dignity and communion with the Father's substance" (12.18). The latter charge is most serious, and is mentioned again in 31.3, a passage where Hilary is thought to be refuting "Arian" contemporaries. The heretical individuals or groups, however, are described as living potentially commendable lives and capable of understanding the Gospels. Given these designations, it seems that the unnamed opponents are a concern to the degree that it suits Hilary's pastoral and didactic purposes, rather than that he is confronting an actual situation that requires urgent refutation. The remarkable lack of hostil-

---

88. *Ep. ad Const. per Luciferum* 4 (CSEL 65.92, lines 5–7). This conciliar letter, Liberius of Rome informs us, circulated throughout Italy, but also almost certainly elsewhere such as Gaul.

89. It cannot be a coincidence that Hilary begins the narrative of *Adversus Valentem et Ursacium* with the events at Arles (353).

90. *De syn.* 91.

91. J. H. Reinkens, *Hilarius von Poitiers* (Schaffhausen, 1884), 5–60; C. F. A. Borchardt, *Hilary of Poitiers' Role in the Arian Struggle* (The Hague: Martinus Nijhoff, 1966), 13–17.

ity, when compared to Hilary's later works, written when he has actually engaged anti-Nicene antagonists, adds further corroboration that they were not the target of the commentary. There is no need to place the commentary chronologically any later than 353.

The most important theological consideration throughout the work is the need to preserve a categorical separation between *spiritus* (that is, divinity) and *corpus*. The great sin of blasphemy against the Holy Spirit, according to the commentary, is to regard the human Christ as man only and not God in the flesh. Hilary never tires of drawing this point out of a large number of Matthean passages. When the devil "heard his name *Satan* as a designation for his crimes, he realized that the Lord his God would have to be worshiped in a man" (*In Matt.* 3.5).[92] "But the Lord's works incited jealousy among the Pharisees, and they took counsel against him because they regarded him with the body as a man, and did not understand him to be God in his works" (*In Matt.* 12.8).[93] Related to, if not part of, their error (that is, in *In Matt.* 14.1) are those who attribute weakness to Christ's divinity because of his sufferings. Hilary warns his readers, in *In Matt.* 6.1, that "it is not appropriate that we treat the Incarnation of the Word of God, the mystery of his Passion, and the power of his Resurrection haphazardly, nor should we present it incompetently or carelessly" because there are those who "would turn it against us, shattering our ignorance and our faith with stinging points of contradiction." Presumably the "points of contradiction" posed are related to impugning the eternal substance with the weakness of the flesh (see *In Matt.* 31.2). We need to ask who the contemporaries are in Gaul asserting this position.

Surely Hilary would have known from the past that another interpretation of what modern writers have called "Spirit-Christology"[94] had often led to "monarchian" interpretations of the Incarnation. Tertullian was an obvious resource to draw

92. *In Matt.* 3.5 (SC 254.118).
93. *In Matt.* 12.8 (SC 254.274).
94. See Alois Grillmeier, *Christ in Christian Tradition*, trans. J. S. Bowden (London, 1965; rev. ed., Atlanta and London: John Knox Press, 1975), vol. 1, 88, who refers to "Spirit Christology" as the identification of the divine element in Jesus as Spirit, and the human element as body or flesh.

upon. The logic of the "adoptionist" position was this: if the Divine is susceptible to suffering, it could not possess the nature of God infinite. Since the Son surely was changed and transformed by his physical nature, he could not share the same divinity as God. One hundred and fifty years before Hilary, Tertullian wrote against one of the monarchian positions:

... we must also enquire about this, how the Word was made flesh, whether as transformed into flesh or as having clothed himself with flesh. Certainly as having clothed himself. God however must necessarily be believed to be immutable and untransformable, as being eternal. But change of form is a destruction of what was there first: for everything that is transformed into something else ceases to be what it was and begins to be what it was not.[95]

As a proponent of spirit-flesh Christology himself, Hilary was already familiar with the problem of using the same Christological "model" for an adoptionism that lent itself to the easy endorsement of a "low Christology," that attributed passibility to the divine Son and so reduced the incarnate Son's divine status in relation to the Father.[96] There are numerous instances of Hilary's opposition to this interpretation. For instance, Mt 10.40, "Whoever receives you receives me, and whoever receives me, receives him who sent me," makes plain that our reception of Christ is the same as receiving the Father because "there is no other in Christ than God himself" (*In Matt.* 10.27). Likewise, in 14.2: "Plainly he was the son of a carpenter who hammers on iron with fire, he who smelts all the power of this world by his judgment, and who gives form to matter all for the benefit of humanity."

Hilary was not simply seeking sanction from theologies of the past as if he were unaware of or ignoring his contemporary situation. Nor was he merely reproducing Tertullian's or Novatian's thought. It is more plausible to envision Spirit (divine)-flesh theology as the norm for "western" Christology prior to

---

95. *Adv. Prax.* 27, trans. E. Evans, *Tertullian's Treatise Against Praxeas* (London: SPCK, 1948), 173.

96. Tertullian, *Adv. Prax.* 27: "They say that the Son is the flesh, that is, the Man, Jesus, while the Father is the Spirit, that is, God, Christ. Those who contend that the Father and the Son are one and the same, now begin to divide them rather than to call them one" (trans. Evans, 172).

the 360s, used with at least two different applications. The first is related to the kind of adoptionism associated with the names of Euphratas (of Cologne) and Photinus (of Sirmium), both of whom were condemned for "Sabellianism" in 345 and 351 respectively.[97] The second application is Hilary's usage of the substantial distinction between spirit and flesh; that is, the "Spirit" refers to the divine element in Jesus.[98] This describes the views of contemporaries such as Potamius of Lisbon, who sided with anti-Nicene theology in the later 350s, and is quoted as teaching that "in the flesh and spirit of Christ, coagulated through Mary's blood and reduced to a single body, was made the passible God (*passibilem Deum factum*)."[99] This is the doctrine that Hilary opposes in the Commentary. Hilary was on guard against a theological exegesis that divided the divine Word from the divine Word in the flesh (the divine Word incarnate). And it is not unlikely that Hilary's condemnation at Béziers had to do with his opposition to the view that Christ was the passible God—a position that fits a pre-Nicene Christological scenario as much as it does a post-Nicene.[100]

97. At the council of Cologne, Euphratas was charged with denying that Christ is God (*Christum Deum negat*), and for asserting that Christ was only a man. Significantly, the council accused him of blaspheming the Holy Spirit by denying that *Christum Deum dei filium*, that is, "Christ is God, the Son of God" (7; 14), which is especially informative in light of Hilary's *In Matt.* 12.17, which states that the blasphemy of the Spirit is *Christo negare quod Dei sit . . . quia et in Christo Deus et Christus in Deo sit* ("to deny that Christ is of God . . . because God is in Christ and Christ is in God").

Against Photinus and his alleged teacher Marcellus, the letter from the eastern bishops from Serdica (343) condemns anyone who says, *Christum non esse Deum, aut ante aevum non fuisse Christum, neque filium dei . . .* ("that Christ is not God, or that he was not Christ before the ages, or that he is not the Son of God"; *CAP* A.IV.2, CSEL 65.73). At the same time as the proceedings were held at Cologne, Photinus was under investigation and twice condemned: in Milan (345) and Rome (347).

98. As one finds in Irenaeus; see Anthony Briggman, "Spirit-Christology in Irenaeus: A Closer Look," *VC* 66 (2012): 1–19.

99. Quoted by Phoebadius of Agen, *Contra Arrianos* 5.1. This is the only indisputable text that comes from Potamius.

100. If we accept Alfred Feder's reconstruction of Hilary's *Against Valens and Ursacius* (in CSEL 65.191–93), the preface indicates that he had been labeled a heretic for his "spurning the company of the wicked and association with the faithless." Instead of "corrupting the Gospel truth with falsehood," he declares that he was happily associated with "my own creed," by which he meant, not Nicaea, but his baptismal formula.

Thus the reader of Hilary's text is rewarded with valuable insights that open a unique, if limited, window into the doctrinal and exegetical milieu of the west some twenty-five years after the council of Nicaea.[101] What one finds is that western bishops either still did not know of the Nicene creed or had little use for such a controversial formula until the kind of ecclesiastical-imperial politics that had plagued the east began to disrupt Latin sees in the mid-350s.

### INCARNATION

While Hilary wants to emphasize that Christ was fully human (*homo totus*),[102] and that our salvation is dependent upon the truth "that he became man to forgive men's sins and to obtain the resurrection of their bodies,"[103] the more dominant preoccupation for Hilary was convincing the reader not to attribute Christ's human qualities and limitations to his divine nature. Because the Son was in and from God the Father, Christ shared the Father's divinity, which meant that there was no limitation of the divine power within him, regardless of the weaknesses of his humanity.

When a great crowd had assembled together, he then climbed up and taught them from the mountain. In other words, having situated himself on the height of the Father's majesty, he laid down the precepts of heavenly life. For he could not have delivered eternal principles had he not been situated in eternity.[104]

Of paramount importance to an orthodox understanding of the incarnate Son of God was avoiding any confusion be-

---

101. For a fuller exposition of Hilary's doctrinal perspective, see D. H. Williams, "Defining Orthodoxy in Hilary of Poitiers' *Commentarium in Matthaeum*," *JECS* 9 (2001): 151–71.

102. Cf. 13.5–7, where the Lord compares himself to a grain of wheat that falls to the ground and dies, or to a treasure buried in a field, signifying how "God has been found in a man."

103. *In Matt.* 8.7. Elsewhere Hilary claims that the entire mystery of our salvation has been accomplished in and through the humanity of Christ. For the Commentary's language of *salus* in Jesus' Incarnation, including his Baptism and Passion, see Thomas Buffer, '*Salus' in St. Hilary of Poitiers* (Rome: Pontificia Universitas Gregoriana, 2002), 33–44.

104. *In Matt.* 4.1.

tween the Son's divine and human selves. As the reader moves through the different parables and events in the Gospel, he should never mistake the Lord's humility for any impotency of his divine power. In fact, the unforgivable sin is making this very mistake. It is denying the Son's divinity by attributing to him human weakness: "For who is so completely beyond pardon as one who denies that Christ is of God, or repudiates that the substance of the Spirit of the Father resides in him?"[105]

An important characteristic that helps in establishing the Commentary's *terminus ad quem* is the way Hilary defines his incarnational theology according to a two-stage Logos, and does not exhibit an awareness of the doctrine of the Son's eternal generation. In the most succinct passage on how the Son came from the Father, in 16.4, Hilary insists that the process of divine birth is "from the eternal God ... God the Son had proceeded, to whom belongs eternity from his eternal Parent." We are then told that the Son "received" (*accepit*) deity from his eternal Parent, and that "he received (*accepit*) that which he was and is born the Word which was always in the Father." All who ponder this mystery should likewise know that "he was born from what he was, and that he possesses that into which he is born because he is himself in possession of what he was before he was born."[106] This is language strongly reminiscent of, if not directly drawn from, Novatian's *De trinitate* 31, where the Son receives his eternality from the eternity of the Father. It has been suggested that Novatian freed the idea of generation from the time of creation, but this is premature. Granted, the Son is not generated simply for creation, and the only source for the Son's generation is the eternal substance of God; nevertheless, procession for Novatian is still linked (as it is for Tertullian) to temporal stages in which the Son came forth as the visible God *after* the Father.

The same suggestion of the twin stages of the Word occurs in *In Matt.* 31.3, where the Son was in the Father before he "proceeded" as an independent entity.[107] Citing Jn 1.1, Hilary writes that "he is himself in possession of what he was before he was born, [namely,] that the one who generated and the one who is

---

105. *In Matt.* 12.17.          106. *In Matt.* 31.3.
107. Hanson, *The Search*, 468.

begotten have the same eternity." It has been rightly noted that Hilary is making a distinction of time in the career of the Word, that is, between "before he was born," that is, that which he was in the Father, and that which he possessed by means of his birth once he proceeded from the Father. Such a position negates the eternal generation of the Son,[108] since he is eternal, not because his birth is eternal, but because by his birth he comes into full possession of the eternal divinity. This undermines the idea that Hilary had been exposed to the terminology and emphases which governed pro-Nicene theology. Significantly, Hilary never discusses or alludes to Jn 6.38, 10.30, 10.38, 14.11, or any of the Johannine proof-texts (except the prologue of John on this one occasion) so commonly employed in "Nicene-Arian" debates and found freely in De trinitate 3 and elsewhere.

There are at least two other themes that imply that Hilary's Commentary, theologically speaking, is just as indebted to and structured around the Christology of the mid-third century as that of the fourth. First, his understanding of the Son originating from the Father is completely ignorant of the fourth century's view of eternal generation;[109] and, secondly, the Logos or Spirit of God temporarily inhabited the flesh produced by Mary. This is most evident when Hilary states (In Matt. 3.2) that the Son's virtus was not affected by the forty days of fasting, but had "abandoned the humanity from his nature," and that Christ's cry unto God from the cross was the voice of the body as it was departing from the Word of God.[110] By all counts,

108. Smulders, La doctrine trinitaire, 78–79: "L'éternité du Fils consiste en ce qu'il est éternel par celui qui l'a engendré, c'est-à-dire du fait que lui a été communiquée la nature éternelle du Père. Ainsi donc, même ici, le Fils ne semble pas éternel par sa propre personnalité, mais parce que le Père lui a donné une nature qui, en elle-même, est éternelle" (p. 79).

109. Hilary makes a distinction of time in the career of the Word: "before he was born," that which he was in the Father; and that which he possessed by means of his birth once he proceeded from the Father. See Smulders, La doctrine trinitaire, 78–79.

110. In Matt. 33.6 (SC 258.254). On the Sermon on the Mount, In Matt. 4.1 (SC 254.120), Christ is said to have "yielded the service of his mouth to the movement of the Spirit's eloquence." See Tertullian, Adv. Prax. 26.4–6 (CCSL 2.1196–97); 27.6–7 (CCSL 2.1198–99); 30.2 (CCSL 2.1203). The sermo dei was not transformed by the Incarnation, but remained unchanged as divine substance.

this is a striking statement for someone to make in the 350s as a means of communicating the separation of the two natures. And indeed, Hilary creates a wide chasm between the divine spirit of Christ and the earthly Jesus in order to protect the integrity of the former. In the Commentary this gulf is most accentuated by his explanation of how the divine Christ could experience human suffering. There were those unnamed persons who claimed that the text clearly showed how "sorrow had occurred in God and the fear of his coming Passion weakened him."[111]

Some want to attach the neediness to his spirit because of the body's weakness, as if the taking of flesh in its feeble condition corrupted the power of his incorruptible substance, or as if eternity received a fragile nature. If he is sad to the point of fear, if weak to the point of pain, if anxious to the point of death, eternity will be subjected to corruption, and thus it will fall ...

Hilary responded by negating the reality of the force of human suffering on the divine self. In no sense was the divine in Jesus affected by his agonies in the garden. Since Hilary worked on the theological assumption that the Divine Logos was the soul of the human body, it was not difficult for him to compartmentalize the legitimate functions of the body and immutable eternity of the Spirit.

In sum, what the commentary says and does not say are equally important. The absence of any pro-Nicene theology, much less a defense of or an attack upon a creed, is noteworthy. Certainly Hilary would have known of the doctrinal tensions of the day. And yet, the commentary, as we have it (the preface and ending are lost), shows no awareness of Nicaea, nor are there identifiable refutations of "Arian" arguments.[112]

### JUSTIFICATION BY FAITH

Throughout the Commentary there is an unambiguous emphasis on the theology that stems from Paul's epistles, especially with regard to the concept of being justified through faith.

---

111. *In Matt.* 31.2.
112. See Williams, "Defining Orthodoxy," *JECS* 9 (2001): 151–71.

Here, some sixty years before Augustine and lacking the Orig-
enist contributions, Hilary follows little or no precedent. About
twenty occurrences of the phrase *fides iustificat* (or *fidei iustifica-
tio*) are to be found expressing an interpretation germane to
an understanding of the Gospel. It would seem that Hilary's
interest involves much more than mere restatements of Pauline
passages. In fact, Hilary is the first Christian theologian explicitly to have formulated what Paul left implicit by referring to
God's work of grace in the phrase *fides sola iustificat:* "Because
faith alone justifies ... publicans and prostitutes will be first in
the Kingdom of heaven" (Mt 21.15).

The Pauline way of expressing faith can also account for Hilary's incarnational theology. For Hilary, as it was for Paul, the
truth of the Gospel cannot be understood if one does not recognize God working in Christ. In 2 Cor 4.4–6 the unbeliever
perishes, being blinded by the devil, because he does not see
"the light of the gospel of the glory of Christ, who is the likeness of God" (RSV). The light of the knowledge of the glory of
God is found in the face of Jesus Christ. This is where the devil
utterly failed in his three temptations of Jesus in Mt 3:

Because the devil was afraid of losing the opportunity of tempting him
whom he regarded as man, he acted rashly. For he had enticed Adam
and led him into death by deception. Yet it was fitting, given the devil's
wickedness and evil deeds, that he should be overcome by a man in
whose death and calamity he gloried. He who had begrudged God's
blessings to humanity was not able to understand that God was in the
man before his temptation.[113]

Hilary is quite conscious of how divine revelation came by
stages through stages of human history. Thus a prominent part
of God's purposes, as Hilary describes it, is God's offer of justification to the pagans or Gentiles as the capstone of salvation
history. For example, the withered fig tree in Mt 21 is said to be
a figure of the chief priests and Pharisees who made complex
the simple way of grace because they "were not justified by faith,
nor did they return through repentance to salvation."[114] Unlike
the Jews, who clung to the Law for righteousness, "the pagans

113. *In Matt.* 3.1.
114. *In Matt.* 21.15.

are made righteous by the entry of the Savior, and he is come for their sakes."[115] The message of salvation is that the bonds of the Law, chained by its acknowledgment of sin, are loosed "when one learns the freedom of the Gospel."[116] While it is true that the Law proclaimed Christ and his coming (Lk 24.44–47), it became a liability when used as an end in itself.

Marcionism poses no threat, but Hilary is careful not to reduce the Old Testament functionally to a position of virtual worthlessness. Paul's description in Romans 11 of Israel's place in God's redemptive scheme is an implicit backdrop to the bishop's thinking. The basis of the Gentiles' salvation is derived from Israel's transgression of disobedience; nonetheless, Israel is still among the elect and will ultimately be saved (Rom 11.25–32). In the parable of the talents (Mt 25.14–30), Hilary shows how true believers in the Old Testament are not made righteous by their devotion to the Law, and yet, by their obedience to the divine precepts of the Law, they do demonstrate a faith that corresponds to the life-giving precepts of the Gospel. Indeed, Hilary points out that the servant who had gained five talents besides the five talents he was given had performed obedience according to the ten precepts of the five books of Moses. The servant was only able to do so because he had acted in faith upon adherence to the Law, through the grace of the Gospel's justification. He is told, therefore, to enter the joy of the Lord; that is, he is received in the honor of Christ's glory (Mt 27.7).

Hilary's emphasis on the bestowal of God's righteousness upon a helpless race before the demands of the Law represents a more pronounced application of this side of Paul's thought than is perceptible in any previous writer. There is the strong likelihood that Hilary's commentary was the earliest stimulus for the revival of Pauline studies in the west during the last decades of the fourth century. Within a decade of Hilary's work a concerted interest in Pauline texts and themes is evident among such widely divergent thinkers as Marius Victorinus, Augustine, the Donatist Tyconius, Pelagius, and Priscillian of

115. *In Matt.* 21.2.
116. *In Matt.* 11.2. Cf. 11.8 ("freedom of life in Christ"); 19.10 ("freedom of the Gospel"); 31.11 ("liberty of the Gospel").

Avila (reputed, albeit wrongly, to be a neo-Manichaean). All of these wrote commentaries on all or some of Paul's letters. Augustine's thought after becoming a presbyter shows that he was a beneficiary of this "revival," and that he stood in a succession of writers who benefited from the repercussions of Pauline theology shaping Latin hermeneutics.[117]

### TITLE OF THE COMMENTARY

Like Hilary's subsequent works, such as *Epistula de synodis*[118] and *De trinitate*,[119] which were entitled (somewhat misleadingly) by a later hand, he never seems to have assigned a definitive name to his first known scriptural exposition. The *incipit* varies widely among the medieval manuscripts, using descriptors in the titles such as *Tractatus, Expositio, Commentarium,* or simply *In* or *Super Matthaeum*. The latter epithet was the only one known to Abelard and Aquinas. John Cassian called Hilary's work an "exposition of the Gospel according to Matthew," whereas Jerome makes reference to it on three occasions using the word *commentarii*.[120] This latter term, however, is always used in the plural and liberally applied by Jerome when speaking of other Latin exegetical works, for example, those of Reticius of Autun (c. 314), Victorinus of Poetovio, and Fortunatianus of Aquileia.[121]

117. Two writers produced commentaries on all the Pauline Epistles: "Ambrosiaster" and Pelagius (in brief form). Marius Victorinus in the 360s wrote on Ephesians, Galatians, and Philippians, and Jerome on Galatians, Ephesians, and Philemon.
118. *De synodis* does not seem to have been used before 1000 CE. In the manuscript tradition, one finds the text designated in several other ways: *Liber XIII* (following *De trinitate libri XII*), *De exilio, Tractatus (sancti) Hilar(i)i, Liber fidei catholicae contra Arrianos et praevaricatores Arrianis adquiescentes, Contra omnes haereses*. See M. Durst, "Die *Epistula de synodis* des Hilarius von Poitiers—Probleme der Textkonstitution," in *Textsorten und Textkritik. Tagungsbeiträge,* 59–87, ÖAW.PH Sitzungsberichte 693 (Vienna, 2002). A critical edition of *De synodis* is forthcoming in the SC series.
119. Smulders, CCSL 62–62A (1979).
120. *Ep.* 20. 1; *De viris illust.* 100; *Hom. Orig. in Lucam,* praef.
121. *On the Song of Songs* by Reticius, c. 314 (see *De viris illust.* 82), which does not survive; Victorinus is said to have written *commentarii* on Genesis, Exodus, Leviticus, Isaiah, Ezekiel, Habakkuk, Ecclesiastes, Song of Songs, and on Revelation (see *De viris. illust.* 74); Fortunatianus's work is described as follows: *in evangelia ... brevi sermone et rustico scripsit commentarios* (see *De viris illust.* 97).

Two small hints come from the text itself which may reveal Hilary's own view of it. Though it is an ambiguous word, Hilary describes his exposition as "our book" when he is making reference to an earlier typology.[122] Another hint comes from 5.1: "De oratione autem sacramento necessitate nos commentandi Cyprianus vir sanctae memoriae liberavit," which shows that Hilary may well have thought of his work as a "commentary,"[123] though certainly not in any formal sense that the word will later acquire. In general, scholars have tended to depend on the usage of Jerome, who also refers to the work simply as *in Matthaeum* when writing his own commentary on Matthew's Gospel.[124] This description, like that of *commentarii*, is another characterization of the work, rather than titular. For lack of a decisive solution we will content ourselves with the Hieronymian usage, which Doignon follows, since its ambiguity seems best in reflecting Hilary's own silence on the matter.

TEXT

With minor corrections, the critical edition used for this translation is that of Jean Doignon, *Hilaire de Poitiers: Sur Matthieu* (Paris, 1978), volumes 254 and 258 of the Sources chrétiennes series. Doignon's achievement represents the first critical edition of Hilary's Matthean commentary since Pierre Coustant's publication of the bishop's extant works in 1693. In the intervening three centuries, four editions of the commentary appeared, though each was either a reimpression or only a slightly edited version of Coustant.[125] Doignon has provided a greater wealth of manuscript evidence for reconstruction of the text[126] than was

---

122. *In Matt.* 2.2.
123. Coustant's *Admonitio* 8 (PL 10:912B).
124. *In Matt.*, praef.: *Legisse me fateor ante annos plurimos in Matthaeum ... Latinorum Hilarii, Victorini, Fortunatiani opuscula* (SC 242.68).
125. *Hilarii (S.) Opera*, Petr. Ant. Bernam et Jac. Vallarsium (Verona, 1730); *S. Hilarii ... opera omnia*, ed. Fr. Oberthür (Würzburg, 1785); *S. Hilarii, Opera: In evangelium Matthaei commentarius*, ed. A. B. Caillau (Paris, 1830); *Sancti Hilarii ... Opera Omnia*, PL 9, ed. J.-P. Migne (Paris, 1844). For a description of texts before Coustant, see Paul Burns, *Christology in Hilary of Poitiers' Commentary on Matthew*, 14 n.23.
126. Some fourteen manuscripts are consulted, and a number of frag-

previously available, using no less than twenty-four manuscripts, eight of these going back to the Carolingian period. There are three other manuscripts containing the commentary listed by A. Casamassa,[127] which are unfortunately not utilized in this edition: Reginensis, Vat. lat. 212 (8th century); Salisbury Cathedral 124 (12th century); and Cheltenham Philipps Library 3733 (13th century). The first one is very fragmentary; nevertheless, any future revisions of Doignon's text will have to take these into account besides any others that come to light.

Doignon rightly removed the *capitula* or *canones* (chapter headings) from the body of the text which Coustant and early manuscripts had incorporated. These are decidedly written by a later hand.[128] Nor do all the manuscripts share the same division of the commentary into thirty-three chapters. At most, one can postulate that because the earlier manuscripts are divided in this way, it is likely that there existed very early, perhaps from the beginning, a breakdown of the work into numbered sections, although they are not always uniform. Following Doignon's edition, I have placed the *capitula* at the end of the commentary, though it must be admitted that they add very little toward a better understanding of the text. In two instances, the content of a *capitulum* is actually misleading, while several others simply quote the opening biblical text with no further information as to what Hilary taught. The numeration of the *capitula* also varies in the manuscript tradition. Some manuscripts join Chapters 27 and 28, whereas others separate the two, resulting in thirty-four *capitula*. For the list of the *capitula*, see Appendix II.

The structuring of the commentary does not consistently

---

ments are discussed, in *Sur Matthieu,* 46–54. Of these, the primary witnesses or "family α" are the four: Laureshamensis, Vatican, Palatine lat. 167 (end of 9th or early 10th century); Reginensis, Vatican, Reg. lat 314a (11th century); Excubiensis, Grenoble, Bibl. mun., 263 (428) (12th century); and Parisinus, Paris, Bibl. Nat., lat 2083 (13th–14th century).

127. "Note sul *Commentarius in Matthaeum* di Ilario di Poitiers," *Scritti Patristici* I, 211.

128. H. Jeannotte, "Les 'capitula' du *Commentarium in Matthaeum* de saint Hilaire de Poitiers," *Biblische Zeitschrift* 10 (1912): 36–45. Coustant includes them in the text though he assembles arguments against their authenticity (PL 10:913A–C).

follow the traditional divisions of the Gospel. After Chapter 19 Hilary no longer matches the chapters of the commentary with the Gospel's chapters. *In Matt.* 20.1 continues with Mt 19.25 and extends the commentary on Mt 19 until 20.5. Whereas Hilary produced long chapters when he dealt with long chapters of the Gospel, he shows no such compunction to keep his work in parallel. In fact, the average length of a chapter is shorter after Chapter 14; in some cases, much shorter. Chapters 28 and 29 of *In Matt.* have only two sections each.

For his reading of Matthew, Hilary used a version of the Old Latin text of the Gospels, although no one of the variations recorded in Adolf Jülicher's book *Itala: Das Neue Testament in Altlateinischer Überlieferung: I. Matthäus Evangelium* is followed consistently.[129] We may safely assume that the version used by Hilary was one shared by fellow clergy in the Provincia Aquitania.

### THE PREFACE

The preface of the commentary was probably lost sometime after the middle of the fifth century. That there originally existed a preface is suggested by 2.1, which opens with "ut quia diximus," and seems not to be in reference to anything said in the first chapter. Since Hilary took care to begin his three other major works with a prologue, it is a likely inference that he would have done the same with this commentary. The habit of prefacing a work is itself part of the rhetorical inheritance that consistently marked Hilary's literary efforts.[130] His other large-scale scriptural exposition, on the Psalms, contains a lengthy prologue,[131] as does *De trinitate,* whose first book serves as a prefatory overview for the rest of the treatise.[132] Hilary's *Tractatus mysteriorum* opens with a short prologue, though now slightly corrupted.[133]

---

129. For Jülicher's own method in distinguishing an "Itala" format from an African ("Afra"), see Philip Burton, *The Old Latin Gospels—A Study of their Texts and Language* (Oxford: Oxford University Press, 2000), 9–11.

130. Doignon, *Hilaire de Poitiers,* 228.

131. PL 9:231D–247B.

132. SC 443.202–73.

133. SC 19.72–75. The preface is corrupt in that immediately following the

Three small portions of the commentary's missing preface
are allegedly preserved by John Cassian, who says he is quoting from it: "To begin with, it was necessary for us that the
Only-begotten God, born as a man, should be known for our
sakes"; "To the end that he who was God should be born as
man which he was not"; and, "Thirdly, then, it was appropriate
that as God was born as man in the world ..." (*Contra Nestorium*
7.24.3).[134] Doignon casts doubt on the accuracy of the passages
since it appears that Cassian's locutions of Christ as "unigenitus" or "genitus" are not found in the lexicography of Hilary's
commentary.[135] With qualification, such skepticism may be warranted since these theological terms are found only later in *De
trinitate*, and used at a time when Hilary's later role as a heroic
"anti-Arian" overshadowed the distinction of his early career.
Doignon also argues that Cassian's use of passages from Ambrose of Milan show the tendency of the former to amalgamate
texts rather than quote them directly—a practice not uncommon for the ancients.[136] While the sentiments expressed by Cassian are in keeping with the Christological and incarnational
purposes of Hilary's commentary,[137] we cannot verify whether
they are sufficiently accurate so as to be considered actual portions of the missing text.

The ending of the commentary seems, likewise, corrupt. It
abruptly ends in a condensed observation about the guards' behavior in Mt 28.11–15. Assuming the final portion of commen-

---

first word there is a lacuna of unknown length which ends in the middle of a
sentence.

134. *erat namque primum necessarium nobis, ut unigenitus deus nostri causa homo
natus cognosceretur ... ad id quod deus erat homo, id quod tum non erat, gigneretur
... tertium deinceps illud congruum fuit, ut, quia deus homo genitus in mundo* (CSEL
17.383). Cf. Doignon, *Hilaire de Poitiers*, 229 n.3. Alcuin also quotes from Hilary's preface, but he seems only to know Cassian's citation (PL 10:912C).

135. *Hilaire de Poitiers*, 229 n.4. Although Hilary uses the verbal form *genuit*
with reference to the Son's eternal birth (31.3). Moreover, Tertullian uses *unigenitus* in *Adv. Prax.* and elsewhere.

136. Thus Doignon calls Cassian's three passages not extracts from Hilary's prologue but florilegia ("florilège hilarien"), a summarized version of
the original text.

137. Less convincingly, Doignon maintains that Cassian's remarks are derived from *In Matt.* 2.5, where the baptism of Jesus is described and where Hilary introduces Jesus' Sermon on the Mount; *Hilaire de Poitiers*, 229 n.3.

tary is missing, it is quite a loss since we do not know how Hilary treated the triadic invocation of God in 28.19. We also do not know whether an epilogue was appended. That none of the extant manuscripts contains an ending beyond what we have could imply that Hilary stopped writing at 28.15, but this is unlikely. The same thing could be said for the prologue, which is likewise missing from all the manuscripts.

## TRANSLATION

In the making of this translation I attempted to render it into idiomatic English without too often violating the original word order and sentence structure. Hilary has a unique rhetorical style that deserves as much preservation as is possible in an English translation. It is inevitable that in trying to do justice to the original phrasing of a sentence, which is crucial for Hilary's own method of interpretation, a more formal approach was needed.

It became apparent from the start of the project that different English words would have to be used for the same Latin term, since certain Latin words (for example, *ratio*) carried nuances that required variation. This is especially the case for well-educated writers such as Hilary. Where I have tried to be more uniform is in the rendering of *potestas* as "authority," and *virtus* as "power" instead of "virtue," which tends to cloud the original meaning. I have also translated *sacramentum* as "mystery" in order to retain the religious diversity of the term, though I have sometimes simply transliterated the word ("sacrament") when it proved to be more useful for conveying the writer's intent. The difficulty with using "sacrament" is that it sounds as if Hilary had a sacramental theology, but this is at best dubious in this commentary.

# COMMENTARY ON
# MATTHEW

# CHAPTER ONE

*[Preface missing]*[1]

HEREAS MATTHEW followed the order[2] of royal succession, Luke reckons it according to priestly origin. Each writer is using a [different] criterion, one tracing the Lord's bloodline,[3] and the other by means of his tribe. It is quite right to present the sequence of the Lord's generation[4] in this way since the association of the priestly and royal ancestry[5] inaugurated by David in his marriage is thereafter confirmed through the lineage[6] of Shealtiel to Zerubbabel.[7]

And so while Matthew established his paternal origin which stemmed from Judah, Luke teaches that the lineage proceeded through Nathan from the tribe of Levi.[8] Each writer in his way has demonstrated the glory of the double genealogy of our Lord Jesus Christ, who is the eternal king and priest, even in his fleshly birth.[9] That his nativity is traced from Joseph rather than Mary does not matter, for there is one and the same bloodline for the entire ancestry.[10] Moreover, Matthew and Luke have given us a model, describing each of the fathers[11] not as much according to lineage as by a race of people who originated from one ancestry and who are encompassed within

---

1. See Appendix I.
2. *gradum.*
3. *cognationem.*
4. *generationis.*
5. Lit., "tribe" (*tribus*).
6. *genere.*
7. Cf. Jer 27.20; 28.4; 1 Chr 3.17. Shealtiel was son of Jeconiah, the King of Judah who had been taken captive by Nebuchadnezzar into Babylonia. From Shealtiel was born Zerubbabel, the leader of the first wave of those who returned from the Babylonian Captivity. "Shealtiel to Zerubbabel" refers to the time from the exile to the repossession of the land.

8. Lk 3.23–38. Cf. 1 Chr 3.5; Zec 12.12.

9. A prominent theme for Hilary in this commentary is that the earthly Incarnation of the Son in no way detracts from his full divinity.

10. *tribus.*

11. That is, the familial names listed in both genealogies.

a family of one succession and origin. For although he must be revealed as the son of David and Abraham, just as Matthew begins: *The book of the generations of Jesus Christ, son of David, son of Abraham,*[12] there is no difference whether someone is classified by an account[13] of their origin and lineage,[14] provided it is understood the families of the world began from one man.[15] Thus, as Joseph and Mary are from the same ancestry, so Joseph is shown to have proceeded from the lineage of Abraham, and the same is true of Mary. In fact, this is the principle,[16] which was preserved in the Law: namely, if the head of a family died without any sons, the next eldest brother of the same bloodline would accept the wife of the dead man.[17] Sons begotten by this arrangement were ascribed to the family of the dead man, and so the order of succession should continue for those who are the firstborn, accomplished either by name or by lineage, through the [acting] fathers of those who were later born.

2. Then there is the issue that (as we said,[18] given the reliability of the facts) the sequence of the Lord's generation agrees neither with the method of enumeration nor its order of succession so that a rationale of the [present] narrative might be sought.[19] There is a reason why the narration makes one kind of emphasis[20] and the facts say another, and yet another [rea-

12. Mt 1.1.
13. *numerus.*
14. In this instance *ordo* is functioning like *genus.*
15. I.e., Adam (Lk 3.37).
16. *ratio.*
17. Dt 25.5. Cf. Ru 4.5–9.
18. I am following here Doignon's reconstruction of the text, *ut, quia diximus* (*Sur Matt.* I.92), instead of PL 9:920A: *ut quia diximus,* in order to agree with *adferatur* and *dico* with an infinitive. This means that Hilary's remark at this point is not in reference to something he said in the (lost) preface, but to what he had just been saying in 1.1.
19. *rei ratio adferatur.* As with other patristic writers, Hilary understands contradictions in the text or seemingly nonsensical passages as grounds for searching for its deeper *ratio* (translated in this volume as "rationale" or "underlying principle"), which often leads to a spiritual or allegorical interpretation. All of Scripture contains a *ratio* instilled by the Spirit and meant for the believer to understand, depending on his or her spiritual ability to comprehend deeper truths.
20. *aliud.*

son] which is related to the whole, and then another is connected with their enumeration.[21] In fact, *from Abraham to David fourteen generations* are counted, and *from David to the deportation to Babylon fourteen generations,*[22] whereas in the books of the Kings seventeen generations are detected.[23] But there is not a problem here of falsehood or fault from an oversight. For three generations have been bypassed according to an underlying principle.[24] Joram begot Ahaziah; then Ahaziah begot Joash; after Joash, Amaziah; and from Amaziah, Azariah. But in Matthew, it is written that *Joram begot Azariah*[25] although the latter is fourth after him. It was done in this way because Joram begot Ahaziah from a pagan woman, that is, from the household of Ahab,[26] and it was declared by the prophet that not until the fourth generation would anyone from the household of Ahab sit on the throne of the kingdom of Israel.[27] By removing the disgrace of a pagan family and bypassing its ancestry, the royal origin of those to follow in the fourth generation is then counted. And although it is written that there are fourteen generations until Mary,[28] and thirteen are found in counting them, there can be no mistake for those who know that our Lord Jesus Christ has an origin not only from Mary, but in the procreation of his bodily nativity, his eternal significance is discovered.[29]

3. The explanation of his generation is simple. That he was "conceived by the Holy Spirit, born of the Virgin Mary"[30] is the

---

21. *in numero.*

22. Mt 1.17.

23. 1 Chr 3.10–15.

24. *ratione.*

25. Mt 1.18.

26. 2 Kgs 8.18, 25–27.

27. 2 Kgs 10.30, 15.12.

28. Mt 1.17.

29. Or some MSS: "in his bodily procreation, they perceive the significance of his eternal nativity." See SC 254, 94–95, n. 6.

30. Very probably a citation from a local credal statement. By way of comparison see (Ps.-) Hippolytus, *Apostolic Tradition* 21.15: *natus est de spiritu sancto* [*et*] *ex Maria Virgine.* This form in Hilary appears nowhere in Tertullian, Cyprian, Novatian, or the later creeds of the fourth century. The phrase *conceptus de spiritu sancto* just before *natus ex Maria virgine* is particularly unique; i.e., it differs from the Old Roman Creed or St. Gall. The latter, Connolly says, drew upon a version of the Apostles' Creed. Ambrose, *Exp. Symb.* 11, has two versions, including a Gallic version that has been expanded, *conceptus spiritu sancto, natus de Maria virgine.* R. H. Connolly, *The 'Explanatio Symboli ad Initiandos': A Work of Saint Ambrose* (Cambridge University Press, 1952), 12. This is not the Roman

message of all the prophets.[31] But many irreligious people and those who are complete strangers to spiritual teachings seize an opportunity in dealing with this matter by entertaining disgraceful notions concerning Mary[32] because it is written: *Before they came together, she was found with child*,[33] and again: *Do not be afraid to take your spouse*,[34] and again: *He did not know her until she gave birth*.[35] They do not remember that she was engaged to be married and that this was spoken to Joseph, who wanted to cast her out because he was a righteous man and did not want her to be judged by the law.[36] So that there would be no uncertainty about her offspring, Joseph therefore becomes a witness to Christ, who was "conceived by the Holy Spirit." It is

text, which is just *natus est de spiritu sancto, et Maria virgine* (cf. Leo, *Ad Flav.* 2). Hilary therefore knows of an older Gallic witness to what will closely resemble the Apostles' Creed and which is presumably functioning as the baptismal confession used at Poitiers. This is not so remarkable if, as generally accepted, the origin of the "Apostles' Creed" is in southwest Gaul or northeast Hispania (*qui conceptus est de spiritu sancto, natus ex Maria virgine*). Substantiation for the existence of a baptismal creed in use at Poitiers is found at the end of *De trin.* 12.57 (PL 10:472A), where Hilary claims fidelity to the "creed of my regeneration" (*quod in regenerationis meae Symbolo*).

31. That is, the message of Christ in the Old Testament (Lk 24.19, 28; 1 Cor 15.1–5).

32. The reference to the "many" who are *irreligiosi et a spiritali doctrina admodum alieni*, represents a specific group that Hilary knows and earnestly refutes. Given the adjectives he uses to describe these opponents, it is unlikely he is talking about the longstanding pagan slur that Mary was impregnated by a Roman soldier. Rather, the allusion is to adoptionist views of Christ as one born completely and only human and who is later imbued by the Divine Spirit. The idea is that Mary was not truly a virgin (Joseph was the father) and Christ's birth was remarkable, but not the birth of God incarnate. Coustant (PL 9:921D–922C) saw a parallel with Tertullian's attack on Hebion, dubiously known for a monarchian adoptionist view, "God ... sent his own son made from a woman ... a virgin, even though Hebion resists this" (*De virg. vel.* 6; cf. *De carne Chr.* 14.5). Hilary seems to have drawn on Tertullian's work at this point also for making the distinction between "woman" and "wife" with the purpose of arguing Mary is called "betrothed," and cannot be a "wife." So too there is a difference between "virgin" and "woman" such that the words are not always interchangeable as the Greek would indicate (*De virg. vel.* 5).

33. Mt 1.18.

34. Mt 1.20. Cf. the fuller quotation of this verse near the end of the paragraph.

35. Mt 1.25.

36. Hilary is saying two things at once: Joseph lived according to the Law and would not wed Mary, and yet he did not want to submit Mary to the religious authorities and to a likely death by stoning.

thereafter, because she had been engaged, that she was taken in marriage, and thus he knew her after the birth.[37] That is, the term *marriage*[38] applies to their relations, for she has been known by Joseph, not merely in terms of being legally related.[39] Finally, when Joseph was warned to cross over into Egypt, it was said: *Take the child and his mother,*[40] and, *Return with the child and his mother,*[41] and again in Luke, "And there was Joseph and his [the child's] mother."[42] However often reference is made to one or the other,[43] she is properly the mother of Christ, for it was not the case that she was called the wife of Joseph because she was not. But this also is the reason why the angel, indicating that she was engaged to Joseph, a righteous man,[44] called her espoused.[45] For as he said: *Joseph, son of David, do not be afraid to take Mary as your spouse.*[46] The name "fiancée"[47] acquired that of "spouse,"[48] and while she was recognized to be engaged *post partum,* she was revealed solely as the mother of Jesus.[49] Just as Joseph was considered righteous for his marriage to Mary, who was a virgin, so in her motherhood of Jesus the sanctity of her virginity was revealed.

4. And yet some very depraved men take from this the basis of their view that there were many brothers of our Lord as a point of tradition.[50] If there had been sons of Mary who were not rather produced from a previous marriage of Joseph's,[51]

---

37. *cognoscitur itaque post partum.*   38. *coniugis.*
39. *admiscetur.*   40. Mt 2.13.
41. Mt 2.20.
42. Lk 2.33. RSV reads, "And his father and his mother ..."
43. That is, to the two references about Joseph.
44. Mt 1.19.   45. *conjugem.*
46. Mt 1.20.   47. *conjunx.*
48. *sponsa.*

49. By this tortuous explanation Hilary is making a distinction between *conjunx,* which could mean espoused (*non cognoscitur*) or engaged, and *sponsa* (*cognoscitur*) or *uxor,* as a consummated espousal. Old Latin versions of Mt 1.24 read *conjunx* or *uxor* (*Itala,* 6). The point is to show Joseph is not the father of Christ because Mary remained a virgin.

50. *habuisse sit traditum.* Hilary never identifies the group of 1.4, but it appears to be a different one from those mentioned in 1.3.

51. An early interpretation that Joseph had sons from a first marriage is found in the *Protoevangelium* or *Proto-Gospel of James* 9.2 and *History of the Death of Joseph the Carpenter* 2.

Mary never would have been transferred to the apostle John as his mother at the time of the Passion, nor would the Lord have said to them both, "Woman, behold your son," and to John, "Behold your mother,"[52] unless perhaps he was leaving his disciple's filial love in order to comfort her who was left behind.

5. The appearance of the star which the Magi first apprehended reveals that the pagans were soon to profess belief in Christ. Men long opposed to a knowledge of divine understanding were about to understand that light which shone forth the moment it appeared.

Then there follows the offering of gifts, which represented their awareness of Christ's full identity:[53] the gold proclaims him as King, the incense as God, the myrrh as man. And so through the Magi's veneration [of him], the understanding of every mystery[54] is summed up concerning his death as man, of his resurrection as God, about his judgment as King. Just as the Magi were prohibited from retracing their route and returning to Herod in Judea,[55] so we ought never to look to Judea for our knowledge and learning.[56] Instead, we are admonished to refrain from following the "route" of our former life by placing all our salvation and hope in Christ.[57]

6. As Herod was plotting the death of the newborns, Joseph was warned by the angel to move the child to Egypt,[58] the same Egypt which is full of idols and venerates monstrous omens of every kind of god.[59] Even now, after persecution from the Jews and the agreement of wicked people who sought to kill him,

52. Jn 19.26–27.

53. *totus qualitatis. Qualitas* is a concept from Stoic logic which Tertullian applied to the Nativity of Christ in *Apol.* 21.9 (*Sur Matt.* I.99).

54. *omnis sacramenti.* Hilary uses *sacramentum* for the three roles of Christ.

55. Mt 2.12.

56. That is, the Law of the Old Covenant.

57. Cf. Fortunatianus of Aquileia, *Commentarii in Evangelia* 2.12–20 (CCSL 9.368). The title or description is taken from Jerome, *De viris illust.* 97, who says that Fortunatianus *in evangelia ... brevi sermone et rustico scripsit commentarios* during the reign of Constantius (II).

58. Mt 2.13.

59. See Virgil, *Aeneid* 8.698: *omnigennoque deum monstra* (*Sur Matt.* I.99, n.11).

Christ passes over to the pagans who are devoted to the most futile religious practices. Forsaking Judea, he is presented to an ignorant world as one worthy of worship, while Bethlehem, that is Judea, overflows with the blood of the martyrs. Indeed, the fury of Herod and killing of the infants are a pattern[60] of the Jewish people raging against the Christians; the former imagining that by the slaughter of the blessed martyrs they are able to wipe out the name of Christ from the faith and the profession of all [believers].

7. But a glorious honor is rendered to the slain through the prophet who said: *A voice was heard in Rama, weeping and great lamentation, Rachel weeping for her children, and she did not wish to be comforted because they were no more.*[61] Rachel, wife of Jacob, was for a long time barren though she lost none of those whom she had borne. In fact, she is presented in Genesis as a type of the Church.[62] It is not therefore her voice and weeping which are heard, since she harbored no sorrow over slain children, but it is that of the Church; for a long time barren, yet now fruitful. This kind of weeping over her children is heard, not because she was grieving that they had been slain, but because they were being slain by those whom she had wanted to preserve as her firstborn sons. In this way, she did not wish to be comforted in her grief. For there is no denial of those who died; yet they were appointed, through the glory of martyrdom, for the gain of eternity. Consolation ought to be offered for a loss, not for a gain.

60. *forma.* A commonly used term in the commentary. Cf. Rom 5.14, where the Greek τύπος ("type") is translated in the Latin Bible as *forma*.
61. Mt 2.18.
62. An exegetical parallel and probable source for Hilary is Cyprian, *Test.* 1.20: *Rachel typus Ecclesiae, quae et sterilis diu mansit.* Cyprian proceeds to push the typology by claiming that Joseph, borne by Rachel, was also a type of Christ. Cf. Tertullian, *Adv. Iud.* 10. Joseph is a figure of Christ particularly because of his sufferings at the hands of his own brothers.

## CHAPTER TWO

NCE HEROD was dead, Joseph was later instructed by the angel to return to Judea with the boy and his mother.[1] And as he was returning, he learned that the son of Herod, Archelaus, was ruling, so he feared to enter there and is warned by the angel to cross over into Galilee and to live in Nazareth, a town of that region.[2] So [we learn that] Joseph is instructed to return to Judea, and having returned, he is afraid; then being admonished in a dream, he is told to cross over into the land of pagans. But it is strange that he should be afraid once he was encouraged to go, or that the initial instructions conveyed by an angel should be changed so readily.

In this case, however, a figurative principle[3] has been observed here. Joseph provides an image[4] of the apostles to whom Christ[5] was entrusted for dissemination far and wide. These men were commanded to preach to the Jews, because even as Herod was being overtaken by death, his people were becoming lost as to the meaning of the Lord's Passion. The apostles had been sent to the "lost sheep of the house of Israel,"[6] but because the domination of a hereditary infidelity persisted, they were afraid and drew back. Joseph was warned in a dream, by which we understand how the gift of the Holy Spirit was directed to the pagans.[7] The apostles now have announced life and salvation for the pagans, introducing them to Christ, who was sent to the Jews.

1. Mt 2.19.
2. Mt 2.22–23.
3. *typica ratio.* See the Introduction on Hilary's use of allegorical and figurative interpretation.
4. *species.*
5. That is, the Gospel of Christ.
6. Mt 15.24.
7. Cf. Tertullian, *De anima* 47.2, who refers to Acts 2 and the Joel 2 prophecy when discussing the way the Holy Spirit is revealed by dreams.

2. *In those days John[8] came preaching in the desert of Judea, saying,*
*"Repent,[9] for the Kingdom of heaven has arrived,"[10]* etc. With John,
the location, the preaching, the clothing, and the food must
be carefully considered in such a way that we should become
mindful of the truth of the facts without distortion, since the
principle of an interior understanding[11] underlies the realization of these facts. Surely there was a more suitable location for
his preaching, and there was more practical clothing and more
appropriate food. A pattern,[12] however, underlies these events
as they occurred, and in this (pattern) there is a deliberate operation at work,[13] which is itself a preparation.[14]

So it was that John came to a deserted Judea; deserted by
the visitations of God, though not of the people; emptied of
the Holy Spirit's dwelling,[15] though not of men so that the location of his preaching should bear witness to the barrenness
of those to whom it was directed. John also called for repentance in light of the approaching Kingdom of heaven, by which
one is turned from error, restored from guilt,[16] and, due to the
shamefulness of sins, decides to give them up.[17] In her deserted
condition, Judea should have recalled that she could have received him in whom is the Kingdom of heaven. She might not
be empty now, if she had purified herself from her ancient sins
through the confession of repentance.[18]

Moreover, a garment woven of camel hair indicates the
strange[19] clothing of John's prophetic preaching. With the garments of unclean animals[20]—to which we bear a resemblance[21]—
the preacher of Christ is clothed. Whatever emptiness or filth
there once was in us, has become sanctified by the prophetical[22]

---

8. Some MSS add *baptista* ("baptizer") in accord with Mt 3.1–2.

9. I am following the typical English usage, which is based on the Greek,
but the Latin literally means, "Do penance" (*paenitentiam agite*).

10. Mt 3.1–2.                    11. *interioris intelligentiae ratio.*

12. *exemplum.*                    13. *operatio.*

14. *meditatio,* i.e., for a deeper understanding than just the facts of the narration.

15. Cf. Mt 3.9–11; Lk 3.7–9, 21–22; Jn 8.39–47.

16. *crimine.*                    17. *professio desinendi.*

18. Mt 3.6.                    19. *peregrinum.*

20. Cf. Lv 11.4; Acts 10.12–15.

21. Cf. Tertullian, *De anima* 32.8; Novatian, *De cib. Iud.* 3.

22. *prophetali*; a neologism of Hilary's (Kinnavey, 8). Cf. *infra,* 23.3.

clothing. The girding around of the [John's] belt, which is effective in every good work,[23] has been provided so that we may be prepared[24] in our desire to serve Christ in every way.

Locusts are chosen as food, which flee from people and fly off any time we come near them. We too [want to] flee from every word of and confrontation with the prophets, as we are represented by those same leaping bodies. With a will that wanders, being unprofitable in works, argumentative in words, in a strange place, we are even now the nourishment of the saints and the sufficiency of the prophets. We who have been chosen, just like the wild honey, will furnish from ourselves the sweetest food, drawing it not from the beehive of the Law but from the trunks of wild trees.[25]

3. It is in such clothing that John preaches and publicly identifies the Pharisees and Sadducees who were coming for baptism as a *race of vipers*.[26] He warns them to bear *fruit which is worthy of repentance* and not to gloat over having Abraham as a father since God is capable of raising up sons of Abraham out of stones.[27] What John seeks is not a carnal succession but the heredity of faith. Worthiness of origin consists in the examples of one's deeds, and the glory of one's race is preserved by the imitation of [one who has] faith. The devil is without faith; Abraham has faith.[28] As the former was a betrayer of man into transgression, so the latter was justified by faith.[29] The characteristics and manner of life of each one are acquired by a proximity of resemblance;[30] that is, those who have faith are the descendants of Abraham because of their faith, whereas those

23. Cf. Eph 6.14.

24. The meaning of this statement is supported by the parallel of the words *praecinctis* ("girding around") and *accincti* ("prepared"); John's belt symbolizes the action of preparation on our part so that we may be used of Christ. Cf. Eph 6.14.

25. An allusion to Rom 11.17–24.     26. Mt 3.7.

27. Mt 3.8–9.

28. Jn 8.33, 44. Cf. Tertullian, *De paen.* 5–6, for the contrast between Abraham believing and the devil unbelieving.

29. Rom 4.9–13; Gal 3.6–7. For the centrality of the theme of justification by faith, see the Introduction.

30. *cognatio*. The same word means "bloodline" or "lineage," which is how Hilary used it in I.1.

who have no faith are transformed by their lack of faith into the offspring of the devil. When the Pharisees are scorned as a *race of vipers,*[31] and their gloating of a holy parentage is checked, it is out of rocks and boulders that sons of Abraham are raised up. The Pharisees are then urged to produce fruit worthy of repentance. They who began with the devil as a father, along with those who are raised up from stones, can become sons of Abraham through faith once more.

4. That *the axe is now placed at the root of the trees*[32] testifies to the prerogative[33] of holy power[34] that is present in Christ which indicates that, by the cutting down and burning of unfruitful trees, the destruction of an unfruitful faithlessness[35] is being prepared for the conflagration of judgment. And because the work of the Law was ineffective for salvation, John had appeared as a messenger for the baptizing of those who repent.[36] It was the duty of the prophets to recall the people from their sins, whereas it now belongs to Christ to save those who believe, [those whom] John says that he baptizes for repentance. Yet, he says, there will come one greater whose shoes he is unworthy to carry in the fulfillment of his ministry,[37] surrendering to the apostles the glory of preaching everywhere, to whose "beautiful feet" it was assigned to proclaim the peace of God.[38] He points to the time of our salvation and judgment when he says of the Lord: *He will baptize you in the Holy Spirit and by fire.*[39] It remains only for those baptized in the Holy Spirit to be brought to perfection[40] by the fire of judgment:[41] *his winnowing fork is in his hand, he will clean his threshing floor, and he will gather his wheat into the barn, but will burn up the chaff with unquenchable fire.*[42] The

---

31. *viperarum natio.*
32. Mt 3.10.
33. *ius.*
34. *potestas.*
35. *perfidia.*
36. Cf. Acts 13.24; Mt 11.12.
37. Mt 3.11a.
38. Rom 10.15 (Is 52.7).
39. Mt 3.11b.
40. *consummari.*

41. It would seem that the baptized believer is also to endure the judgment of fire. Hilary accepted the view that the faithful are judged according to their deeds. The point might be in reference to Tertullian's *De bapt.* 10.7, according to which the baptism of a "stable and true faith" is of the Spirit, whereas a "pretended and weak faith" is a baptism of fire, namely, unto judgment.

42. Mt 3.12.

job of the winnowing fork is to separate that which is fruitful from the unfruitful. That fork which is in the Lord's hand indicates the resolve[43] of his power for storing up the wheat into his barns, that is, the perfected fruit of believers. But the chaff of those who are unprofitable as well as the uselessness of those who are unfruitful are [bound] for the fire of burning judgment.

5. *Then Jesus arrived from Galilee at the Jordan coming to John in order to be baptized by him,*[44] and so on. In Jesus Christ there was complete manhood,[45] and so, having assumed a body as a servant of the Spirit, he accomplished in himself the entire mystery of our salvation. In this way he came to John: born[46] of a woman, fashioned under the Law,[47] made flesh through the Word.[48] There was no need for him to be washed [baptized] since it was said concerning him: *He committed no sin,*[49] and where there is no sin, remission of it is thereby superfluous. Nevertheless, he had assumed both the body and the name of our created condition, and although it was not necessary for him to be cleansed, the purifying[50] water that cleanses us had to be sanctified by him.[51] He then instructed John, who refused to baptize him as God, that it was necessary for him to be baptized as a man. For *all righteousness*[52] had to be fulfilled by him through whom alone the

43. *arbitrium.*
44. Mt 3.13.
45. *homo totus.* There is not a theory about Christ's human soul behind this remark. Hilary means that Christ as man endured all the limitations and frailties that concern his humanity though without human sin.
46. *natus.*
47. Gal 4.4.
48. A rearrangement of Jn 1.14, "the Word was made flesh." Since the Word for Hilary made all things (Prv 8.30a; Col 3.16), it also created the body of Christ.
49. 1 Pt 2.22 (Is 53.9).
50. *purgatio.*
51. Cf. Lactantius, *Div. Inst.* 4.15. Compare with Hilary's interpretation of Christ in the Garden of Gethsemane. In no way was Christ baptized for his own sake but for ours, just as he did not suffer for his own sake, but for ours (*infra,* 31.2–3). In the present passage Hilary seems to be saying that the very process and means of baptism were sanctified by Christ's partaking of it. All believers, therefore, follow his pattern.
52. Mt 3.15.

Law could be fulfilled. And thus, on one hand, he had no need for washing according to the prophetic testimony,[53] though, on the other hand, he perfected the mysteries of human salvation by the precedent[54] of his example, sanctifying humanity by his assumption and washing of it.[55]

6. Moreover, the plan[56] of the heavenly mystery[57] is portrayed in him. After he was baptized, the entrance of heaven was opened, the Holy Spirit came forth and is visibly recognized in the form of a dove. In this way Christ is imbued by the anointing of the Father's affection.[58] Then a voice from heaven spoke the following words: "You are my Son, today I have begotten you."[59] He is revealed as the Son of God by sound and sight, as the testimony of his Lord by means of both an image[60] and a voice; he is sent to an unfaithful people who were disobedient to their prophets. As these events happened with Christ, we should likewise know that following the waters of baptism, the Holy Spirit comes upon us from the gates of heaven, imbuing us with the anointing of heavenly glory. We become the sons of God by the adoption[61] expressed through the Father's voice.[62] These actual events prefigured an image of the mysteries established for us.[63]

53. Mt 3.3.

54. *auctoritate.*

55. See Doignon, "La scène évangélique du baptême de Jésus commentée par Lactance et Hilaire de Poitiers," in *Epektasis* (Paris: Editions Beauchesne, 1972), 63–73.

56. *ordo.* It might be understood here in the Tertullianic frame of reference as "economy."

57. *arcani caelestis.*

58. *pietatis.*

59. Lk 3.22. Hilary incorporates this passage from Luke, which is lacking in Matthew, in order to emphasize the divine epiphany that the passage announces. Cf. Tertullian, *De bapt.* 8.3, who also conflates the images from Mt 3.17 with Lk 3.22.

60. *contemplationis.*

61. An implicit contrast is established here, which Hilary will make clearer: namely, the distinction between the Son of God, whose divine nature is declared by the Father, and us who are sons of God by adoption, called by the Father's voice.

62. Cf. Tertullian, *De bapt.* 8.3.

63. *dispositi in nos sacramenti imaginem.*

# CHAPTER THREE

**HEN JESUS** *was led into the desert by the Spirit in order to be tempted by the devil.*[1] The passage[2] into the desert, the forty days of fasting, the hunger after fasting, the temptation of Satan, and the response of the Lord have been fulfilled in accordance with the realization of a great and heavenly plan. That he was led into the desert indicated the prerogative of the Holy Spirit, who exposed his humanity to the devil at that moment by allowing him to be tempted. This provided an opportunity which the Tempter would not have had unless it had been given to him. Accordingly, the devil had a suspicion generated by fear, not derived from insight.[3] Though the Lord was weakened by fasting for forty days, he knew nevertheless that in just as many days the waters had erupted from the depths,[4] that the land of promise had been scouted out,[5] that the Law of Moses was written by God,[6] and that the people who dwelt in the wilderness, living a life like that of the angels,[7] had completed this number of years.[8] But because the devil was afraid of losing the opportunity of tempting him whom he regarded as man,[9] he acted rashly. For he had enticed Adam and led him into death by deception. Yet it was fitting, given the devil's wickedness and evil deeds, that he should be overcome by a man in whose death and calamity he gloried. He who had begrudged God's blessings to humanity was not able to understand that God was in the man before his temptation. For this reason, the Lord was tempted immediately after his baptism, indicating that, while the devil's temptations[10] are meant to un-

---

1. Mt 4.1.   2. *traductio.*

3. *cognitio.* The devil does not know of the "great and heavenly plan," the Incarnation, though he is not unfamiliar with the Son's power (Mt 4.3).

4. Gn 7.11–12.   5. Nm 13.25; Neh 9.21.

6. Ex 24.18.   7. Ps 78.25.

8. Ex 16.35.   9. Cf. *infra*, Chapter 10, n.143.

10. *tentamenta.*

dermine us—especially believers[11]—God more greatly wishes that the victory be won by his saints.

2. The Lord hungered not for the food of man but for their salvation. In fact, he was hungry after the forty days, not during that forty-day period, just as Moses and Elijah were not hungry when they fasted for the same amount of time.[12] Although the Lord hungered, his abstinence from food did not undermine him, since his power,[13] which was not affected by his fasting for forty days, handed over his humanity to its own nature.[14] It was necessary to defeat the devil, not by God, but by the flesh, which the devil would never have dared to tempt unless he had recognized the weakness that hunger brings to human nature. This, at least, is what the devil discerned in him when he began with the words, *If you are the Son of God.*[15] The statement is an uncertain one: *if you are the Son of God.* Even though the devil saw him going hungry, he was growing frightened of him who fasted for forty days.

According to the ordering of these events, the Gospel indicates that following his experience[16] of forty days, during which Christ would remain in this world after his Passion, he possessed a hunger for the salvation of humanity. In that time he brought back humanity, which he had assumed, as his appointed service to God the Father.

3. Now we must consider the matter of how the devil conducted the examination of Christ. He said: *If you are the Son of God, tell these stones to become bread.*[17] The devil, who is deceitful and most cunningly skilled in leading anyone astray, knew that Christ held complete power.[18] Even though the devil realized

---

11. *in sanctificatis nobis maxime.*            12. Ex 34.28; 1 Kgs 19.8.

13. *virtus.* This reading is contested, but Doignon has made a convincing case: "L'*argumentatio* d'Hilaire de Poitiers dans l'*exemplum* de la Tentation de Jésus," *VC* 29 (1975): 296–308.

14. *naturae suae homilem dereliquit.* Proper to the Son's nature is his divinity which assumes humanity. Cf. Tertullian, *Adv. Prax.* 30.1–2: *Sed haec vox carnis et animae ... propterea emissa est ut impassibilem Deum ostenderet, qui sic Filium reliquit dum hominem eius tradidit in mortem* (CCSL 2.1203).

15. Mt 4.3.                          16. *conversatio.*
17. Mt 4.3.                          18. *posse omnia.*

that his hunger as man stemmed from this period of fasting, he was unaware for what Christ hungered.

By tempting him in this way, the devil was establishing tests by which he might learn the power of Christ's divine authority:[19] as God, by changing stones into bread; as man, by taking advantage of his patience as he fasted from food. But the Lord hungered not for bread as much as for the salvation of men, saying, *Man shall not live by bread alone*[20] because he was not man only, but also God. While he abstained from the earthly food at the time of his temptation, he was nourished by the Spirit of God. The Lord shows that we must put our hope, not in bread itself, but in the Word of God—the nourishment of eternity.

4. After this examination the devil took him up to the top of the Temple: *If you are the Son of God, throw yourself down,*[21] etc. He sought to draw the Lord by temptation from the heights down to the depths by placing him on the top of the Temple, that is, by placing him high above the Law and the prophets in order to confine him among the lowest. For the devil knew the ministrations of angels were ready to serve the Son of God and that the latter could not fall against an offensive stone.[22] On the contrary, the Lord was going to tread upon the asp and cobra and trample on the lion and the serpent.[23] The devil was silent concerning these things that were said, but as he recalled what happened earlier, he wanted to elicit the Lord's obedience by whatever kind of temptation in order to derive glory [for himself] from this. It was necessary only that the Lord of majesty surrender his trust to him. But no opportunity for such a deception came to pass for the devil, as the Lord testified at a later point, *The ruler of this age is coming and has found nothing in me.*[24] An appropriate response from the Lord is thereby given to this impudence of his: *You shall not tempt your God and Lord.*[25] After foiling

---

19. *virtutem potestatis.*                    20. Mt 4.4.

21. Mt 4.6.                                   22. Ibid.

23. Ps 90 (91).12–13. A prophetic statement made in reference to Christ's final victory.

24. Jn 14.30.

25. Hilary reversed the word order of the verse, which in the Old Latin reads, *dominum deum tuum*, perhaps in order to lay greater stress on the Son's divinity.

the efforts and attempts of the devil, he affirms that he is both God and Lord, teaching us that arrogance (like the devil's) has no place among the faithful. Although all things are possible for God, we still should not provoke temptation such as this.[26]

5. But now, for the third time, all the ambition of the devil's power[27] was being shaken. When he placed the Lord at the top of a mountain, he offered him all the kingdoms of the world and their glory if only the Lord would worship him.[28] By this time the [Lord's previous] two responses confirmed the grounds for suspicion.[29] The devil had seduced Adam[30] by means of food and led him away from the glory of paradise into the place of sin, that is, into the region of the forbidden tree.[31] On this third occasion, the devil sought to corrupt the Lord with expectation of the divine title by promising him that he would become like God.[32] All worldly authority is presented before the Lord, and possession of this universe is offered to its Creator.[33] In this instance, the devil did not seduce him with food nor a [glorious] place, but now—in keeping with the pattern[34] of the ancient deception—he tried to corrupt him with ambition. But the Lord's response took the approach[35] in keeping with what he had done earlier, saying, *Begone Satan, for it is written, "You shall worship the Lord your God, and him alone shall you serve."*[36] The devil was dealt with in a way appropriate to his great audacity. When he heard his name *Satan* as a designation for his crimes, he realized that the Lord his God would have to be worshiped in a man.[37]

26. *nihil tamen in temptationem eius audendum sit.*

27. *potestas.*

28. Mt 4.8.

29. *Supra,* 3.1: *Erat igitur in diabolo de metu suspicio, non de suspicione cognitio.*

30. Hilary is drawing on a familiar contrast between Adam, who was seduced by the devil, whereas Christ, the second Adam, did not succumb and freed mankind from the devil's power. 1 Cor 15.21–24; Irenaeus, *Adv. haer.* 3.23.6–7.

31. Gn 3.24. The idea is that Adam was seduced into thinking that he would be like God (3.5) if he ate the forbidden food.

32. *diis futurum simile.*  33. Cf. Col 1.16.

34. *ordo.*  35. *graduum.*

36. Mt 4.10.

37. Compare with 3.1. The temerity of the devil when he began to tempt

Given his effective responses, the Lord presents us with a wonderful example: by spurning the glory of human authority and disregarding the ambition of this age, we may remember to worship only the Lord God[38] because all the honor of this age is the devil's affair. Following the flight of the devil, the angels ministered to Christ showing that once we have conquered and trampled upon the head of the devil, the services of angels and aid of heavenly power[39] will not be lacking for us.

6. *When Jesus heard that John had been taken into custody, he withdrew into Galilee.*[40] The crossing into Capernaum and the prophecy of Isaiah are the order of events as they happened.[41] By choosing fishermen,[42] the role of their future service is made clear from their profession: just as they drew fish from the sea, so they would draw men one by one[43] from this age to a higher place, that is, into the light of a heavenly dwelling.[44] By their abandonment of their profession, their country, and homes, we who will follow Christ are taught not to be bound by concern for life in this world or by attachment to our family's home.[45] In the choice of the first four apostles, apart from the evident veracity of the facts (for this is how it happened), the number of the future evangelists is prefigured. Christ went around Galilee preaching in the synagogues about the Gospel of the Kingdom and healing the infirmities of all the sick.[46] He revealed himself by these deeds so that he would be recognized as the one whom the Jews had long read about in the books of the prophets.

---

Jesus was based on his erroneous conclusion that Christ was man only. The exegetical exercise of 3.1–5 is to show that Christ is the Lord God in a man, though this is *not* the point of the spiritual application that Hilary makes in the conclusion (3.5). It indicates *not* a polemical argument, but a pastoral one.

38. *Deum et Dominum.*                    39. *virtus.*
40. Mt 4.12.                              41. Mt 4.13–16.
42. Mt 4.18–22.                           43. Lit., "in succession" (*deinceps*).
44. See *infra,* 13.9. Cf. Tertullian, *De bapt.* 1.3.
45. *paternae domus.*
46. Mt 4.23–24.

# CHAPTER FOUR

HEN A GREAT CROWD had assembled together, he then climbed up and taught them from the mountain. In other words, having situated himself on the height of the Father's majesty, he laid down the precepts of heavenly life. For he could not have delivered eternal principles had he not been situated in eternity. And so it is written: *He opened his mouth and began to teach them.*[1] It would have been easier to say that he was the one to speak, but because he dwelt[2] in the glory of the Father's majesty and taught about eternity, it is clear that he had yielded the service of his human mouth over to the movement of the Spirit's eloquence.[3]

2. *Blessed are the poor in spirit, for theirs is the Kingdom of heaven.*[4] The Lord had taught by his example that we should forsake the glory of human ambition when he said, *You shall worship the Lord your God, and him alone shall you serve.*[5] And when he had announced through the prophets that he was going to choose a lowly people who trembled at his words,[6] he laid the foundations for this perfect beatitude in the humility of spirit. He has placed in possession of his heavenly Kingdom those who possess the character of humility, that is, those who remember that they are but men.[7] They are conscious that they have been formed by him from the lowest and most insignificant elements, yet fashioned and created into the form of a perfect

---

1. Mt. 5.2.  2. *institerat.*
3. ... *ad motum Spiritus eloquentis oboedisse ostenditur humani oris officium.* Cf. Lk 4.18; Mt 12.18.
4. Mt 5.3.  5. *Supra,* 3.5 (Mt 4.10).
6. Is 66.2.
7. What follows in the text is a sketch of the creation of mankind in Gn 2 designed to reinforce our dependent and therefore humble condition before God.

body.[8] As they progressed under God's direction, they came to have the capacity of feeling, thinking, discerning, and acting. They are conscious that there is nothing which belongs to anyone, nothing of one's own, but to each one the gift of one Parent[9] is offered in the same way, both in bestowing the origins of life and for enjoying the means of this life.[10]

Through the example of that greatest blessing[11] that is abundantly given to us, we ought to be emulators of the goodness[12] he has displayed in us. Let us show goodness to all and consider that everything is common to all lest anything corrupt us; neither the insolence of the world's arrogance, nor the desire of wealth, nor the ambition of vainglory. Rather, let us be subject to God, and on account of a common nature[13] of our being, let us embrace a common life of love toward all people. Let us recognize that we are born into that greatness[14] along with future prospects of divine goodness and that we must merit this reward and honor by our works in the present life. Through this humility of spirit, therefore, as we remember what God has done for us—endowed with all things and with the hope of greater things to come—the Kingdom of heaven will be ours.

3. *Blessed are the meek, for they shall inherit the earth.*[15] To the meek the inheritance of the land is promised, that is, the inheritance of his body, which the Lord himself assumed as his dwelling. Because Christ will have dwelt in us through the gentleness of our disposition,[16] we also will be clothed in the glory of his bodily splendor.[17]

---

8. Cf. Gn 2.7. Perhaps an echo of Tertullian's contrast between *homo* and *humilitas*; see *Apol.* 18.2.

9. *parentis unius.*

10. *ea substantiam ministrari.*

11. *optimi illius.*

12. Following the reading of PL 9:932B: *esse aemulos oportere.*

13. *communia.*

14. *magnum.*

15. Mt 5.4. In accord with several Latin readings available to him, Hilary interposes the order of vv. 4 and 5.

16. *mentis.*

17. *clarificati eius corporis.* Cf. 1 Cor 15.40, 53.

4. *Blessed are those who mourn, for they shall be comforted.*[18] For those who are mourning, the comfort of eternal consolation is offered. We do not lament over losses or injuries or misfortunes, but by weeping for past sins and from the awareness of the transgressions[19] that defile us, there is this consolation carefully prepared in heaven.

5. *Blessed are those who hunger and thirst for justice, for they shall be satisfied.*[20] To those who thirst and hunger for justice, he bestows blessedness, indicating that the eagerness of the saints, increased by the teaching of God, will be fulfilled by the goodness of a perfect satisfaction in heaven.

6. *Blessed are the merciful, for God shall be merciful to them.*[21] For those who are merciful, he prepares gifts of his mercy. God is so delighted by the compassion of our kindness to all people that he will grant his mercy to the merciful.

7. *Blessed are the pure in heart, for they shall see God.*[22] To those who are pure in heart—one who follows after nothing polluted or filthy contrary to divine splendor and, in seeking the vision of God, does not allow his sensitivity to be dulled by a defiled conscience[23]—he promises the vision of God. In other words, those who endure for the sight of and encounter with God through the brightness of the soul and purity of life become capable of beholding him. Not until we are perfected in spirit and changed into immortality,[24] will we discover what has been prepared only for those who are pure in heart, that which is immortal in God.

8. *Blessed are the peacemakers, for they shall be called the sons of God.*[25] The blessedness of peacemakers is the benefit of adoption that they should abide as the sons of God. For God is the

---

18. Mt 5.5.                          19. *criminum.*
20. Mt 5.6.
21. Mt 5.7. Hilary's citation, *quoniam ipsis Deus,* reflects one of several versions. Cf. the reading, *quoniam ipsi misercordium consequentur* (or *consequuntur*), found in the Vulgate.
22. Mt 5.8.                          23. *acies obsoletae mentis hebetatur.*
24. 1 Cor 15.53.                     25. Mt 5.9.

one Parent[26] of all, and not one of us will be permitted to assume[27] the name of his family except through the forgetfulness of those things done against us,[28] [so] we may live in the fraternal peace of mutual[29] love.

9. *Blessed are those who suffer persecution for the sake of righteousness,*[30] etc. In the end, he rewards those with perfect blessedness whose will[31] is devoted to suffer all things for Christ who is himself righteousness.[32] It is for them that both the Kingdom is reserved as well as abundant rewards in heaven are promised,[33] because they, in contempt of the world by the loss of all present things, are poor in spirit. And by their rejection of shameful words and opposition to the evil of man, they are confessors of heavenly righteousness. And therefore, as glorious martyrs of God's promises, they have devoted their whole lives to the witness of his eternity.

10. *You are the salt of the earth. If the salt becomes tasteless, it has no effect on whatever is salted.*[34] Salt, I do believe, is not "of the earth." Why then does he call the apostles to be "the salt of the earth"? A proper understanding must be sought in the use of the words that will show both the function of the apostles and the nature of salt itself. Salt is an element containing within itself water and fire, and from these two comes the one element.[35] Produced for the particular use of the human race, it bestows incorruption on bodies that have been sprinkled with it, and it is most suitable for completely preserving flavor. So too, the apostles are the preachers of heavenly matters, and sowers of eternity, planting seeds of immortality[36] in all bodies on which their word has been sprinkled and perfected (John [the Baptist] is the best witness on this) by the sacrament of water and fire.[37] Therefore, the *salt of the earth* has rightfully been

26. *parens.*
27. Lit., "come into" (*transire*).
28. Mt 5.23–24.
29. *invicem.*
30. Mt 5.10.
31. *pronus.*
32. 1 Cor 1.30.
33. Mt 5.12.
34. Mt 5.13. Hilary's citation of the first part of this verse differs slightly from the word order of other Latin MSS (*Itala*, p. 21).
35. Cf. Pliny, *Nat.* 31.7 (39), 73 (*Sur Matt.* I.127, n.5).
36. Cf. 1 Cor 15.38–44.
37. Mt 3.11 (Mk 1.8; Lk 3.16).

declared through the power of the Apostle's teaching, preserving bodies for eternity by means of salting them.

The nature of salt, however, is always the same; it is never capable of alteration. Yet humanity is subject to change,[38] and he alone is blessed who will have persevered unto the end in all the works of God.[39] Thus, those who have been called the *salt of the earth* he admonishes to endure in the power of divine authority[40] handed over to them, lest by becoming insipid they produce no saltiness. They who have lost their taste are unable to renew[41] that which has spoiled, and, after being thrown out from the storehouse of the Church[42] with the ones they salted, they are trampled underfoot by those walking over them.[43]

11. *You are the light of the world.*[44] It is in the nature of light to emit radiance wherever it moves. Once it has been introduced into a house, darkness is dispelled by its overwhelming brightness. In like manner, the world is reckoned outside of the knowledge of God, enshrouded by the darkness of ignorance.[45] Through the apostles, the light of understanding is brought into it, and illuminated by the knowledge of God. Wherever the tiny particles of light have gone, darkness is dissipated.[46]

12. *A city built upon a hill cannot be hidden, nor do they who light a lamp place it under a bushel,*[47] etc. The Lord calls the flesh that he had assumed a *city* because, just as a city is composed of a variety and multitude of inhabitants, so too there is contained in him, given the nature of his assumed body, a union[48] with the whole human race. Thus he becomes a *city* from our union with him, and we, through union with his flesh, are the dwelling-place of his *city*. He cannot, therefore, be hidden now that he is situated on God's highest of heights. He is raised up in order

38. *conversioni.*
39. 2 Tm 2.12.
40. *potestatis uirtute.*
41. *vivificare.*
42. Image reflects Ps 143 (144).13 as applied to the Church. *Infra,* 26.5.
43. Mt 5.13.
44. Mt 5.14a.
45. *obscurabatur ignorantiae tenebris.*
46. Lit., "light is served by the darkness" (*lux tenebris ministratur*). Cf. Seneca's definition, *Nat.* 1.15.2. (*Sur Matt.* I.130, n.13).
47. Mt 5.14b–15.
48. *congregatio.*

to be perceived[49] and understood by all in wonder of his good works.

13. But neither should a lamp, once it is lit, be concealed under a bushel. What benefit is it to possess something that provides light in a confined area? Yet the Lord appropriately compared a bushel to the synagogue, which, as it eagerly welcomed the fruits[50] that were brought, maintained a sure means of measuring all its observances. Despite all the fruit that was brought, it was empty, though not capable of hiding the light.

And thus the lamp of Christ should not be hidden under a bushel or under the concealing cover of the synagogue. Rather, it is highlighted in his sufferings on the tree,[51] offering eternal light to those who will dwell in the Church.[52] By a similar light the apostles are also admonished to shine so that in admiration of their works, praise may be rendered to God.[53] It is not appropriate to seek glory from human beings when everything has been done in honor of God. Let our work, even if it is ignored, shine among those with whom we live.[54]

14. *Do not claim that I came to abolish the Law and the prophets: I came not to abolish but to fulfill.*[55] The power and authority of these heavenly words contain a lofty[56] significance. For the law of works was established and encompassed everything pertaining to the faith that would be revealed in Christ:[57] both his teaching and his suffering, the eminent and profound decision of the Father's will.[58] Moreover, under the veil of spiritual

---

49. *contemplandus.*

50. *Fructus* is translated in this passage as "benefit" and "fruit" (i.e., produce) in order to accommodate Hilary's emphasis on the synagogue, which received the fruit of the people and gave no benefit.

51. I.e., cross. *In ligni passione.* Cf. Tertullian, *Adv. Marc.* 3.18.1–4, for a discussion of OT types of the Lord's cross. "And of course it was especially important that this mystery should be expressed figuratively in prophecy" (*Adv. Marc.* 3.18.2; trans. mine); see *Tertullian: Adversus Marcionem, Books 1 to 3*, ed. and trans. Ernest Evans (Oxford: Clarendon Press, 1972), 224.

52. Cf. Cyprian, *De unit. eccl.* 5, for the Church–light of the Lord metaphor.

53. Mt 5.16a.                        54. Mt 5.16b.

55. Mt 5.17.                         56. *grandia.*

57. Gal 3.23.

58. *grande et profundum est paternae uoluntatis arbitrium.* Cf. Eph 1.5.

words, the Law spoke of the Nativity of our Lord Jesus Christ and of his Incarnation,[59] and of his Passion, and of his Resurrection. It was decreed even before the times of the ages and the time of our age, frequently mentioned by prophetic and apostolic authority.

After the period of fasting for forty days, Satan—who was troubled with much suspicion—undertook the very bold move of tempting Jesus because he feared in him the mystery of great heavenly preparations.[60] In fact, "Jesus" is the name given to the flesh of our Lord. And so both his Incarnation[61] and his suffering are the will of God and the salvation of the world. It is beyond the eloquence of human speech to describe how he is God from God, Son of the Father's substance, and dwelling within the substance of the Father,[62] how at first he was incarnate as man, then subject to death in his human condition, how after three days he returned from death to life, how he brought to heaven the matter of the body that he assumed,[63] already united to the Spirit and in the eternality of his substance.[64]

15. Lest we should think that there is in his works anything that is not contained in the Law, he declared that he did not come to abolish the Law but to fulfill it.[65] Whereas heaven and

---

59. *corporalitatem.*

60. *pertimescens caelestis molitionis arcanum.* See *supra,* 3.1.

61. *corporalitas.*

62. *Deum ex Deo, Filium ex Patris substantia atque intra Patris substantiam consistentem.* Cf. *infra,* 10 n.143.

63. Cf. Victorinus of Poetovio's *Commentary on the Apocalypse,* 5.8, 9, and 11.1, which tells of the Son of God who ascended into heaven with his body.

64. It is likely that this sequence is presented by Hilary as a kind of *regula fidei* similar to that found in Tertullian, *De praescr. haer.* 13; 1–5; *Adv. Prax.* 2.1; and *De vel. virg.* 1.3. Clearly Hilary is drawing upon the language of Tertullian's *Apol.* 21.21–23: *Sed ad tertium diem concussa repente terra et mole revoluta, quae obstruxerat sepulcrum, et custodia pavore disiecta, nullis apparentibus discipulis nihil in sepulcro repertum est praeter exuvias sepulturae. Nihilominus tamen primores Iudaeorum, quorum intererat et scelus divulgare et populum vectigalem et famularem sibi a fide avocare, subreptum ad discipulis iactitaverunt. Nam nec ille se in vulgus eduxit, ne impii errore liberarentur, sed ut fides, non mediocri praemio destinata, difficultate constaret. Cum discipulis autem quibusdam apud Galilaeam Iudaeae regionis ad quinquaginta dies egit docens eos quae docerent. Dehinc ordinatis eis ad officium praedicandi per orbem, circumfusa nube in caelum est ereptus multo verius quam apud vos asseverare de Romulis Proculi solent* (ed. Dekkers, CCSL 1.126–27). The credal-like pattern in this passage may also reflect the baptismal creed that Hilary cited in 1.3.

65. Mt 5.17.

earth, the greatest of elements as we imagine, will be destroyed, it is still not possible for the least of the commandments of the Law to be left uncompleted[66] since all the Law and the prophets are fulfilled in him. During his Passion and on the verge of delivering his spirit, no less certain of this great mystery within him, he took a drink of sour wine and declared that all was finished.[67] Everything that was once spoken by the prophets was summed up in the affirmation[68] of his deeds. And so it was established by God that not even the least of the commandments of God should be abolished (except [the statutes] concerning sacrifice). He warned that those who abolish the least of these will be the least; that is, they will be last or of no account at all.[69] For no one can be less than those who are the least.

And yet the suffering of the Lord and his death on a cross are the least of all. If anyone will not acknowledge it, as if he were ashamed of it, he will be the least. But to the one who acknowledges it, there is promised the glory of a great calling to heaven.[70]

16. *I say to you that unless your righteousness surpasses that of the scribes and the Pharisees, you will not enter the Kingdom of heaven.*[71] Providing a marvelous introduction to the subject,[72] he begins to surpass the role of the Law, not in order to abolish it, but to rise above it through the steps of a higher advancement.[73] He warns that the apostles will not be admitted to heaven unless they should surpass the righteousness of the Pharisees with equity. Once he established those things that were prescribed by the Law, he surpassed it by advancement, not by abolition.

17. The Law, which prohibited killing, sought to expiate the one accused of homicide with a severe judgment.[74] But the same attitude toward punishment in the Gospels may be found in an evil intention toward another brought on by anger. According to the precept of faith, an angry person is said to be no less guilty, barring an accepted reason, than a murderer

---

66. Mt 5.18.
68. *fides.*
70. Mt 10.32; Lk 12.8.
72. *pulcherrimo ingressu.*
74. Mt 5.21.

67. Jn 19.28–30.
69. Mt 5.19.
71. Mt 5.20.
73. *profectu potiore.*

under the Law. *And whosoever shall say to his brother, "Raca," he will be guilty before the council.*[75] *Raca* is an insult of calling someone "useless";[76] and whoever accuses someone full of the Holy Spirit with the false charge of "useless" becomes guilty before the assembly of saints. For he will have to atone for the outrage committed against the Holy Spirit through the condemnation of the saints' judgment.[77] *Also whoever says, "Fool," he will be guilty of the fire of Gehenna.*[78] There is danger of great impiety in attacking someone by making him look like a fool whom God has called "salt," or by insulting one who is salting the foolish with intelligence, by insulting foolish intelligence.[79] In this way such a person will become fodder for eternal fire. In sum, whatever the Law has not ruled out by its own works, the faith of the Gospels in its words [above] condemns as an outrage.

18. Binding all people together in a mutual love, he allows no one to offer a prayer without the spirit of peace. If one remembers while offering his gifts at the altar that he harbors some grudge against his brothers, he is commanded to make reconciliation with a human peace before returning to divine peace and so cross over from the love of humanity to the love of God.[80]

19. Because the Lord allows that there should always be opportunity for conciliation, he commands us [at every turn] on every road of our lives[81] to be reconciled quickly with our adversary in goodwill. By making a slow return to favor we arrive at the moment of death without having made peace, and the adversary delivers us to the judge, and the judge to the warden, and we are not released [from prison] until we pay up the last cent.[82] According to the precepts of the Lord's Prayer, we pray

75. Mt 5.22a.                                   76. *vacuitatis.*
77. This reading slightly alters Doignon's text from *sanctorum iudicum* to *sanctorum iudicium* as in PL 9:937C (*Sur Matt.* I.136).
78. Mt 5.22b.
79. This word play is inspired by 1 Cor 1.20–25.
80. Mt 5.23–24.
81. *in omni vitae nostrae via.* I am following Perrin's text emendation of *via* instead of *viae;* see M. Perrin, "Comptes Rendus," *Mélanges de science religieuse* 38.3 (1981): 146.
82. This is a very rough quotation of 5.25–26, rendered in the first person plural.

for the forgiveness of our sins following his example. After we have granted pardon to our adversaries, we seek his pardon.[83] So he will refuse this to us if we will refuse it to others, and we are subject to our own judgment if, at the time of judgment, we should not have renounced our grievances. The adversary delivers us to the judge because the wrath of our grievances, which stand opposed to him,[84] is used in accusation against us. Knowing that love covers a multitude of sins[85]—the devil is a solicitous advocate[86] before God of our errors—we will pay off the "last cent" of our punishment, unless the blame of our weighty transgressions[87] is redeemed by his reparation.

What many writers have clarified in this chapter [of Matthew],[88] I have decided not to treat. Here, when we are ordered to be reconciled to our adversary out of goodwill, they [that is, earlier writers] have related it to the harmony of body and spirit, which are naturally opposed to one another. While observing the order of the teaching, and considering how the work of the Law is surpassed by the advancement of the Gospel, we should not sever a continuation of [their] understanding [with our own].

20. *You have heard that it was said, "Do not commit adultery,"*[89] etc. The order of this precept is reported in its proper course as the works of the Law are bypassed. Now the eye that wanders, being equated to adultery in the Gospels, ought to be cut out,[90] and the lustful gaze upon someone's appearance is punished as an act of fornication.[91]

21. *If your right eye offends you, pluck it out and cast it from you,*[92] etc. There is a higher progression to purity[93] here, as faith takes

---

83. Mt 6.12.

84. *manens in eum simultatis nostrae ira nos arguit.* The meaning is not entirely clear, but it seems the wrath (*ira*) that we deserve is also lodged against our adversary, the devil, who accuses us before God (1 Tm 5.14; 1 Pt 5.8).

85. 1 Pt 4.8b.                           86. *patrona.*

87. *criminum.*

88. Probable allusion to Cyprian, *De orat. Dom.* 16, and Tertullian, *De anima* 40.2.

89. Mt 5.27.                           90. Mt 5.29.

91. Mt. 5.28.

92. Mt 5.29.                           93. *innocentiae.*

a step forward. Not only are we told to abstain from personal vices, but also from that which assaults us from without. It is not because our bodily members have sinned that their removal is prescribed; for the left eye goes astray no less than the right one. Certainly a foot, which lacks awareness of concupiscence, does not need to be cut off since the reason for punishment will not fall upon it. Although the members [of the body] are different from one another, we are all nevertheless a single body.[94] We are told to eject, or rather pluck out, those intimate things[95] whose names are most dear to us. We should discern in them any sort of way in which they bring us into the company of their wickedness because of our familiarity with them. It is better for us to surrender useful and even necessary things, like an eye or a foot, than to cling with affection to a corrupted complicity with the fellowship of Gehenna. In fact, the cutting-off of a member is useful if there is an indictment of the heart.[96] When a pervasive concupiscence is manifest, the loss of the body is superfluous since the impulse of the will remains.[97]

22. *It is said that whoever separates from his wife, let him give to her a certificate of separation,*[98] etc. Establishing equity for all people, the Lord instructs the spouse to remain above all in marital harmony. By adding many things to the Law, no part of it is diminished. Nor can one reasonably find fault with the progress made [by the Gospel]. Whereas the Law had granted the freedom to give a certificate of separation on the authority of the document, now the evangelical faith not only proclaimed its desire for concord to the husband, but also imposed guilt for forcing his wife into adultery. If, out of the necessity of separation, she marries another with no other reason than for end-

94. Cf. 1 Cor 12.12–27; Col 3.15.
95. *propinquitates.*
96. Cf. Tertullian, *De paen.* 3.8–11: "[E]very sin is either an action or a thought, so that what is done is done bodily because an action, like a body, can be seen and touched.... is not the will the origin of the action?" (ed. Borleffs, CCSL 1.325).
97. Mt 5.31. The point is that the will, not the flesh, is the locus of sin. While not explicitly anti-docetic, this theological emphasis had become a settled part of the Church's tradition by Hilary's time.
98. Ibid.

ing the first marriage, it is said that she dishonored her [new] husband because of his union with a prostitute wife.[99]

23. *Again you have heard that it was said by the ancients: You shall not make false witness,*[100] etc. The Law has established a penalty for making false witness because the taking of an oath was supposed to repress a fraudulent conscience. In like manner, simple folk and the inexperienced make frequent mention of their god by habitually swearing an oath. Yet faith removes the habit of oathtaking and establishes the affairs of our lives in the truth. Once we have rejected an inclination toward deceit, a straightforward manner of speaking and hearing is prescribed so that whatever is the case, it is what it is, and whatever is not the case, it is not, because there exists between *yes* and *no*[101] a possibility for deceit, *and whatever is beyond these, is complete evil.*[102] For whatever is, is always what it is of itself, but whatever is not, is by nature not to be.[103] For those who come in the simplicity of faith, there is no need for the observation of an oath;[104] what is "yes" is always "yes," and what is "no" is always "no." For these reasons, every work and word of theirs is trustworthy.

24. *Nor shall you swear by heaven since it is the throne of God,*[105] etc. Not only does the Lord not permit us to render oaths unto God, because all of God's truth ought to be retained in a straightforward manner by our words and deeds, but he also condemns the superstitious pride of the ancients.[106] Among Jews there was an observance of swearing by the names of the elements in heaven and the earth, of Jerusalem, and of their own heads. In this way they offered veneration with an oath; [however, it] served as an insult to God. What was the impulse for swearing by heaven, the

99. Mt 5.32. Cf. 1 Cor 7.11.  100. Mt 5.33. *Non periurabis.*
101. *inter "est" et "non."*
102. Mt 5.37. *Sit autem sermo vester: est, est, et non, non: quod autem abundantius* [or *amplius*] *est hoc, a malo est.*
103. This recalls the definition of the being of God in Tertullian, *Adv. Hermog.* 12.4: "But the eternal Lord cannot be any other thing than what he always is" (ed. Kroymann, CCSL 1.407).
104. *iurandi religio.*  105. Mt 5.34.
106. Lit., "the superstition of the ancients' pride" (*superstitionem contumaciae veteris*).

throne of God, or swearing by the earth—the footstool of his feet—or swearing by Jerusalem, a city which was soon going to be destroyed on account of its inhabitants' arrogance and sins? Had not that *city of the great king*[107] been established especially as a prefiguring[108] of the Church, that is, the body of Christ?[109] Why do they want to swear by their own heads? Is there a chance of changing even one hair by swearing, when nature (as effected by God) assigns a color to every person?[110] The Lord therefore shows that their confidence in making an oath is full of impiety since they are participants of a religion of works,[111] having ignored or neglected their Maker.[112]

25. *You have heard that it has been said: an eye for an eye, tooth for a tooth,*[113] etc. The Lord wants the hope of our faith, which stretches toward eternity, to be proven by our own deeds[114] so that the tolerance of overlooking an injury may serve as a witness to future judgment. By using fear, the Law controlled an unfaithful Israel in a climate of fear, as the desire to commit injury was checked by the threat of injury in kind. Faith, however, does not allow resentment so grave from an injury that it seeks for revenge, nor should anyone avenge an insult brought against him. In God's judgment there is greater consolation for those who have suffered injury and more severe punishment for those who commit injuries. Not only do the Gospels command us to abstain from iniquity, but they also exact our forbearance from avenging an injury. Upon receiving a slap on the cheek we are ordered to offer the other cheek,[115] and after carrying a burden for one mile, to go the distance of two miles.[116] With the increase of injury will come the increase of [divine] retribution.[117] The Lord of the heavenly powers[118] offered himself, his

107. Mt 5.35.
108. *praeformationem*, a neologism of Hilary. Cf. *infra*, 6.3; 21.10; 24.7.
109. Col 1.18; Eph 1.22–23.
110. Mt 5.36. Cf. Tertullian, *De cult. fem.* 2.6, which quotes Mt 5.36 against those who dye their hair a color different from how God made them.
111. *religio operibus.*                    112. Rom 1.25.
113. Mt 5.38.
114. Or, "by the events themselves" (*rebus ipsis*).
115. Mt 5.39.                    116. Mt 5.41.
117. *ultionis.* That is, for those who do injuries to others.
118. *virtutum caelestium.*

cheeks to the palms [of hands] and his shoulders to the whip, for the advancement of his glory.

26. Not only are we told that the decisions of human judgment must be shunned, but that we also should avoid the desire of inflicting loss, in such a way that we should also hand over our cloak to the one wishing to take our tunic.[119] By despising worldly goods on account of a hope for future benefits, we denounce the foolish desire of the pagans and the vanity of their unproductive greed. The Lord commands that we give to each one what he asks and that we not turn away our attention or inclination[120] from the requests of someone wanting to borrow from us.[121] The purpose is that they may be satisfied through our generosity by the things they lacked and that we may prevent either their thirst with a drink, or their hunger with food, or their nudity with the provision of clothing.[122] And thus we may be found worthy of the good things that we seek from God since the practice of liberality is linked to the right of possession.[123] Moreover, in the process of administering his kindness, which we have received, it shows that we must be given to generosity. By the gracious administration of freely doing good,[124] we may not deny the one who wishes to borrow from us what we are borrowing from God. In this way we will always perform our office of sharing without the liability of possessing things.[125]

27. *You have heard that it was said, "You shall love your neighbor, and you shall hate your enemy,"* [126] etc. He has bound all things together perfected by his goodness. The Law demanded love of one's neighbor and gave license to the hatred of one's enemy. Faith, however, commands us to love our enemies.[127] The disposition of love toward all people breaks the headstrong activity of human impulse, not only by quelling the anger of taking revenge

---

119. Mt 5.40.
120. *os atque animum.*
121. Mt 5.42.
122. Mt 25.35–36.
123. *obtinendi meritum.*
124. *boni gratuiti sit dispensatio gratuita.*
125. *habendi damno.* Cf. *supra,* 16.11; 17.1.
126. Mt 5.43.
127. Mt 5.44.

but also by mitigating the effect of an insult through love. To love those who love you is characteristic of the pagans, and to esteem those who esteem you is commonplace.[128] Instead, he calls us into God's inheritance, as well as to the imitation of Christ at his coming,[129] both for the good and for the unjust [people], and into the mysteries of baptism and of the Spirit even as he confers on us the sun and the rain.[130] Thus the Lord establishes us in a life perfected by this mandate of goodness toward everyone, just as we are to imitate our perfect Father in heaven.[131]

28. *Beware of practicing your righteousness before the eyes of men,*[132] etc. He removes every concern about our offering [physical] things, telling us to be inspired only by a future hope. We are not to pursue the favor of others by a display of our goodness,[133] nor to vaunt our religion by demonstrative prayer before the public.[134] Rather, the fruit of good works must be supported within the conscience of one's faith. When the eager pursuit of human praise strives for that alone which comes from others, it will have its reward. Whereas the expectation of one who seeks to attain God will obtain the reward of [God's] long patience.

Furthermore, the left hand should ignore the action of the right hand. But does the nature of the body permit this? Don't the functions of the hands respond to the direction of our intelligence? In order that our actions may be grounded on knowledge of God, may our understanding, when we perform those actions with our members,[135] be a protection within us and with us.[136]

---

128. Mt 5.46.
129. That is, Christ in his Incarnation.
130. Mt 5.45.                      131. Mt 5.48.
132. Mt 6.1.                       133. Mt 6.6.
134. Mt 6.5.
135. Lit., "under the name of our members" (*sub nuncupatione membrorum*), that is, our right and left hands. See Mt 6.3.
136. Or, "prevent us from doing the wrong" (... *conscientia arceatur*).

# CHAPTER FIVE

E ARE INSTRUCTED to pray with the door of our room closed,[1] and likewise taught to offer our prayer in every place since the prayers of the saints were undertaken in the midst of wild beasts, in prisons, within flames, from the depth of the sea, and from the belly of the monster.[2] We are told to enter the secret places, not of a house, but of the room of our heart. Enclosed within the privacy of our mind, we are to pray to God, not with copious speaking, but with our understanding, because every such prayer is superior to the words of our speech. Concerning the sacrament[3] of prayer, Cyprian, the man of blessed memory, has freed us from the necessity of making comment.[4] And although Tertullian wrote a most competent volume on this matter,[5] the subsequent error of the man has detracted from the authority of his commendable writings.[6]

1. Mt 6.6.

2. *bestia.* Probably a reference to Jonah praying from the belly of the sea monster (Jon 2.2). Cf. Tertullian, *De resurr.* 32.3–4, who speaks of Jonah in the fish as prefiguring the persecution of Christians.

3. *sacramento.*

4. The Cyprian mentioned here was the bishop of Carthage from ca. 248 to 258, martyred under the reign of Decius. Among his surviving writings is *De dominica oratione,* a brief and apparently well known set of observations on the Lord's Prayer.

5. Tertullian, *De oratione.* Tertullian, a layman who also lived in Carthage, focuses on the Lord's Prayer in Chapters 2–8 of this work.

6. The negative reference is to Tertullian's embrace of the New Prophecy later in his life. By Hilary's day, the New Prophecy, or Montanism, had become completely discredited as a heretical movement. See Jerome, *De viris illust.* 26, 40, 41, 53; Augustine, *De haer.* 26–27. Vincent of Lérins cites this passage of Hilary's in *Comm.* 18.46, slightly altering it to read, "by his subsequent error he undermined the authority of his commendable writings" (PL 50:664). Hilary's attitude toward the value of Tertullian's contributions is probably typical. The latter's theological and biblical work was utilized extensively, but despite its importance, the writer is never regarded *in nomine* as an authority.

2. *Whenever you fast, do not put on a gloomy face as the hypocrites, for they neglect their appearance in order to be seen fasting by men.*[7] He teaches us that the benefit of fasting is gained without the outward display of a weakened body, and that we should not curry the favor of the pagans by a display of deprivation. Instead, every instance of fasting should have the beauty of a holy exercise. For oil is the fruit of mercy according to the heavenly and prophetic word.[8] Our head,[9] that is, the rational part of our life, should be adorned with beautiful works because all understanding is in the head. Impurities on our face are washed off so that no one is appalled by its disheveled appearance. There is, however, a greater grace of [his] radiance in our encounter:[10] once we are purified for the clarity of a good conscience and have been anointed with oil[11] for the grace of works of mercy, our fasting commends us to God. Even when we shun the attention of others by fasting with our heads anointed, we will be more pleasing[12] and be acknowledged.[13]

3. *Do not lay up treasure for yourselves on earth,*[14] etc. Bypassing the concern for human glory and riches, the Lord shows that we should make every effort to please God. Because detraction by envious people distorts human glory[15] as do the vices of the body, the result is that a treasury of money here on earth is in danger of being either lost or stolen. Heavenly glory, however, is eternal; it cannot be seized by robbery, nor destroyed by a moth, nor deteriorated by the rust of envy.[16] Whether the locus of treasure that we seek is held in our heart[17] or in the light

7. Mt 6.16.
8. Ps 44.8 Vg. (Ps 45.7).
9. The head is the part anointed with oil.
10. I.e., with God, as suggested by Coustant, PL 9:943D. Cf. Hilary, *In Matt.* 4.7 and *Tract. Ps.* 140.9.
11. *delibutos.*
12. *ridiculi,* literally meaning "absurd" or "laughable." The choice of words here may be Hilary's attempt to be ironic; that is, the results of fasting present a beauty seen only by God.
13. I.e., by God. Cf. Tertullian, *De ieiun.* 9.2 (CCSL 2.1265), discussing the appearance of Daniel and his friends, who preferred water and vegetables over the king's rich food, yet were "better-looking" (*formosiores*) than the others.
14. Mt 6.19.     15. *laudem.*
16. Mt 6.20.     17. Mt 6.21.

of our understanding, [our choice] is going to be either with money (which is lost to robbery) or with the eternal God.

4. *The lamp of your body is your eye.*[18] Perception is the chief feature [of the eye]. It is through the functioning of the eye that light within the heart is portrayed. If it remains uncompromised[19] and clear, it will bestow to the body the clarity of eternal light and will pour the splendor of its source[20] into the corruption of the flesh. But if it becomes obscured by sin and by a vile willfulness, the nature of the body will be subjugated to the vices of the mind. And if that light within us should turn to darkness,[21] how great must that darkness be! In this case, a corrupted source of earthly flesh has already been accustomed to dominate dangerously over the nobility of the soul. Sins of the body grow worse over time, especially if they are sustained by the desires of the soul. For this reason, our bodies will become darkness beyond that which is their nature if the light of the mind is extinguished within them. But if we have preserved the simplicity of spirit, then its light is sure to illuminate the body.

5. *No one is able to serve two masters.*[22] Servitude to two masters is disloyalty: one cannot be equally concerned with both the world and God. It is unavoidable that there should be disdain for one and love for the other, [since each master desires different work]; doing the same work according to the wishes of different masters is not appropriate. Nor can the poor in spirit,[23] who are pleasing to God, be made suitable for the vanity of this world.

6. *Therefore I say to you: do not concern yourself with what you shall eat nor how you shall clothe your body. Is not your life more than food and the body more than clothing?*[24] In all the preceding words, Jesus had prescribed contempt for the world and confidence in the future. When he commanded us to be open to insult,

18. Mt 6.22.
19. *simplex.*
20. That is, the origins of the heavenly glory, 1 Cor 15.40.
21. Mt 6.23.                              22. Mt 6.24.
23. Mt 5.3. *Supra,* 4.2.                 24. Mt 6.25.

and willingly accept loss, and to be indifferent about taking revenge, and indiscriminate about those whom we love, and unconcerned for human glory, he was urging us to set our hopes courageously on eternal gain.[25] Both the love of present things[26] and anxiety about things to come foster uncertainty in many people, either captivating them by enticements or confounding them through their disbelief. He wants us, therefore, to put our hope, without any ambiguity of an uncertain will, in the Kingdom of heaven, which the prophets announced, John preached, and our Lord declared was found in himself. If faith is doubtful, how can there be justification by faith?[27] For this reason, the Lord instructs us to have no care about clothing or about food, saying that life is more valuable than nourishment and the body more valuable than food.

7. It is certainly wonderful to devote attention only to divine matters in contempt of present things. The pronouncement[28] with its meaning[29] from on high has descended and is broadened to an understanding of heavenly speech, confined, as it were, to words.[30] The Lord has prescribed that our treasure be established in heaven, and he has also promised splendor for the body from the light of the eye.[31] He affirmed that no one can please two masters, and, following this, he said: *Therefore, I say to you, do not concern yourself with what you shall eat nor how you shall clothe your body.*[32] These latter words do not really correspond with the previous statements. Is not a servant of one master able to be anxious over clothing and food? Will not the

25. *confirmari nos in spem bonorum aeternorum laborat.*

26. *amor praesentium.* Cf. 5.12, *cura saecularis substantiae;* 10.5, *saeculi gaudia;* 14.8, *saecularis luxus.*

27. *Infra,* 26.5. On Hilary's theology of justification by faith and the possibility that his commentary may have contributed to the revival of Pauline studies in the west after the middle of the fourth century, see P. Smulders, "Hilary of Poitiers as an Exegete of St. Matthew," *Bijdragen* 44 (1983): 82.

28. *sermo.*

29. *ratio.*

30. In other words, the reader should seek the *ratio* of the passage in a spiritual interpretation.

31. Mt 6. 22.

32. Mt 6.25

body, on account of illness, have the light in its eyes dimmed and be placed in darkness? For what light of the body can there be except from the eye? Will nudity or hunger alone be able to store up treasure in heaven?

8. Because there is a view, corrupted as it is, among those who deny the faith[33] when it comes to the matter of future things—what kind of bodies they will have at the resurrection, and what is the sustenance of [their] eternal substance—amidst the complexities of useless questions,[34] they have sought a certain reason for the enjoyment of pleasures in the present. Lingering in a futile fear over reverence shown to God, they pass into the joys of this world.[35] When service is rendered to two masters, it is unfaithful to one of them. Despite their lofty disposition toward piety, the Lord has declared about the aforementioned gravest danger of the lack of faith,[36] as he warns: *Is not life more than food and the body more than clothing?* In these words there is the truth of God, as well as all effectual power for the work of creation in his word. For this reason, there is no uncertainty about what he has promised, nor ineffectiveness about what he has spoken. There is nothing that is not corporeal in its substance and in its creation,[37] while the elements of all things, whether in heaven or on the earth, whether visible or invisible, have been formed. For all kinds of souls,[38] whether they possess bodies or are departing from them, possess a corporeal substance according to their nature[39] because everything that is created must be within something.

With reproach, God does not allow the absurdity of their useless disputations;[40] seeing how soul and body must be placed

33. *infidelium.* Cf. 2.3; 5.12; 7.6; et passim.

34. The same questions are mentioned *infra,* 22.4.

35. Cf. 1 Cor 15.32.

36. *diffidentia.* Cf. Tertullian, *De resurr.* 2.3.

37. See Tertullian, *De carne Chr.* 11.4: *Omne quod est, corpus et sui generis. Nihil est incorporale, quod non est;* see E. Evans, ed., *Q. Septimii Florentis Tertulliani de carne Christi liber* (London: SPCK, 1956), 42.

38. *animarum species.*

39. Cf. Tertullian, *De anima* 5.6, 36.2, and *De resurr.* 18.6, who espoused the corporeality of the soul. Hilary seems to be accepting this idea, though he will reject it in later works. See *Tract. Ps.* 129.4–5.

40. Presumably this is in reference to the "view ... among those who deny

in an eternal substance,[41] our hope of a resurrection would be minimized over concern over future food and clothing. Since there is such a high price of restoring them, namely, body and soul, no blame should be imputed to the ones who place less value on food or clothing.

9. *Look at the birds of the sky; although they do not sow, nor gather into barns, your heavenly Father feeds them. Are you not worth more than they?*[42] The Lord instructs us by the example of unclean spirits under the name of *birds.* They live without any worries of acquiring and stockpiling, but to them are provided the resources[43] drawn from the power of his eternal wisdom.[44] Since it was appropriate that this reference should be used of the unclean spirits, he added, *Are you not of greater worth than they?*— showing from the efficacy of a comparison[45] a distinction between wickedness and holiness.

10. *But who among you is able to add a single cubit to his stature? And why are you anxious concerning what you will wear?*[46] From the pattern[47] drawn from these principles,[48] he has bolstered confidence in the vitality of our [bodily] substance. As it concerns our (body's) future condition, he rejects the commonly held understanding.[49] Because he is the one who grants the particularities of all bodies that possess life, [making] one whole and perfect man,[50] he alone is capable of bestowing height to each one, whether it be one, two, or three cubits. How greatly do we

---

the faith," above (5.8). Hilary never specifies whom he has in mind here. Not being a polemical document, no erroneous or heretical group is ever identified throughout the commentary.

41. I.e., the incorruptibility and immortality of 1 Cor 15.50–54.

42. Mt 6.26. Part of the verse is omitted: *quoniam non serunt neque metunt neque congregant . . . (Itala,* 34).

43. *substantia.* See Kinnavey, 259–62, for Hilary's use of *substantia.*

44. *consilii.*

45. *praestantia.* Some MSS read *distantia.*

46. Mt 6.27–28a.

47. *documento.*

48. Reading *spirituum* (Perrin, 146) instead of Doignon's *spiritum (Sur Matt.* I.158).

49. Viz., that we ought to be concerned about our clothing and our physical appearance.

50. Cf. Ps 8.5.

insult him when we worry about our garments, that is, the aspect of our bodies! He will add to human bodies just the right measure in order that he may realize equality and uniformity for all humanity.

11. *Consider how the lilies of the field grow; they do not labor nor do they weave. Yet I say to you that not even Solomon in all his glory was clothed as one of these,*[51] etc. The lilies do not labor, nor do they weave, nor was Solomon, a great prophet[52] and deservedly esteemed before God for his love of wisdom, clothed in their glory. Of course, lilies bloom instead of being covered [with clothing]. Clothing is a covering[53] for the body; it is not the body itself. According to the perception of human understanding, the splendor of clothing is able to rival the color of the lilies. But the lilies, not by labor or weaving, must be understood to signify the radiance of the heavenly angels. Upon them the splendor of glory has been bestowed by God, quite beyond the industry of human knowledge or payment for doing work (lest anyone should think that he had appropriated it by his own labor or artistic ability). Although men will be like the angels in the resurrection,[54] the Lord desires that we put our hope in the covering of heavenly glory, following the example of angelic radiance.

Now there is in the nature of the lily a fitting comparison to the heavenly substance of angels. When its blossoms are plucked off its stalk, which is grounded by the roots in the soil, the vitality of its nature,[55] even if it seems to have withered, is hidden. But after the season returns, the plant is clothed once more with the honor of its lily. For within itself, it is rejuvenated and blossoms, and its being[56] is indebted neither to the root nor to the soil since the sap within is derived from itself. And so the plant emulates the vitality of a heavenly substance,[57] according to the pattern of this annual verdancy, given that it receives only what is within itself to produce a flower. For this reason, there-

---

51. Mt 6.28b–29.
53. *coopertio.*
55. *naturae suae virtutem.*
57. *virtutem caelestis substantiae.*

52. *propheta magnus.*
54. Mt 22.30.
56. Lit., "what it is" (*quod est*).

fore, the lilies do not labor nor weave, just as the vitality of the angels—who always exist—receives what they obtained in accordance with the state of their origin.

12. *If, indeed, the grass of the field, which exists today and tomorrow is thrown into the fire, is thus clothed by God, how much greater are you, who have little faith?*[58] By the weight[59] of these examples[60] he encourages the unshakeable assurance of our faith. Inasmuch as doubt holds great danger, so the heavy weight of anxiety seizes every occasion of disbelief. Grass is not produced to be thrown into the fire, nor does God have special concern for clothing that will be burned up. Rather, under the name of grass we find that God frequently designated the pagans.[61] They are like a plant which, after it has lost the blossom of its vitality,[62] withers in the heat of the sun. Thus there will be given no rest to the pagans nor will the onset of death bring the peace they desire.[63] Instead, their bodies are destined to suffer eternally because their punishment of eternal fire will be physical. What they endure, along with everything else destined for eternity, will have no end. If pagans are given a body destined for eternity in order to suffer the fire of judgment, how great is the impiety of those saints who doubt the glory of eternity since eternal punishment is certain for sinners![64]

The Lord expects all our hopes[65] will be placed in the certainty of his promises and in the power of his might,[66] in order that, having ceased to worry about what we lack, we should look forward to receiving all things from him, from whom our very life had its beginning. We should seek the Kingdom of God[67] through the service of our life.[68] And this is the reward for those who live a righteous and perfect life: to be transformed

---

58. Mt 6.30.   59. *auctoritate.*
60. Such as lilies and grass.
61. *Supra,* 2.4. Cf. Ps 37.2 (36.2 LXX); Is 40.6; 1 Pt 1.24.
62. *virtutis suae.*
63. *compendio quies dabitur.* Cf. Cicero, *Tusc.* 1.97 (*Sur Matt.* I.163, n.12).
64. *iniquis.*
65. Lit., "expectation" (*exspectationem*).
66. *virtutis suae.*   67. Mt 6.33.
68. *vitae nostrae stipendiis.*

from the corruptible matter of this body into a new and heavenly substance; for earthly corruption to be changed into heavenly incorruption.[69] It follows that the pagans in their unbelief are anxious about their affairs[70] since they are captured by the love of this age and absorbed in the delights of the body. They do not seek nor desire the way to the heavenly Kingdom through faith and praise of God.[71]

13. *Therefore, do not be anxious about tomorrow. For tomorrow will be anxious about itself. Sufficient for the day are its own evils.*[72] It is generally understood that a day is a lapse of time which is illuminated by the light of the sun, and in which night intervenes, dividing and preparing for another day to follow. And yet, the significance of the future[73] is contained in tomorrow.[74] God forbids us to be anxious about the future. Release from worry through indifference is not negligence, but faith. Why should we be anxious about tomorrow when tomorrow is anxious for itself? Therefore, the anxious day itself dispels our worries for us. But worry, as I think of it, is a sentiment unique to human beings; for worry provokes this feeling on account of concern, fear, or sorrow. But a day's segment is a lapse of time, and only those who have obtained foreknowledge[75] undergo a sense of anxiety. A "day" thereby must be construed as a living creature[76] that is wary, keeps watch, and frets, and its own evil is sufficient to itself without the addition of sin heaped up from elsewhere. And when one is [inwardly] burdened with sin, nothing further need be added to someone so impaired.[77] But the nature of things does not suppose that the state of our mind should be determined by a day. For the day has its own worries,[78] and its own evils suffice for it. Since we are prohibited from being anxious about tomorrow, everything [that concerns

---

69. 1 Cor 15.50–53.

70. Mt 6.32.

71. Mt 6.33.

72. Mt 6.34.

73. *futuri temporis.*

74. On classical wisdom regarding the relation of day to night and the future of tomorrow, *Sur Matt.* I.165, nn.13–14.

75. *providentiam.* A quality unique to God.

76. *Animal.*

77. *neque extrinsecus accidenti sit.*

78. *sibi ipsa sollicita est.*

us] is contained by the significance of the heavenly words. We are instructed not to have doubt about what is to come.[79] There are enough evils in our life, and the sins in which we live daily are sufficient that all our preoccupation[80] and effort may be engaged with purging of and expiation for these [evils and sins]. If we should lose confidence in future good, we would be guilty of unforgivable disbelief. Once our worry has come to an end, those future things which had preoccupied us[81] will give way to the good things bestowed on us by God's goodness. On that day we will no longer be anxious.

14. *Do not judge, lest you be judged. For by whatever judgment you have judged, you will be judged.*[82] God utterly rejects every element of judging, nor does he allow a place for it at all. Yet the latter part of the verse[83] appears to be opposed to the former when it states: *By whatever judgment you have judged, you will be judged,* while it says above: *Do not judge, lest you be judged.* Is it not appropriate to accept the decision of a good judgment? Indeed, he declares that we should be judged according to the terms of our judgment and that everyone should be measured by the terms he has used to measure [another]. There will never be a righteous judgment if there is no judging at all. But as it was already acknowledged much earlier,[84] there is nothing in the words of God that is treated lightly or in vain, and in this case too every word goes beyond the understanding of pagan ears.[85] In effect, God has forbidden that his promises should be judged. Just as judgments among men are founded upon uncertainties, so we must not annul a judgment that is contrary to God on the basis of the doubt of someone's thought or opinion, and that deeply repels us, so that we may be more confident[86] about our [own] faith. If there is sin that corresponds to our having made a wrong judgment, we are surely guilty[87] in this instance for casting judgment upon God.

79. Mt 6.34.
80. *meditatio.*
81. *ipsa in officio suo.*
82. Mt 7.1–2.
83. *subsequentia.*
84. *Supra,* 4.14.
85. That is, those who do not understand that Scripture contains meanings that go beyond the surface or literal level of interpretation.
86. *constans potius fides.*
87. *criminis.*

15. *Why do you notice the speck in your brother's eye and not notice the plank in your eye?* etc.[88] In what follows the Lord taught that only blasphemy against the Spirit will be beyond pardon,[89] whereas there will be leniency for all other sins according to the generosity of God. A sin against the Spirit is to deny the fullness of power[90] to God and to abrogate the eternal substance in Christ,[91] through whom God came into man, so man will become as God.[92] Just as there is a great difference between a speck and a plank, so a sin against the Spirit supersedes other charges of guilt. When unbelievers put the blame on others for the wrongs [committed] in the body, they do not see the load of sin in themselves. This causes them to doubt the promises of God, because they do not see that a plank is fixed in their eye, as it is also [lodged] in their faculty of understanding.[93] For it often happens that we usurp authority for ourselves by accusing others without any opportunity[94] for personal reform. We prefer to boast that we are able to heal the blindness of another, while we ourselves are found in darkness, our eyesight[95] ruined. Since it is difficult for anyone to offer what he lacks, it is best to teach by example rather than words. Care must therefore be used in dealing with one's own blindness, because it is the nature of things that no one can be a teacher capable of removing a speck from his brother's eye before he has rejected from his own eyesight of understanding[96] the plank of an onerous faithlessness.[97]

---

88. Mt 7.3.

89. *veniam.* Cf. *infra*, 12.15–17.

90. *virtutis potestatem.*

91. Cf. *infra*, 12.15–17.

92. Cf. Irenaeus, *Demonstratio* 31: "So He united man with God and brought about a communion of God and man" (*St. Irenaeus: Proof of the Apostolic Preaching,* trans. J. P. Smith, ACW 16, 167). Hilary's emphasis is not merely soteriological, but christological and incarnational; *infra*, 10.27; 12.17–18; 24.1; *De trin.* 1.13; 10.7.

93. *mentis acie.*

94. *exemplo.*

95. *luminis.*

96. *de mentis suae lumine.*

97. Mt 7.4–5.

# CHAPTER SIX

O *NOT GIVE to dogs what is holy nor throw your pearls before pigs,*[1] etc. Nothing is more valuable and more holy than the precepts and promises of God, which confer upon us, who are sanctified, the treasure of immortality. We are not permitted to distribute those sacraments and powers[2] to the pagans or to discuss them with heretics. For *dogs* are the pagans, so called[3] because they bark in rage against God. But the name *pig* is given to heretics because, although they have a cloven hoof, they nevertheless reconstitute the knowledge of God they received without chewing it.[4] And thus it is not appropriate that we treat the Incarnation of the Word of God,[5] the mystery of his Passion, and the power of his Resurrection[6] haphazardly, nor should we present it incompetently or carelessly. If we lack the instruction of a complete knowledge,[7] they may mock and despise our ignorance and ridicule the weakness of God in his Passion.[8] They would turn it against us, shattering our ignorance and our faith with stinging points of contradiction.[9]

1. Mt 7.6.

2. *virtutes.* In this case, *virtus* is the divine work of God in the believer's life.

3. Cf. Mt 15.27; Mk 7.28; Rv 22.14–15.

4. Lv 11.3; Dt 14.6. Only animals that have a cloven hoof and chew their cud are considered clean. Cf. Novatian, *De cib. Iud.* 3. Believers who have both things are considered clean, whereas heretics have one but not the other, and the pagans have neither.

5. *concorporationem verbi Dei.* Cf. *De trin.* 4.27, where Hilary uses *concorpatio,* i.e., the Word who assumed a body.

6. *virtutem resurrectionis.* Phil 2.10; Hilary, *De trin.* 5.33; 8.42; 9.56.

7. Cf. 1 Cor 2.6.

8. This is one of many warnings that Hilary raises about those who criticize any view of Christ's Incarnation that results in attributing weakness or want to God. *Supra,* 3.1–3; *infra,* 8.2; 12.8; 23.6, 8; 24.1; 31.2–3.

9. The probable source of Hilary's comments here are found in Cyprian, who begins his address to a pagan critic, Demetrianus, against whose "sac-

2. In these matters of which we are ignorant the way is opened for us to pursue truth, obtainable only through periods of prayer.[10] So that we may perceive and believe all things, and cast off any uncertainty of a doubtful will, we have to ask, to seek, and to knock,[11] discovering mercy by asking, progress in seeking, and an open door in making the attempt.[12] It is indeed with this hope of obtaining what we ask, seek, and knock that we are taught by an example of human affection. Just as we will not offer a snake or a stone to our children who seek fish or bread,[13] how much more will our highest and most excellent Father bestow gifts of complete faith to those who beseech him?[14] Nor is he going to offer a stone of pagan callousness[15] instead of the food of life, or give a serpent of poisonous heresy instead of the protection of our baptism.[16] Accordingly, he accomplished everything according to the model of his goodness, joining all people together in the peace of mutual love, which constitutes within it the commandments of the Law and the prophets, so that we may be good to all, desiring that all will be good to us.[17]

3. *Enter through the narrow gate. How wide and spacious is the way that leads to perdition!*[18] The journey on the way to heaven is a difficult one, and its entrance is narrow and small,[19] whereas

---

rilegious mouth and impious words against the one and true God," "we are, moreover, bidden to keep what is holy within our own knowledge, and not expose it to be trodden down by swine and dogs, since the Lord speaks, saying, 'Give not that which is holy unto the dogs, neither cast ye your pearls before swine, lest they trample them under their feet, and turn again and rend you.' For when you used often to come to me with the desire of contradicting rather than with the wish *(voto)* to learn, … you shouted with noisy words …" *Ad Demetrianum* 1.1 (ANF 5.457–58; CSEL 3.1, p. 351).

10. Cf. Cyprian, *De orat. dom.* 1–2, regarding the discovery of the way of truth in prayer.

11. Mt 7.7.

12. Reading *temptamento aditum* with Doignon's text, instead of *testamento adytum*, found in some MSS.

13. Mt 7.9–10.

14. Mt 7.11.

15. *duritiae gentiles.*

16. Cf. Tertullian, *De bapt.* 1.2 (CCSL 1.277): "vipers, and asps and basilisks generally prefer arid and waterless places. But we, little fishes, are born in water after the example of our Ἰχθύς, Jesus Christ."

17. Mt 7.12.                    18. Mt 7.13.

19. Mt 7.14.

the way of perdition is wide. There are many who acquire this latter way, but few who find the other. For these few, the loss of present things is a blessing.[20] To overcome the lusts of the soul, to tame the body, and to bypass the enticements of all attractions provided by all the powers of the age:[21] this is for them the greatest gain of heavenly hopes. But for those whose only good is to engage in fornication, to squander, to strive for gain, to act arrogantly, to be haughty, to have hatred, and to plunder,[22] there is a very large company going on such a journey.

4. Because there are few who find the narrow way,[23] the deceit of those who imagine they are seeking it is exposed: *Watch out for false prophets who come to you in sheep's clothing,*[24] etc. The Lord warns that flattering words and the pretense of innocence[25] should be weighed according to the fruit of one's works.[26] We do not depend only on the kind of person who represents himself by words, but on one who proves himself by deeds. There are many whose wolf-like fury[27] is cloaked in sheep's clothing. It follows that just as thorn bushes do not produce grapes, nor thistles produce figs, so bad trees do not bear edible fruit.[28] Thus he teaches that among these kinds of people the production of good works does not occur, and, for this reason, all ought to be known by their fruit. Indeed, they do not reach the Kingdom of heaven solely by the use of words, nor will whoever should say, *Lord, Lord,*[29] inherit it.[30] For what is to be gained by calling the Lord "Lord"? Will he still not be the Lord unless we call him that? And what name[31] can be applied to one's holy service[32] when it is rather one's obedience to the will of God, not the name, that charts the way to the Kingdom of heaven?

---

20. *cara.*
21. *totis saeculi viribus.*
22. Cf. *infra,* 27.2.
23. Mt 7.14.
24. Mt 7.15. The Old Latin reads, *Attendite vobis a falsis prophetis* … ("Guard yourselves from false prophets who come to you in sheep's clothing"), which makes slightly better sense than Hilary's *Adtendite a pseudoprophetis qui veniunt* …
25. *mansuetudinis simulationem.*
26. Mt 7.16.
27. *rabies lupina.*
28. Mt 7.17–18.
29. Mt 7.22.
30. *coheres illius.*
31. *nominis nuncupatio.*
32. *officii sanctitas.*

5. *Many will say to me on that day, "Lord, Lord, did we not proph-esy in your name?"*[33] etc. He again condemns the deceitfulness of pseudo-prophets and the pretense of hypocrites who attri-bute glory to themselves by the power of their words[34] in pro-phetic teaching, expelling demons and exercising powers of this kind. They promise themselves the Kingdom of heaven as if anything which they speak or do is unique,[35] and as if the power of God, when summoned,[36] does not accomplish every-thing. It is, however, the reading[37] that brings about knowledge of doctrine, and it is the name of Christ that empowers[38] the expulsion of demons.[39] Therefore, we must merit that blessed eternity, and we must offer something of ourselves in order that we should desire the good, avoid every evil, and submit to heavenly instruction with all our heart. By such service we may be known to God[40] and pursue what the Lord desires rather than what brings glory to ourselves.[41] He repudiates and expels those who, through their own knowledge, would turn to works of iniquity.[42]

6. *Therefore, everyone who hears my words and does [them], I will make him like the wise man who built his house upon a rock,*[43] and the rest. An understanding of this passage is linked to what has preceded. Repudiating the boasts of false prophets and the fabrications of hypocrites, the Lord describes a man who has perfect faith by means of an example of comparison. The man who hears his words and acts on them is built upon a rock and supported on a stable and firm foundation. He cannot be dislodged by the force of the storm when it occurs, since the

---

33. Mt 7.22.                    34. *ex verbi virtute.*
35. *proprium.*                 36. Or "invoked" (*invocata*).
37. The "reading" is probably of Scripture, though Doignon suggests it is a reference to the reading of saints' letters (e.g., *Life of Cyprian* 2).
38. *exagitet.*                 39. Mt 7.22b.
40. Mt 7.23.                    41. *quod potest gloriemur.*
42. Hilary's contrast between the two uses of "knowledge" (*cognitio*) here is not as obvious in the English. There is knowledge of one's own abilities ex-ercised for one's own glory versus the power given by God that brings the ac-knowledgment (or knowledge) of those that yield their abilities as gifts.
43. Mt 7.24. This verse has a number of variations in the versions of the Old Latin Bible. Most common is, "Therefore, everyone who hears these my words and does them is like a wise man" (*Itala,* 39).

Lord indicates [with the words] *on a rock* that he himself is a strong foundation of the highest building. Moreover, this person who has grown to be a towering construction[44] based on the Lord will not be moved by rain nor by flames nor by wind[45] (by *rain* he indicates the enticements of smooth talkers[46] and of those who gradually slip into sensuality,[47] which is how their faith initially becomes "wet" through the open cracks [of their "house"]). Despite the onset of rushing waters (that is, the swirling of deep desire[48] as an aggressive force), and all the force of the wind whipping around and raging furiously—namely, the assault of every spirit of diabolical power[49]—the person established on the foundation of the rock will stand fast and cannot be dislodged.[50] But the foolish person, ignoring the words that he heard, is similar to a work of construction[51] that rests upon sand. It stands insecurely,[52] to be quickly undermined by the falling rains, to be destroyed by flames, and to be knocked over by the winds. Given the properties of sand on which it was built, it is broken down into a heavy pile of ruins.[53]

7. And so, by the example of the preceding comparisons, the Lord wants us also to do what he commands, and to believe what he has promised. Once all these things were accomplished, the crowds were amazed at his teaching[54] because he taught them not in the manner of the scribes and Pharisees.[55] For it was in the power[56] of his words that the efficaciousness of his authority[57] was measured.

44. *in sublime opus excreverit.*          45. Mt 7.25.
46. *blandarum.*
47. *illabentium voluptatum.* Cf. Tertullian, *De bapt.* 5.14.
48. *cupiditatum.*                          49. *diabolicae potestatis spiritus.*
50. Mt 7.25.                                51. *opus aedificationis.*
52. Mt 7.26.                                53. Mt 7.27.
54. Mt 7.28.                                55. Mt 7.29.
56. *virtutibus.*                           57. *effectus potestatum.*

# CHAPTER SEVEN

ND WHEN *he came down from the mountain, large crowds followed him. And behold, a certain leper came and entreated him, saying, "Lord, if you are willing, you can make me clean,"*[1] etc. In the beginning of this account we warned about thinking that anything should be omitted perchance from the factual events[2] of faith. So we teach that the events themselves contain the development[3] of the facts in their order.[4] For nothing is omitted from the truth, since the truth is what we follow in imitation. In all of his earlier words the Lord had delivered the precepts of the faith, and he had surpassed the Law, indicating, by surpassing it, that it was useless and ineffective. He repudiated the observance of the commandments; he required a most confident hope in his promises.[5] What he first did after these words needs to be considered.

2. The leper is present, asking to be cleansed. With a touch,[6] he is cleansed by the power of the Word[7] and ordered to be silent, although he is told to show himself before the priest and offer a gift that Moses prescribed as a testimony.[8] In the leper is shown to the crowd the healing of one who hears and believes and comes down from the mountain with the Lord.[9] The leper, who has been defiled by the corrupting ruin of his body and then heard the preaching of the Kingdom of heaven, asks that he be healed. Through bodily contact, he is healed by the power of the Word.[10] In order that this salvation should not be

---

1. Mt 8.1–2.  
2. *rerum gestarum.*  
3. *profectus.*  
4. *consequentium.* See Introduction for Hilary's method of biblical interpretation.  
5. Cf. *supra,* 4.20–28.  
6. Mt 8.3.  
7. *Verbi potestate.*  
8. Mt 8.4. Cf. Lv 14.1–32.  
9. Mt 8.1.  
10. *Verbi virtute.*

proffered[11] but sought after, he is ordered to be silent and told to present himself before the priests. The man whose healing is discernible in the works and acts announced in advance by the Law, but for whom the Law is shown to be weak, the power of the Word[12] is understood in him. Moreover, the man [now] purified offers to God a gift for the healing he received. This was not a gift of birds for sacrifice,[13] but the man offered himself, cleansed from the stains of his sinful body and transformed as a sacrifice to God,[14] because what Moses had prescribed in the Law as a testimony was not effective.

3. *After these things, when he had entered into Capernaum, a certain tribune[15] approached him, entreating him with the words, "My servant[16] lies paralyzed at home,"[17]* etc. Following the cleansing of the leper is the healing of the paralytic servant. But what does this mean when the tribune, master of the servant, professes that he is not worthy for Christ to enter his house, or to look upon the servant, or to offer aid in person? He has authority over soldiers, he says, and orders whatever he wants, and many obey him because of his place of power. Is not the Lord likewise able to effect healing by his word?[18] Concerning the tribune, it is enough for me to think of him as the precursor[19] of those pagans[20] who will eventually believe. Who is this leader to whom many men are subject and who wishes to know the song of Moses in Deuteronomy[21] and Ecclesiasticus, the book of Solomon,[22] where he reads what has been spoken of the scattering of the pagans? To us, it is only an account about a servant.[23]

4. Then, after the restoring of the paralytic in the person of the servant, there follows the salvation of the pagans[24] in the

11. *non offerretur.*     12. *Verbi virtus.*
13. Lv 14.4.     14. Rom 12.1–2.
15. The Old Latin has "centurion." This is yet another indication that Hilary is using an otherwise unknown Latin version of Matthew.
16. Lit., "boy" (*puer*).     17. Mt 8.5–6.
18. Mt 8.8–9.     19. *princeps.*
20. *gentium.*     21. Dt 32.43.
22. Sir 47.16.     23. A touch of irony here.
24. *salus gentium.*

healing of the people who came down from the mountain.[25]
The servant was lying in a humble house, dissolute and dying.
Even though the house was falling apart and unworthy of the
Savior's entry, he was, nevertheless, in need of the Savior's coming. The tribune knows his servant can be healed by a word—
the salvation of all pagans is by faith, and life for all people
is found in the precepts of the Lord. The pagans should be
reckoned as those "bed-ridden"[26] in the world, dissolute with
the sickness of sin, all their limbs completely atrophied[27] and
incapable of performing and executing their duty.[28] The sacrament of their salvation is fulfilled in the servant of the tribune,
although Christ does not go into the "house." Although he[29]
[Christ] lingered in this world, he did not enter upon worldly
vices and sins.

5. Amazed at his faith, Jesus then said: *I have not found such
great faith in Israel.*[30] This tribune was not of the pagans.[31] How
was such a faith not found in Israel when he who had believed
was an Israelite?[32] There is a reason underlying the words[33] of
this truth which emulates a future likeness, namely, that such
a great faith as among the pagans is not to be found in Israel
and that the most foreign pagans will find rest with Abraham,
Isaac, and Jacob in the Kingdom of heaven.[34] Indeed, the reality of healing in the servant is fulfilled because of the faith
of the one who believed. The efficacy of this present situation,
however, also points to an image of the future: concerning the
tribune who believed and the servant who was healed, no such
faith was found in Israel. Fellowship with Abraham in the Kingdom of heaven is appointed for the pagans.

---

25. Mt 8.1. Hilary skips over the healing of the leper (8.2–4) and continues
with the tribune and his servant.

26. *iacentes.*                                    27. *fluidis.*

28. Cf. *infra,* 9.10; 15.4.                        29. Presumably the tribune.

30. Mt 8.10.

31. I.e., because of his faith in Christ.

32. The meaning is not clear here, although the point seems to be that the
tribune was located in the land of Israel.

33. *verbi ratio subiecta .*

34. Mt 8.11; cf. Lk 13.29.

6. *When Jesus had come into the house of Peter, he saw his mother-in-law lying down with a fever.*[35] We should understand in Peter's mother-in-law a diseased disposition of unbelief that is associated with a freedom of the will,[36] and links us to her in a kind of bonded fellowship. Thus, with the Lord's entry into Peter's house, that is, in his body, he cured the unbelief of those who are burning in the heat of their sins and who are dominated by the illness of their wickedness. Soon afterwards, now healed, she performs a servant's role. Peter was the first to believe and has the primary apostolic place.[37] Although faith was formerly weak in him, he grew strong by the ministry of the Word of God because the Word undertook the work of salvation for all.[38] This parable taken from Peter's mother-in-law is rightly adapted for showing the disposition of unbelief which we will consider in a later place concerning the daughter-in-law and mother-in-law.[39] But at this point we will refer to Peter's mother-in-law as unbelief because, to the degree that Peter believes, he is held back by the slavery of his own will.[40]

7. *When evening had come, they brought to him many who had demons, and he cast out the unclean spirits.*[41] In those evening hours we can recognize in his indiscriminate healing of that assembly [the following:] those whom he taught after his Passion,[42] remitting all sins, expelling the infirmities of all, and casting out the provocative elements[43] of our deep-seated, evil desires. Moreover, he assumed the weaknesses of our human helplessness [witnessed] by the Passion of his body[44] according to the words of the prophets.[45]

35. Mt 8.14.
36. Heresy or unbelief is attributed by Tertullian to the self-determination of the will in *De praescr. haer.* 2.
37. *apostolatus est princeps.* Cf. Cyprian, *Ep.* 71.3, which places a link between Peter's confession in Mt 16 and his primacy in the Church's foundation.
38. *ministeris tamquam publicae salutis operatum est.*
39. Cf. *infra*, 10.22.                    40. Mt 16.22–23; 26.69–75.
41. Mt 8.16.                              42. Lk 24.47; Mk 16.14.
43. *incentiva.*
44. For Hilary, it was Christ's human body alone that endured the sufferings of his Incarnation. See *De trin.* 10.27–29.
45. Mt 8.17 (Is 53.4).

8. *When Jesus saw the great crowd gathered around him, he gave orders for his disciples to go across to the other side of the sea. And a certain scribe approached him and said, "Teacher, I will follow you wherever you go,"*[46] etc. Many things happened that invite an ordinary interpretation.[47] We do not contrive an understanding since the events themselves produce the understanding for us. Nor does the reality of events accommodate[48] itself to our understanding, but understanding is accommodated to the reality. The crowd is large, and the Lord instructs the disciples to go across the sea to the other side. I do not think that it was a lapse in the Savior's goodness that he wanted to leave those who were around him and to choose a secret place for the imparting of salvation.[49] Then a scribe approached him saying that he was going to follow the Teacher wherever he might go. We read that the scribe said or did nothing offensive. The Lord responds that while there are holes for foxes and nests for the birds of the air for rest, there is no place for the Son of Man to rest his head.[50] When a disciple asked that he be given time in order to bury his father, it was refused because the religion of human piety and service was forbidden.[51] We should clarify two things here: the reason for such important and diverse events contained in the text, as well as the profound causes of its truth, so that an understanding of interior significance may be explained.[52]

9. The name of *disciple* should not be applied to the twelve apostles only. For we read that there had been a great many disciples besides the apostles. Out of the entire crowd, a particular election is prescribed, that is, of those who come forward[53] and follow the Lord through the many dangers of this age. For the Church is just like a ship—as it has been called in numer-

---

46. Mt 8.18. Some Latin texts of the passage read "one from the crowd approached him and said ..."

47. *sensum communem.*                    48. *subsecundat* (a neologism).

49. The "secret place for the imparting of salvation" has gnostic overtones.

50. Mt 8.20.                            51. Mt 8.21–22.

52. We see that Hilary consistently acknowledges a historical or literal ("ordering") interpretation as well as an allegorical or "interior" one for the same passage.

53. *iactationes.*

ous places[54]—a ship which, having taken on board a very great diversity of races and nations, is subjected to everything: the blowing of the wind and the motion of the sea. Accordingly, the Church is buffeted by the attacks of the world and of unclean spirits. Even though it is exposed to so many dangers, we enter the ship of Christ, that is, the Church, knowing that we have to be tossed about by the sea and the wind. In order to make a figurative meaning[55] coherent and to make sense of the proportion of believers who board the ship and the crowd from those unbelievers who remain behind, the role[56] of the scribe and that of the disciple are joined together.

10. The scribe, who was one of the teachers of the Law, asked about following the Lord as if Christ, whom he was willing to follow, was not found in the Law. Thus a spirit of unbelief is expressed under [the cloak of] a mistrustful question, whereas the acceptance of faith should not be questioned, but followed. So that the same question of unbelief might be chastised appropriately,[57] the Lord responded that foxes have their holes and birds of the air their nests where they rest, yet the Son of Man has nowhere to lay his head. Now the fox is a cunning animal that hides itself near the holes of dwellings, lying in wait for birds that live there.[58] We read that it is by this name[59] that pseudo-prophets are called in several places.[60] Concerning the birds of the air we have often observed that unclean spirits are described in this way.[61]

The Son of God, noticing that his followers were few and that the teacher of the Law was uncertain about following him, reproached the pseudo-prophets with the terms of "holes" and "nests" in reference to unclean spirits. Because they are not

54. Cf. *In Matt.* 8.4; 13.1; 14.9; 15.10; and Tertullian, *De bapt.* 12.7.

55. *typicae significantiae.* For uses of *typicus*, see 2.1; 8.8; 12.24; 14.10; 17.8; 19.1,3; 20.11; 33.3.

56. *persona.*                                    57. *indicio.*

58. Cf. Horace, *Ep.* 1.7, 29 (*Sur Matt.* I.190, n.10).

59. I.e., "fox."

60. Ezek 13.4.

61. *Supra,* 5.9. Since Hilary has only mentioned it once before, his comment "we have often observed" may be an indication that Hilary has preached on other Gospel passages (cf. Mk 4.4; 4.13).

on board the "ship," that is to say, they are placed outside the Church where the abode of the pseudo-prophets and the dwelling of demons are established and where the Son of Man—the one of whom God himself is the head[62]— is not found. In him the knowledge of God resides and rests.[63] While everyone has been invited into the Church to board the ship, it happens that only a few will follow because of their fear of the sea, that is, fear of the world.

11. Then there approached a disciple who did not ask whether he should follow the Lord (since he already believed that he ought to follow). Rather, the disciple wanted to be allowed to bury his father.[64] We have learned from the beginning of the Lord's Prayer that we ought to first pray: *Our Father, who are in heaven.*[65] Because the disciple represents those persons who believe, he is told to remember that his living Father is in heaven. And he is told to follow the Lord, as he wished to do, in such a way that the dead would bury the dead. But I think that the dead cannot expect this service.[66] In what way will the dead inter the dead? In the first place, it shows that a perfect faith in itself is not obligated by the scruple[67] of rendering service to the one or the other in the world. The prerogative that belongs to the name of father is not upheld when it comes to the difference between a believing son and an unbelieving father.[68] As the Lord refused the man's entreaty to bury his father, he added, *Let the dead bury their own dead,*[69] encouraging us not to mix the unbelieving dead with remembrances[70] of the saints. In any case the [unbelieving] dead are those who live apart from God. For this reason the duties performed for the dead should be abandoned so that the dead may be buried by the dead, as it were, just as it is necessary for the living to adhere to the living one through faith in God.

---

62. 1 Cor 11.3.

63. Mt 8.21.

64. Ibid.

65. Mt 6.9.

66. *officium.* Cf. 23.4.

67. *religio.*

68. It seems Hilary's exegesis is built on the assumption that the disciple's father was an unbeliever and Jesus' words have to do with rejecting the ties of earthly paternity.

69. Mt 8.22.

70. *memoriis.*

## CHAPTER EIGHT

ND WHEN *he got into the boat, the disciples followed him. And behold, a great storm arose on the sea,*[1] etc. After the disciples entered the ship, a storm arose, the sea was agitated, and the passengers were thrown into commotion. Having fallen into a deep sleep, he was aroused by their nervous fearfulness; they begged him to do something.[2] After he once more scolded the disciples because of their small faith, he commanded the wind and the waves to be quiet.[3] To their amazement, the wind and the sea obeyed his orders.[4] It stands to reason that churches which have not followed the Word of God will be shipwrecked.[5] This does not happen because Christ is relaxed in sleep, but because he is put fast asleep in us by our own sleep.[6] That happens most often when we put our hope in God chiefly out of fear or worry [resulting] from danger. Even if our hope comes late,[7] there is the assurance that it can evade the danger, because the power of Christ is awake within it![8] So the Lord leaves for us a perpetual memory of his rebuke when he said: *Why are you fearful, men of little faith?*[9] In other words, when faith in Christ is awake, there is no need to fear the commotion of the world.

2. Thereafter follows the amazement of the men who said: *What kind of man is this that the wind and the sea obey him?*[10] This

1. Mt 8.23–24.
2. Mt 8.25.
3. Mt 8.26.
4. Mt 8.27.
5. Cf. Cyprian, *Ep.* 59.6, who spoke of the shipwrecks of the Church.
6. A similar explanation is given *infra,* 31.7, with regard to Christ's fear in the garden.
7. As it did for the disciples in the boat who were at first afraid.
8. Cf. *infra,* 12.17: *virtus* of Christ is of God who dwells in the man (8.6).
9. Mt 8.26.
10. Mt 8.27.

statement comes not from the disciples but from the pagans, as it were.[11] As the text had said earlier that only the disciples boarded the ship and the Lord was awakened only by the disciples, so it indicates that men were amazed, men who spoke in their amazement of *the* man. By this turn of phrase, it is understood that all of Christ's works and powers[12] should be praised as those of God. Pagan sacrilege and the foolishness of their wretched error show how they called him a man corresponding with the humility of his Passion, rather than God on account of his powers.[13]

3. *And when he had come to the other side into the region of the Gerasenes, two men who were demon-possessed went out to meet him as they were leaving the tombs; they were exceedingly dangerous,*[14] etc. The encounter of the two men, the longevity of their demonic possession, the danger of the road for those passing by, the begging of the demons to take refuge in the pigs,[15] and, once the men were restored, the fall of the herd headlong into the sea,[16] then the flight of the herdsmen into town,[17] the procession of the people out of the city and the delegation which besought the Lord not to enter their city,[18] and his return to his country,[19] and the entreaty of the paralytic lying on a bed there, and at that moment the remission of his sins,[20] and the murmur of the scribes,[21] and the pronouncement of power,[22] and the return of the paralytic to his home bearing his cot,[23] and the amazement of the crowd[24]—all have a good purpose.

4. In the beginning of the human race, it was divided into three parts, specifically, from the sons of Noah according to the prophecy of Genesis.[25] Shem was chosen to be God's possession. But outside the city, that is, outside the Synagogue of

---

11. Presumably because such wonder was fitting for pagans, not disciples.
12. *virtutes.* Cf. *infra,* 12.17.
13. See *supra,* 5.15, n.92.                    14. Mt 8.28.
15. Mt 8.31.                                         16. Mt 8.32.
17. Mt 8.33.                                         18. Mt 8.34.
19. Mt 9.1.                                          20. Mt 9.2.
21. Mt 9.3.                                          22. Mt 9.6 (*confessio virtutis*).
23. Mt 9.7; lit., "under the load of his cot" (*sub onere lectuli*).
24. Mt 9.8.                                          25. Gn 9.26.

the Law and the prophets,[26] the demons bound fast two men among the tombs. These are the origins of the two races who occupied the places of the deceased and the remains of the dead. These two molested those who were passing along the way of the present life.[27] In these events we find a complete preparation for future events. That the two men encountered the Lord at his coming is a way of indicating the desire of those who hasten to salvation. But the demons in the men cried out, [asking] why the Lord begrudged them their place and why he molested them before the time of judgment.[28] To those two races of pagans, the mass of the Sadducees[29] are also joined, who are derived from Shem, whose heresy from among the Jews is the sacrilege of denying the resurrection.[30] The demons, seeing that he was not going to leave them among the pagans, begged him to let them stay among the heretics.

As soon as they entered the pigs, the whole herd pitched headlong into the sea by a sudden impulse.[31] In other words, in a desire for the world instigated by demonic forces one is thrown head first into deep waters—one will experience death along with the rest of the pagans in their unbelief. Here also a figurative reason[32] is observed, since it was not enough to say that they were thrown head first into the sea unless it was also added: "and they died in deep waters."[33]

The local leaders and herdsmen were so troubled by the occurrence of such events that they went to the city and announced what had happened. That city provides an image[34]

26. The Law and the prophets are the legacy of the people of Shem (the Jews).

27. Mt 8.28.

28. Mt 8.29.

29. *Adiacebat etiam eis duobus gentium populis[,] plebs ex Sem genere Sadducaeorum.*

30. Among the known Jewish groups in the first century, the priestly class, or Sadducees, were known for denying a bodily resurrection for the believing Jew. See E. Ferguson, *Backgrounds of Early Christianity* (Grand Rapids: Eerdmans, 1989), 326–27.

31. Mt 8.32.

32. *typica ratio.*

33. *in aquis multis.* Unlike the Old Latin versions in our possession, Hilary's version of Mt 8.32 seems to have included *multis.*

34. *speciem.*

of the Jewish people who, once they heard about the works of
Christ, came out against their Lord,[35] preventing him from
reaching their borders and their city (for, in fact, the Law does
not accept the Gospels). After being rejected by them, he returned to his own city.[36] The city is the faithful people of God.
It was in this place, therefore, that he boarded the ship, that is,
the Church.

5. In the case of the paralytic who needed healing, pagans
everywhere are represented, and the words that led to the
man's cure should be considered. It was not said to the paralytic, "Be healed," nor, "Get up and walk," but, *Take courage, my
son, your sins have been forgiven.*[37] In the one man, Adam, the
sins imputed to all the pagans are forgiven.[38] He is accordingly
presented as one who required care by ministering angels; he is
called *son* because he is the first work of God,[39] through whom
the sins of the soul are forgiven and by whose pardon there is
an indulgence for the first transgression.[40] We do not accept
the idea that the paralytic had committed any sin, especially
because in another place the Lord said that blindness from
birth had been brought about neither by the man's own sin nor
from his parents'.[41]

6. A pattern of the truth is followed in these events, even as
an image of the future is fulfilled in the words. It disturbed
the scribes that sin was forgiven by a man[42] (for they considered that Jesus Christ was only a man)[43] and that he forgave sin,

35. Mt 8.34.
36. Mt 9.1. Cf. Gal 4.25–27, on the two Jerusalems.
37. Mt 9.2.
38. See Rom 5.12–21, here and for what follows. Despite the fact that sin
entered the world through one man, the gift of grace of the new Adam, Jesus
Christ, brings forgiveness.

39. *primum Dei opus.* Cf. Prv 8.22–23. Referring to Christ as "first made" or
"first work" is another indication that Hilary has yet to become familiar with
"Arian" usage.

40. Rom 5.17. The point of the sentence turns on Hilary's Christology, that
Christ, though in his condition as man, provided healing as God for all humanity.

41. Jn 9.3.                                    42. Mt 9.3.
43. See *supra*, 8.2; 10.27, n.143.

for which the Law was not able to grant absolution, since faith alone justifies.[44] When the Lord discerned the murmuring of the scribes,[45] he said that it was easy for the Son of Man to forgive sins on earth.[46] For truly no one is able to forgive sins except God alone. He who forgave, therefore, is God because no one can forgive except God. For the Word of God which abides in that Man offers to a man healing, and there was no difficulty for him to do and speak since it is given to him[47] to perform everything that he said he would do.[48]

7. So that we might understand that he became man[49] to forgive men's sins and to obtain the resurrection of their bodies, he said, *In order that you may know the Son of Man has power on the earth to forgive sins, he said to the paralytic, "Rise, and take up your bed."*[50] It had been enough for him to say *Rise,* but because each thing that was done needed to be explained, he added: *Take up your bed and [go] to your home.* First he granted forgiveness of sins; then he displayed the power of the resurrection. By raising the man from his cot, he taught that sickness and sorrow will affect our bodies no more. Finally, the man returning to his own home showed that the way to paradise will be recovered for believers, from which Adam, the father of all humanity, separated himself and departed through the ruin of sin.

8. *Upon seeing this, the crowd was afraid.*[51] Admiration, not fear, ought to have resulted from this act [of raising the paralytic], but even now does the order of mystery[52] abide. That an image of the future might be joined to the truth of present circumstances, the crowd feared the power of the words and deeds of the Lord. The source of great fear, if one is not forgiven of

44. Rom 3.20, 28.

45. Mt 9.4.

46. Mt 9.6.

47. *subest.*

48. Cf. *supra,* 5.8, 11–14; 12.7, 10; *infra,* 23.3–4.

49. *in corpore positus.*

50. Mt 9.6.

51. Mt 9.8. Hilary's wording here varies from that of other Latin versions.

52. *ordo mysterii.* Used in relation to the next sentence. The use of *ordo* has significance for Hilary as a pattern inherent to God's revelation in Christ, which is in the process of unfolding the truth meant to be recognized by believers. Cf. other uses of *ordo:* 2.6 (*arcani*); 8.6 (*veritatis*); 14.16 (*typicus*); 21.2 (*futuri*).

his sins by Christ, is the dissolution of death, because no one who has not been pardoned from sin may return to his eternal home.[53]

*And they glorified God who had given such authority*[54] *to men.*[55] Everything was accomplished in its order. Once the fear of despair subsided, honor was rendered to God because he had given such great authority to men. To Christ alone the prerogative belonged to do such things, because he was the only man to have communion with the Father's substance.[56] It was not about admiration for what he could do—for is not God believed to be capable?—otherwise, the praise would have come from one man, not many. But the reason for this honor ascribed to God is that the authority, and the way of the remission of sins, of the resurrection of the body, and of return to heaven, may be given by his Word to men.

53. Cf. Cyprian, *De mortalitate* 26.
54. *potestatem.*
55. Mt 9.8.
56. *paternae substantiae.* Cf. *infra,* 12.18; Tertullian, *Apol.* 21.11; Novatian, *De trin.* 31.2.

# CHAPTER NINE

**N**D AS JESUS WENT on from there, he saw a man sitting at the tax booth, by the name of Matthew, and he said to him: "Follow me,"[1] etc. He commands Matthew the publican, sitting at his tax booth, to follow him. And going to his house, Matthew prepares a dinner, where with Jesus was seated a group of publicans and sinners.[2] At this, the Pharisees rebuked the disciples, asking why their teacher dined with publicans.[3] To them he responded, it is not the healthy who need a doctor but the sick who require treatment.[4] And he commanded them to *go and learn* what is meant by, *"I desire mercy rather than sacrifice."*[5]

2. The name "publican" comes from the life of those who abandoned the works of the Law and preferred to comport themselves according to common and public practice. Thus it is from his house, that is, from the sins of the body, that the Lord called Matthew in order to enter his mind and recline at its "table." This is the self-same writer of this Gospel, and, upon leaving the home of his sin, he accepted the Lord, who illuminated his innermost dwelling place. In this place, a dinner is richly prepared from the food of the Gospel[6] for sinners and publicans. It was then that a spirit of jealousy agitated the Jews because of the Lord's communion with sinners and publicans. He unveiled their talk about keeping the Law[7] as but veiled coverings for unfaithfulness, showing that he was bringing aid for them because they were sick, and was providing medicine for them because they needed it, though they thought they were healthy and in no need of treatment. But so that they would

1. Mt 9.9.
2. Mt 9.10.
3. Mt 9.11.
4. Mt 9.12.
5. Mt 9.13; Hos 6.6.
6. *evangelicis cibis.*
7. Mt 9.11. Cf. 2 Cor 3.15.

understand that none of them were healthy, he warned them to learn what is meant: *"I desire mercy, not sacrifice."* In other words, he means that because the Law is bound up with offering sacrifices it is not able to be of help. Salvation for all people is preserved through the gift of mercy.[8]

*For I am come not to call the righteous, but sinners to repentance.*[9] If he had come for all people, why then did he say that he had not come for the righteous? Was it not necessary that he should come for those that were there? But no one is made righteous by the Law.[10] He shows that it is a worthless display of justice, although mercy was necessary for all those who, placed under the Law, offered feeble sacrifices for salvation. In fact, if justice had come from the Law, forgiveness through grace would not have been necessary.

3. *Then the disciples of John came to him and asked, "Why do we and the Pharisees often fast, whereas your disciples do not fast?"*[11] The Pharisees and disciples of John were fasting, and the apostles were not. But he responds to them in a spiritual manner[12] and reveals to John's disciples that he is the bridegroom.[13] For John had vowed that his whole life's hope was placed in Christ, and while he is still preaching his disciples cannot be received by the Lord. Unless the Law be completed[14] and the Law and the prophets are wholly found in him, none of them would pass over to faith in the Gospel.[15] For while the bridegroom is present,[16] he responds that it is not necessary for the disciples to fast, showing clearly the joy of his presence and the sacrament of holy food,[17] with which no one will lack his presence. In other words, they possess Christ in the light of the mind.[18] After

8. *misercordiae indulgentia.* In his usual fashion, Hilary is drawing on Pauline theology (Rom 11.30–32) in his interpretation of Christ's words and actions.

9. Mt 9.13. Some Latin versions of this verse do not contain "to repentance" (*in paenitentiam*).

10, Rom 5.                                    11. Mt 9.14.

12. *spiritaliter.*                          13. Mt 9.15.

14. Allusion to Mt 5.17.

15. Cf. Tertullian, *Adv. Marc.* 4.33.8; 5.3.8.

16. Cf. Mt 9.15.

17. *sacramentum sancti cibi.* I.e., the Eucharist.

18. *in conspectu mentis.* Cf. 1 Cor 2.14–16: "But we have the mind of Christ" (v.16, RSV).

he is taken from them, he says, they will have to fast,[19] because all who do not believe that Christ was resurrected will not be entitled to the food of life. For it is by faith in the resurrection that the sacrament of the heavenly bread[20] is received, and whoever is without Christ, will be left in want[21] of the food of life.

4. That they may understand that these perfect sacraments of salvation cannot be bestowed upon those who are located among the old ways,[22] he makes use of a comparison. An unused piece of cloth is not to be sewn onto an old garment,[23] because the strength[24] of a piece of unused cloth sewn onto an old and fragile garment will tear it. Nor should new wine be poured into old wineskins,[25] since the heat of the new wine fermenting will break the old wineskins. In other words, both souls and bodies weakened by the disability of sin do not possess the sacraments of new grace. For what is torn will become worse, and the wine poured into old wineskins will be lost. There will be then a double fault of those in this situation if, along with the disability of their sin, they will not appropriate the strength of new grace. And thus, both the Pharisees and the disciples of John will not accept what is new until they themselves become renewed.[26]

5. *While he was saying these things, a ruler approached and knelt before him saying, "Lord, my daughter has just died; come and place your hand upon her."*[27] The entreaty of the ruler, the faith of the woman,[28] the crowd assembled in the house,[29] the shouting of the two blind men,[30] the dumb and deaf demoniac brought to him,[31] contain an order of understanding that is linked to the words spoken earlier.

---

19. Mt 9.15b.
20. Cf. Tertullian, *Adv. Marc.* 4.40.3; 4.43.6.
21. Lit.,"in fasting" (*in . . . ieiunio*).  22. I.e., the Law.
23. Mt 9.16.  24. *virtus.*
25. Mt 9.17.
26. *nova non accepturos esse, nisi novi fierent.*
27. Mt 9.18.  28. Mt 9.20–22.
29. Mt 9.23.  30. Mt 9.27–31.
31. Mt 9.32–33.

This ruler is understood to be the Law, which was itself fostered[32] by Christ and declared the expectation of his coming, and which now beseeches the Lord on behalf of the people to bring life back to the dead. In fact, we do not read that the ruler had believed; from this the person of this ruler who sought the Lord should rightfully be construed as a symbol[33] of the Law. The Lord promised his help to him and followed him in order to grant it.[34]

6. First of all, [we see how] the crowd of sinners is saved with the apostles. Although it was necessary to abide by the primary place of election, as predestined by the Law,[35] salvation is rendered to publicans and to sinners, however, in the form of a woman,[36] And so the woman is confident that by making contact with the Lord as he passed along she would be healed from her bloody flow with a touch of his garment. So the woman, polluted by the filth of her body and dying from the uncleanness of sins within, hastened to touch the hem of his garment through faith. In other words, she with the apostles[37] reached out for the gift of the Holy Spirit from the body of Christ in the form of a garment's hem as he walked by, and she is immediately healed. Thus the salvation has been brought for one while it is removed from another. The Lord praises her faith and perseverance because what was prepared for Israel, the people of the Gentiles assumed.

7. The great wonder[38] of the Lord's power[39] is found in a simple explanation as the power[40] residing in his body conferred an efficacious healing to the frailty of (her) body[41] in the procession of divine activity through the hem of garments. God was not, of course, divisible or comprehensible that he should be enclosed in a body. For he divided his gifts in the Spirit,

---

32. Lit., "nurtured" (*nutriuerat*).　　　33. *typum.*

34. Mt 9.19.　　　　　　　　　　　35. Rom 11.28.

36. Mt 9.20.

37. Here and in the beginning of this section, the salvation that comes to specific individuals is shared by the apostles, seemingly based on 9.19.

38. *admiratio.*　　　　　　　　　39. *virtutis dominicae.*

40. *potestas.*

41. Lit., "the perishable members" (*rebus caducis*).

rather than being divided in his gifts. Faith follows anywhere his power is, because it is everywhere and is absent nowhere. And the assumption of a body did not constrain the nature of his power,[42] but his powers assumed the frailty of a body for the body's redemption. His power is freed to the degree that it is infinite, so that the operation of salvation for humanity may be contained in the hem of his garment.[43]

8. Afterwards the Lord entered the home of the ruler, that is, the synagogue, throughout which resounded a hymn of mourning,[44] as found in the songs of the Law. And many laughed at him.[45] For never would they have believed that God was in man, just as they laughed instead at the proclamation of the resurrection of the dead.[46] Taking the girl by the hand, whose death was sleep in the presence of the Lord, he returned her to life.[47] And so that we may understand here that the number of elect of those who believe, coming from the Law, are few, the entire crowd was ejected from the house. The Lord had wished at least these would have been saved, but by laughing at his words and deeds, they were not worthy to participate in the resurrection. And from there his fame went throughout the whole land,[48] and after that salvation of election the gift and the works of Christ were proclaimed.

9. Then as the Lord went about, he was soon followed by two blind men.[49] But to what degree were the blind men able to know his direction and the name of the Lord?[50] As a matter of fact, they called him the Son of David and asked that they be healed.[51] In the two blind men, the reason for the whole

42. *naturam virtutis.*

43. The Christology exhibited in this section seems dependent on Tertullian, *Adv. Prax.* 27.5 and *De carne Christi* 5.6–8, which state that the divine and the flesh each have their own and different natures, and that the divine is not subject to the limitations of the flesh, nor to the limitations of his own body.

44. Mt 9.23.                                   45. Mt 9.24.

46. Cf. Acts 17.32, although the reference is not concerning Jews.

47. Mt 9.25.                                   48. Mt 9.26.

49. Mt 9.27.

50. The "name of the Lord" is the "Son of David" (v.27).

51. In Latin, the word "to save" and "to heal" is *salvare,* and Hilary will join the two meanings in this paragraph.

preceding prefiguration[52] is made clear. For it is by these events that the daughter of the ruler is revealed, as well as the Pharisees and disciples of John, who together had tested the Lord earlier.[53]

Although the blind men did not know who it was from whom they sought salvation, the Law indicated and showed them that their savior[54] would be from the race of David. And because they were blinded by their former sins, they did not see Christ until they were spoken to by him who introduced the light of the mind. By these things, the Lord shows that faith should not be expected from salvation, but salvation should be expected through faith. Because the blind men had believed, they saw— not that because they had seen, they then believed[55]—which means we must understand that what is sought for has to be gained by faith, not that faith is to be achieved by accomplishments. The Lord promised sight if they believed, and once they believed, he told them to be silent[56] since it was the role of the apostles to preach.

10. After this, it is clear that the pagans are presented in the mute and deaf demoniac as a people who need an all-encompassing[57] salvation. Continuously besieged by every kind of evil, the demoniac was shackled by the entirety of bodily sins. In him a pattern of the facts[58] is preserved. For instance, the demon is at first cast out, and then the rest of the bodily functions came into their own.[59] Through knowledge of God the insanity of all superstition is put to flight, while the sight and hearing and the word of salvation takes its place. In its astonishment at what had been done the crowd declared: *Nothing like this has ever appeared in Israel.*[60] The demoniac, for whom no help at all could come through the Law, was saved by the power of the Word;[61] the dumb and deaf man declared everywhere the prais-

---

52. *praefigurationis.* A neologism (cf. *infra,* 16.2; 20.12; 21.4; 29.2), but commonly used by Hilary.

53. *Supra,* 9.3, 5.

54. Lit., "their savior in the body" (*salvatorem suum in corpore*).

55. Jn 20.29.                          56. Mt 9.30.

57. *totius salutis.*                   58. *rerum ordo.*

59. *succedunt* (Mt 9.33).              60. Mt 9.33b.

61. *Verbi virtute.*

es of God.[62] Now that salvation had been given to the pagans, all cities and villages[63] were illuminated by the power and presence[64] of Christ, and they were delivered from[65] every infirmity of their ancient illnesses.

62. Mt 9.31.

63. Mt 9.35.

64. *ingressu.*

65. Lit., "they escaped" (*evadunt*).

# CHAPTER TEN

*EEING THE CROWDS, he had compassion on them because they were harassed and helpless,*[1] etc. It is appropriate to examine the authority[2] of his words no less than his deeds, because, as we said,[3] there consists the same important significance in his words as in his actions. The Lord had compassion on the harassed and helpless crowd just as a flock is scattered about without a shepherd.[4] And he said: *The harvest is plentiful, the workers are few, pray that the Lord of the harvest send out many workers into the harvest.*[5] Once he called his disciples together, he gave them authority[6] to drive out unclean spirits and to cure every kind of sickness and disability.[7] While these events were pertinent to their present context, it is necessary to consider what significance they have for the future.[8]

2. No troublemaker had stirred up the crowd, nor were they harassed or made helpless by some calamity or disturbance. Why did the Lord have pity on those who were harassed and helpless? Clearly, the Lord took pity on the people troubled by the oppressive violence of the unclean spirit and disabled by the weight of the Law because they still had no shepherd who would restore to them the guardianship of the Holy Spirit.[9] Although the fruit of this gift was most abundant, nothing had yet been harvested.[10] For the Spirit's abundance surpasses the multitude of those who draw on him. If everyone gathers as

1. Mt 9.36.
2. *virtutes.*
3. *Supra,* 8.6.
4. Mt 9.36b.
5. Mt 9.37–38.
6. *potestatem.*
7. Mt 10.1.
8. This is a fine example of the double hermeneutical principle that governed Hilary's exegesis. The words and deeds of Jesus had meaning, both for the moment and for times to come.
9. Recalls 1 Pt 2.25.
10. Cf. Mt 9.37–38.

much as he needs, there is always enough to give generously.[11] It is useful that the Lord ministers through many; he urged nonetheless that we ask the Lord of the harvest to send forth many workers into the harvest, that is, that we ask God to grant an abundance of harvesters who utilize the gift of the Holy Spirit which was prepared. Through prayer and supplication God pours his bounty upon us. In order to indicate that this harvest and the many harvesters would be drawn first from the twelve apostles,[12] he gave to those gathered together the authority[13] for expelling spirits and for healing every kind of sickness. By the powers[14] of this gift they were able to expel the Troubler[15] and cure illness. It is appropriate that we consider the significance of each point of this teaching.

3. The disciples are told to keep away from the ways of the pagans,[16] not because they were not also sent for the salvation of pagans, but so that they should keep themselves apart from the activities and lifestyle of ignorant pagans. They were [also] forbidden to enter the cities of the Samaritans.[17] Yet did he not himself heal a Samaritan? But they are told not to enter churches of heretics,[18] for there is no difference between ignorance and perversity. They are sent instead to the lost sheep of the house of Israel,[19] even though they [the lost sheep] fiercely attack the Lord with the tongue of the serpents and the jaws of

11. That is, the bestowal of the Spirit. Cf. Cyprian, *Ad Don.* 4.

12. Mt 10.2–4. Apparently, Hilary was not interested in discussing the apostles named here, perhaps because his focus was on the way the message was delivered rather than the messengers.

13. *potestatem.*

14. *virtutibus.*

15. *turbator.* I am taking this term as a personification of the devil on Hilary's part, just as he does elsewhere. Cf. *infra*, 12.3 (*habitor*); 11.5 (*vexator*).

16. Mt 10.5.

17. Ibid.

18. *ecclesias haereticorum.* In contrast, the catholic Church is called *ecclesia catholica* (*infra*, 10.9). *Haereticus* is a term Hilary uses far more in *De trin.*; although it is found *supra*, 6.1, *et passim*, it is in distinction to "pagan." And it seems in this occurrence, Hilary marks a difference between the two when he states in the very next sentence: "For there is no difference between ignorance and perversity." It is not clear that "pagan" represents the biblical past, whereas "heretic" is contemporary to Hilary.

19. Mt 10.6.

wolves. As the Law[20] was bound to receive the higher status of the Gospel, Israel had less of an excuse for its wickedness when it might have heeded the warning with greater zeal.[21]

4. At this point all authority of the Lord's power is transferred to the apostles, those who in Adam had been formed[22] in the image and likeness of God, and now shared in the perfect image and likeness of Christ.[23] Their power differs in no way from that of the Lord, since they who were once earthbound are now of heaven.[24] They preach the coming of the Kingdom of heaven;[25] they have now acquired the image and likeness of God in the fellowship of truth—as all the saints, who are called of heaven, may reign with the Lord;[26] they heal the sick, raise the dead, cleanse the lepers, drive out demons;[27] and, whatever Adam's evils incited by Satan are brought against the body, they cleanse again because they share the Lord's authority.[28] So that they will completely realize the likeness of God according to the prophecy of Genesis,[29] they are commanded to give freely as they have freely received.[30] In other words, for a gracious gift let there be a gracious offering of service.[31]

5. They are prohibited to keep gold, silver, or copper in their belts,[32] nor allowed to carry a wallet for the journey, nor take two tunics or two pair of shoes or take a staff in hand, for the worker is worthy of his earnings.[33] It is not wrong, I think, to

20. *legislatio.*
21. The exact meaning here is obscure, but the idea seems to be that since Israel has not hearkened to the prophetic warnings, including that of Christ, it remains lost in its ignorance.
22. Cf. 1 Cor 4.8.
23. Cf. Tertullian, *De bapt.* 5.7; 1 Cor 15.49. Adam was formed in the image and likeness of God whereas Christ is the perfect image and likeness of God. A seemingly small distinction, but it is representative of a fundamental contrast Hilary draws between Christ, who is the image by nature, and humanity, which comes to share in that image by adoption.
24. 1 Cor 15.48; Col 3.2–4.     25. Mt 10.7.
26. Cf. 1 Cor 4.8.     27. Mt 10.8.
28. *dominicae potestatis.*     29. Gn 1.26.
30. Mt 10.8: *dare gratis quod gratis acceperunt.*
31. *ministratis.* Cf. *infra*, 15.10.     32. Mt 10.9.
33. Mt 10.10.

have money[34] in one's belt. Why, then, does he wish to prohibit them from the possession of gold, silver, and copper in their belts?[35] The belt is a piece of equipment for service, and the waistband for practical reasons.[36] By this we are warned not to let anything in our ministry be for sale,[37] nor should we have a need for possessing gold, silver, or copper in the execution of apostolic service.[38]

*Nor a wallet for the journey.*[39] Our preoccupation with worldly goods[40] must be left behind. Because all treasure on earth is insidious, our treasure will be stored in our heart.

*Nor two tunics.* It is enough that we have put on Christ but once;[41] we are not to be dressed a second time in the clothing of heresy or of the Law through a depraved understanding.[42]

*Nor shoes.*[43] Is not the frailty of the human foot due to the condition of its nudity? But on holy ground, which is not choked with the thorns and briars of sin, we must stand with bare feet, as Moses was told to do;[44] we are told to take no other footwear for our journey than what we have received from Christ.

*Nor a staff in your hands;* that is, the authority of an external power of Law.[45] If we hold in a worthy manner the staff that is from the root of Jesse[46]—for whatever other authority there may be, it will not be of Christ[47]—we will be fully prepared, as we said earlier, for completing the journey of this life with grace, with provisions, with clothing, with shoes, with his [Christ's] au-

34. *thesaurus.*

35. Mt 10.9.

36. Lit., "the performance of work" (*efficaciam operis*).

37. That is, our purpose in ministry should not be focused on monetary value.

38. *apostolatus* (lit., the office of an apostle). See *infra,* 10.29.

39. Mt 10.10.

40. *substantiae.*

41. Gal 3.27; Cyprian, *Ep.* 63.8. Orthodox Christians were baptized only once.

42. Cf. Tertullian, *De bapt.* 15. Some heretical groups would rebaptize new converts.

43. *Calceamenta* has also been translated as "sandals."

44. Ex 3.5; cf. Nm 33.55.

45. *potestatis extraneae iura.*

46. Using alternative reading: *virgam quae est.*

47. Is 11.1; Cyprian applies the image of a staff drawn from the root of Jesse to Christ (*Test.* 2.11).

thority. Following these instructions, we will be found worthy of our reward.[48] By paying attention to these matters, we will receive the rewards of a heavenly hope.

6. *In whatever city you shall enter, search for whoever is worthy there,*[49] etc. Perhaps we will think the Lord gave to the apostles trivial instructions with the purpose of humbling them by his directions for their entering, dwelling, tarrying, and leaving. This simple understanding agrees with the modesty of the saints,[50] that hospitality may be offered to one who is worthy, and that the saints must not be polluted through negligence or ignorance by living with a disgraceful family. Accordingly, he commands them upon entering a city to search out a worthy person and stay with him until their departure, and that his home should be greeted in peace by those entering it.[51] If a home is worthy, it is also worthy of the communion of peace; if it is unworthy, let that peace be likewise rescinded. If anyone does not receive them or their words, the apostles are supposed to shake the dust from their feet,[52] and leave the seeds of an eternal malediction.[53]

7. These matters prompt our need for understanding in no small way. If the apostles would not receive hospitality unless they first sought out who was worthy, how can a home later be found unworthy? And what about those who do not listen to their words and do not receive them? Either the righteous man has nothing to fear, or, if he is found unworthy, they cannot enter and share his house in fellowship. And why should the apostles seek out and inquire who is worthy, if punishment is prescribed against an unworthy host? The Lord instructs the apostles not to be implicated with such homes or have association with those who persecute Christ or do not know him, and to seek out in any city whoever is worthy of their staying with

---

48. Mt 10.10.

49. Mt 10.11.

50. Cf. Cyprian, *Ep.* 5.2, who points out how the confessors displayed *modestia* (unassuming conduct, humble dignity) in their behavior. Cf. Rom 12.16.

51. Mt 10.12.          52. Mt 10.14.

53. Mt 10.15.

them. In other words, wherever is the Church, Christ dwells therein.[54] If it is a worthy home and there is a righteous host, there is no need to leave it for somewhere else.

8. The Lord commands that a house should be greeted by those entering by saying aloud: *Peace be on this house.*[55] If a home is found worthy, peace should come upon it; if it is unworthy, peace should be returned to those who offered it. Once, however, peace is already offered in the form of a greeting upon first entering the house, how will it come upon it, or how will it then be returned? For either peace should not have been offered before determining whether it was worthy, or, if it was worthy and greeted with words of peace, the situation[56] of both entering into and reversing the terms of peace cannot reasonably agree with what has preceded.[57] It is necessary, therefore, to show the suitability of this passage.

9. There were going to be many Jews who had such great affection for the Law that, although they believed in Christ out of admiration for his works, they still clung to the works of the Law. There were others, curious about exploring the freedom which is in Christ,[58] who apparently passed over from the Law to the Gospel. But many of these also crossed into heresy through their distorted understanding.[59] All those who deceive and flatter their listeners are lying in saying that they possess the Catholic truth.[60] The Lord therefore directs the apostles in

54. *Christus habitator.* Cf. Church as a house(hold) in Cyprian, *De unit. eccl.* 8.
55. Mt 10.12.
56. *condicio.*
57. Viz., Mt 10.12–14. Hilary's problem is with the logic of the text; if the apostles find a worthy house (host), it is worthy because the host is righteous and possesses the peace of God. Why is it necessary to bring peace into a house that should already have it? The same applies to the opposite scenario.
58. Gal 2.4.
59. In accord with the heresiological opinion of the day, Hilary understands that some Jewish groups who turned toward Christianity became heretical because of the way they continued to embrace the Law. See Filastrius of Brixia (Brescia), *Diversarum hereseon liber* 4–9.
60. According to Doignon this expression, *veritatem catholicam,* is a new arrangement of words but based on Tertullian, *De monog.* 3.1, and *Adv. Marc.* 3.22.6 (*Sur Matt.* I.225, n.13).

the preceding passage about the necessity of seeking a worthy person with whom one should live. Because it is possible for the ignorant to meet a host through deceptive words, so it was important to find a house cautiously and carefully which is called *worthy*, that is, a church which is [rightfully] named Catholic.[61] They are supposed to greet a house with a peaceful disposition where peace is [already] spoken instead of being given; this is why the Lord directs them to greet it saying, *Peace be on this house.* The peace of the greeting should be bestowed by words and by the expression of works. Peace itself, however—which is found in the very midst of mercy—should not enter a house unless it is worthy. If a worthy house cannot be found, the sacrament of heavenly peace[62] should dwell within their own [the disciples'] conscience.

10. Against those who spit out the apostolic instructions after hearing the preaching of the Kingdom of heaven, the disciples departed and shook the dust from their feet,[63] leaving an eternal malediction for them. Frankly, I do not know how there can be communion for one who remains fixed in one place with that place in which he is fixed, and how there could be established between the two a joining of body and of the land.[64] Every sin of those living inside the house is abandoned by shaking the dust from their feet. In this way nothing of the sanctity of the apostles' journey might be altered. By their arrival and entrance, the iniquities of earthly origin are destroyed, and by their testimony, unfaithfulness with all its earthly dust is judged. *It will be more tolerable for the lands of Sodom and Gomorrah in the day of judgment than for that city,*[65] because it is less serious for those who are misguided on account of their ignorance of Christ than it is inexpiable for those who did not accept what

61. In the west, *catholica* had become a proper name; cf. Tertullian, *De praescr. haer.* 26.9; Cyprian, *Ep.* 50.4; 71.2.

62. See Tertullian, *De orat.* 18.1–2.

63. Mt 10.14.

64. That is, a person cannot be attached to a particular location. Doignon (*Sur Matt.* I.229, n.18) observes that this is a celebrated expression of this kind of "communion" in Cicero, *Leg.* 2.3.

65. Mt 10.15 (i.e., "that city" which rejects the apostolic preaching).

was preached, or for those who preached what was accepted but was neither holy nor catholic.

11. When the Lord says that he is sending them out like sheep in the midst of wolves,[66] he indicates that there will be many of those who will rage against the apostles with an insane fury. But the Lord preaches that they ought to be simple as doves and wise as serpents. Whereas the simplicity of a dove is already established,[67] the wisdom of the serpent has to be considered.

I do not know how the serpent could be regarded as wise or thoughtful.[68] Even if certain writers have reminded us of certain points from this,[69] we understand that whenever a serpent comes within a man's reach, he always strikes off its head, and, once the body is gathered up, he buries it in the ground[70] or throws it into a pit to get rid of the bloody remains. According to this example it is necessary that should any persecution occur, we would hide in our head (that is, Christ).[71] Once we have delivered ourselves to all the tortures by sacrificing our body, we may participate in that faith which we received from him.

12. Everything the Lord says here concerns Jews and heretics: *Brother will betray brother, and a father his son, and children will rise up against their parents;*[72] that is, a family of the same house will be divided among themselves. Whereas the names of the parents and their bloodline signifies a former unity, they are now separated by hostility and hatred for one another, intent on betraying one another to the judges and kings of the earth, who will attempt to extort either our silence or our cooperation.[73]

For we will present ourselves as witnesses before them[74] as

---

66. Mt 10.16.    67. Cf. Tertullian, *De bapt.* 8.3.
68. *consiliique.*    69. Cf. Virgil, *Georg.* 2.473–74.
70. *in orbem corpora.*
71. Eph 4.15. That is, take refuge in Christ.
72. Mt 10.21.
73. There is a sudden move on Hilary's part to the first person plural, presumably induced to make the text "personalized" for his hearers and readers.
74. Mt 10.18 (i.e., judges and kings).

well as before the pagans. Because we bear witness, our persecutors will not be able to claim they are ignorant of God.[75] The
way of faith in Christ preached shall be opened to the pagans
by the tenacious voices of the confessors amidst the tortures of
cruel men.[76] So the Lord urges upon us the necessity of being
instructed by the wisdom of the serpent.

13. This creature, before he betrayed Adam, was already declared to be wise according to Genesis,[77] having a sagacity that
is evident through the scheme of its deceitful plan. For at first
it attacked the soul of the weaker sex, and then seduced her
by the hope and promise of sharing in immortality. By these
enticements, the serpent accomplished the work of its plan
and its will. Once it had scrutinized the character and will of
the man and the woman, its sagacity provided it with the right
words at the opportune moment. It spoke about future blessings and presented the heavenly rewards of a perfect faith—a
lie of the serpent. But in truth we preach that those who believe will become like the angels according to the promise of
God.[78] Through the promises of the heavenly Kingdom, let us
obtain the simple and perfect minds of its citizens[79] despite the
raging[80] of wolves[81] and heretics. With the simplicity of a dove,
let us provide the truth of these matters through the wisdom of
a serpent.

14. The Lord also instructs those who have been "handed
over"[82] to have no concern about how they should respond, but
rather wait upon what the Spirit of God will say.[83] When our

---

75. *divinitatis.*

76. Although the systematic persecution of Christians had long ceased by
Hilary's day, the persecution of heretical Christians did not. Of course, the
different emperors backed differing confessional groups. When Hilary is himself thrust into exile in 356, he says he will be willing to be counted among the
martyrs; *In Const.* 11 (SC 334.190).

77. Gn 3.1.                          78. Mt 22.30.

79. *plebium.*                       80. *circumsaevientibus,* a neologism.

81. "Wolves" are the image of pagan persecutors; cf. Lactantius, *Inst.* 5.23.4;
*De mort.* 52.2.

82. *traditis,* the same verb used in v.19.

83. Mt 10.19–20.

faith has been attentive to all the precepts of the divine will, it will be taught how to respond. We have Abraham, for example, of whom Isaac was demanded for sacrifice, yet he was given a ram to be the victim.[84]

Then the Lord counsels the disciples to flee from one city to another.[85] When his preaching had initially been forced out of Judea, it passed over to Greece, where the apostles were persecuted and suffered in different ways within the Greek cities, and thirdly, it [the preaching] remained with the pagans everywhere.[86] In order to show that the pagans were going to believe in the apostolic preaching, while the rest of Israel would believe only at the occurrence of his [second] advent, he said: *You will not finish going through the cities of Israel until the Son of Man comes.*[87] In other words, once the full number of pagans is added,[88] the rest of Israel will be placed in the Church at the future advent of his glory in order to complete the number of saints.[89]

15. *A student is not above his teacher nor a servant above his master.*[90] Knowledge of imminent events greatly helps us to endure, especially if our will is anticipated by a model of patience.[91] Our Lord, Eternal Light, Leader of believers, and Parent of immortality,[92] sent encouragement to his disciples in advance for their coming suffering, so that no disciple should imagine that he is better than his teacher, and no slave that he is above his master. For if they call the master of the house by the surname of a demon[93] because of their jealousy,[94] how much more will they

84. Gn 22.13.
85. Mt 10.23. Hilary's words literally read "from one to two cities" (*ex una . . . in duas urbes*).
86. Doignon notes that the historical course of the Apostle's preaching is an apologetic scheme found in Tertullian, *Apol.* 21.25 and *De praescr. haer.* 20.4 (two stages: Judea and the world), and *De praescr. haer.* 36.2 (three stages: to Greece, Asia, and Rome). *Sur Matt.* I.233, n.25.
87. Mt 10.23.
88. Rom 11.23–25; i.e., are converted.
89. Cf. Rom 11.25–27.
90. Mt 10.24.
91. *exemplo.* Cf. Cyprian, *Ad Fort.*, pref.
92. *immortalitatis parens.*
93. I.e., Beelzebub.
94. Mt 10.25b. Hilary skips over 10.25a: "it is enough for the disciple to be

commit all kinds of injury and outrage toward the household servants? But they do not at all frighten us with these insults if we, rather than grabbing a position of glory,[95] place ourselves on the same level with our Savior when it comes to suffering.[96]

16. *There is nothing concealed that will not be revealed.*[97] He is referring to the day of judgment, which will reveal the hidden conscience of our will. Those things that they thought were covered up, he will uncover in the light of open acknowledgment. He tells us, therefore, that we should not be afraid of threats, schemes, or the power of our persecutors, because the day of judgment will reveal that those things were really of no account and unfounded.

17. *And what I tell you in the dark, speak it in the light; and what you hear in your ear, proclaim on the rooftops.*[98] We read that the Lord was not accustomed to making pronouncements at night or teaching in the dark. In fact, every word of his is darkness to carnal persons, and his word is night to unbelievers. Whatever he has said must be spoken with a freedom of faith and confession by each one. For this reason, he commands that those words spoken in darkness should be proclaimed in the light. Whatever the Lord entrusted to their hearing in secret, let it be heard on the rooftops, and the speaker's declamation may be heard from on high.[99] For the knowledge of God must be faithfully announced,[100] and the teaching of the Gospel's hidden depths must be revealed in the light of the apostolic preaching. We do not fear those who, though they possess bodily abilities,[101] have no law over the soul. Rather, we fear God who has power of destroying both soul and body in Gehenna.[102]

---

like his teacher, and the servant [or *slave,* according to RSV footnote] like his master" (RSV), which helps the reader tie the meaning of vv.25–26 together.

95. Following Coustant's edition for this sentence (PL 9:972B).

96. Cf. Mt 10.25a.                         97. Mt 10.26.

98. Mt 10.27.                               99. *excelso.*

100. *constanter enim Dei ingerenda cognitio est.*

101. *licentia.*

102. Mt 10.28.

18. *Are not two sparrows sold for a penny, and not one of those falls to the ground without the will of your Father?*[103] There is no crime or fault, I think, in trapping and selling sparrows. When the Lord said: *Not one of those falls to the ground without the will of your Father,* it seems to run contrary to the apostolic dictum that says, "It is not about the oxen that God is concerned."[104] Most of the Apostle's authority would be negated if a different view were expressed other than the one handed down in the Gospels.[105] Nor is much dignity accorded to the apostles if they are [not] more valuable than the sparrows.[106] This passage is a continuation of the idea found in the earlier passages. The sins are multiplied[107] of those who are going to betray us, who are going to persecute us, who are going to force us to flee, who hate us on account of the Lord's name, who exercise all their power[108] over the body alone, possessing no power of the soul. These are the ones who sell two sparrows for a penny. That which has been sold under sin,[109] Christ redeems from the Law.[110]

Since the body and the soul are sold, it is sin to sell them to someone else. Because Christ redeems us from sin, he is the Redeemer of the soul and the body. Those who sell two sparrows for a penny, therefore, are similar to those who sell themselves into sin for the lowest price, even though they were born to fly and be carried up to heaven on spiritual wings.[111] And yet, they are held captive by the price of present pleasures. To gain the luxury of the world, they all have undertaken to market themselves for sale.

19. But we must ask what it means that not even one of these sparrows will fall to the ground[112] without the will of God. The will of God is the means by which one of them may fly higher,

---

103. Mt 10.29.
104. 1 Cor 9.9b.
105. We may be hearing here an echo of the Marcionite criticism of the Gospel, the criticism that claimed that 1 Cor 9.9 revealed another God than the one found in the Gospels. Cf. Tertullian, *Adv. Marc.* 5.7.10.
106. Cf. Mt 10.31.  107. Cf. Mt 10.28.
108. *ius.*  109. Rom 7.14.
110. Gal 3.13; 4.5.
111. A classical poetic expression; see Virgil, *Aen.* 6.15.
112. Cf. Mt 10.29b.

whereas the Law, issued from the ordinance of God, determines which one of these will fall.[113] Yet, if they were to fly, they [the two] would be one. In other words, a body has crossed over to the nature of the soul, when the weight of its earthly matter is abolished in its flight to the substance of the soul, as it becomes instead a spiritual body.[114] In the case of those, however, who are sold by the price of their sins,[115] the simplicity of the soul[116] grows heavy as it passes to a bodily nature, and from the filth of its vices, it draws earthly matter together and becomes one of those who fall[117] to the earth. When the Lord says they are more valuable than many sparrows,[118] he reveals that the election of the faithful takes precedence over the multitude of the unfaithful. For the latter, there is a fall to the earth; for the former, there is flight to heaven.

20. Bringing anything together in order to count it has to be done carefully with diligence and solicitude. So too, counting things that will perish is not a worthwhile task. So that we may know that we are not going to perish, because we are worth much more than many sparrows, the Lord states that the very number of our hairs is counted.[119] Because we are going to be completely saved, whatever is innumerable in us must be preserved so that by his favor and power, it may be counted. We need not fear the fall of our bodies, nor should the destruction of our flesh give us any reason for sorrow. Once the body has been dissolved in keeping with the condition of its nature and its origin, it will be re-established in the substance of a spiritual soul.[120]

---

113. Cf. Cyprian, *Ad Demet.* 3.

114. Cf. 1 Cor 15.53; Tertullian, *De resurr.* 53.15.

115. *Supra,* 10.15.

116. *animae subtilitas.*

117. Lit., "is handed over" (*tradatur*). In Hilary's vocabulary, *traditio* and *tradere* are sometimes connected with death and the departure of the soul. *De trin.* 10.11.61 (4); 62.

118. Mt 10.31.

119. Mt 10.30.

120. *spiritalis animae.* Cf. Tertullian, *De resurr.* 53, who discusses the spiritualization of the body at the resurrection.

21. Once we have been confirmed in this teaching, we may rightfully possess a steadfast freedom in our confession of God. The Lord comments also about our situation: he will deny before the Father in heaven the one who has denied him before men on earth.[121] Whoever personally acknowledges the Lord before men will be acknowledged by him in heaven. Whatever sort of witnesses to his name we have been before men, the same testimony will be used before God the Father about us.

22. *Do not suppose that I came to bring peace to the earth. I did not come to bring peace, but a sword. For I came to turn*[122] *a son against his father, and a daughter against her mother, and daughter-in-law against her mother-in-law, and one's enemies will be members of his household.*[123] What is this division about? For the first precepts of the Law, we receive: "Honor your father and your mother."[124] The Lord himself said, "My peace I give to you, I leave my peace with you."[125] What does he want for them, seeing that he has brought a sword to the earth and separated a son from his father, and a daughter from her mother, and daughter-in-law against her mother-in-law, and a man's household become his enemies? Were civil authority to follow along these lines, it would be regarded as an impiety.[126] Everywhere there is hatred, everywhere there are wars, and the sword of the Lord rages furiously between a father and his son and between a daughter and her mother![127] There is the statement in Luke on this same point: "From now on there will be five in one house divided; three will be divided against two, and two over against three."[128] Can the family on the father's side of the household be expanded to a greater number? Or is the situation limited according to the prescription of the time when there were only five in one household and these five were divided? Thus we ought to consider how it is that he brings a sword to the earth,

---

121. Mt 10.33; 2 Tm 2.12.          122. *separare.*
123. Mt 10.34–35, quoting Mi 7.6.          124. Ex 20.12.
125. Jn 14.27.
126. In the Roman mind *impietas* involved disloyalty to the gods, which was tantamount to disloyalty to the state and the well-being of social order.
127. Hyperbole.
128. Lk 12.52.

what is the property of the names mentioned, what is the reason for the number five, and in what way three should be divided against two and two over against three, and to what extent a
man's household is supposed to become his enemies.

23. First of all, it is necessary to explain the nature of the
individual particulars and of the overall issue [in this passage]
so that we will have a proper perspective on what has preceded
as well as what follows.

The sword is the sharpest weapon of all which serves as the
emblem of authority,[129] due to the severity of its judgment and
the punishment of evil-doers. The very name of this weapon refers, by the prophets' authority,[130] to the preaching of the new
Gospel so called.[131] We remember that the Word of God is signified as a sword—the sword which was brought to earth—that is,
the Lord's preaching that has penetrated the bodies of men.[132]
It is this sword that divides the five inhabitants in one house,
the three against the two and the two over against the three.[133]

In a man we find only three things: body, soul, and will.[134]
As the soul has been given to the body, so also there is granted
him the power of using both [body and soul] as he wishes. This
is the reason that Law was intended for the will. It is understood that in those who first were made by God, the origin of
life's beginnings in them was not transmitted[135] from any other source.[136] But as a result of the sin and unbelief of the first
parents, in following generations sin began to be the father of
our body, and unbelief the mother of our soul. From these two
we received our beginning, through the transgression of our

---

129. Doignon notes the juridical reference of Hilary's remark to the Roman expression *ius gladii* (*Sur Matt.* I.243, n.41).

130. Cf. Hilary's *Tract. Ps.* 149.6.          131. Eph 6.17.

132. Heb 4.12.                                 133. *Supra*, 10.12.

134. *corpus et animam et voluntatem.*

135. *traductus.* A technical term as seen in Tertullian, *De anima* 36, who argues that the soul is given by God but transmitted by the seed of the parents,
body and soul being conceived at the same moment. Hilary will seemingly
reject this view in his later thinking, when he declares in *De trin.* 10 that each
soul is given directly by God.

136. Tertullian, *De paen.* 3, claims that the origin of sin stems from the will,
from which comes every deed.

first parents. Now their will is subjoined to every one of us.[137] So there are five persons for one house: sin, the father of our body; unbelief, the mother of our soul; and our free will, which is between them, attached to every person by a certain kind of conjugal law. The will's mother-in-law is unbelief, who accepts us as her own children, as we wander away from the faith and from God. She holds us, clutched between unbelief and pleasure, in the ignorance of God by attracting us to every vice.[138]

24. When we are renewed in the laver of baptism through the power of the Word, we are separated from the sins that come from our origin, and are separated from its authors.[139] Once we have endured a sort of excision by God's sword, we are cut from the dispositions of our father and mother. Casting off the "old man" with his sins and unbelief,[140] we are renewed in soul and body by the Spirit,[141] rejecting our inborn habits and former ways.[142] Because the body itself has been mortified through faith,[143] it rises to the nature of the soul, which comes from the breath of God (although it still subsists in its own physical form); a communion between the two is brought about by the Word. For this reason, the body begins to desire to be made one and the same with the soul, that is, with what is spiritual. For both, a freedom of the will from its *mother-in-law;* that is, it is separated from unbelief, and yields all of its own law, with the result that what was freedom of will is later on the power of the soul.[144] The result will be serious dissension in one household, and the "new man's"[145] enemies will be the members of his [own] household. Now separated from the others by the Word of God, he will rejoice to remain, both inside and outside, that is, both his soul and body, in the newness of the Spirit.

As a result of these inborn qualities and what we might call

137. Probably a remark that reflects Pauline theology, as do many places in Hilary's commentary. See Introduction, 30–33.

138. An unclear and labored passage of exegesis.

139. Adam and Eve.

140. Col 3.9–10.

141. Cf. Tertullian, *De anima* 41.4; *De carne Chr.* 4.4; Cyprian, *De hab. virg.* 23.

142. Col 3.5–8.          143. Rom 8.13.

144. Cf. Cyprian, *De orat. Dom.* 16.          145. Col 3.10.

an antiquity of lineage, they[146] still desire to remain in those things which gave pleasure to them: the origins of their flesh and the origin of their soul and their free will.[147] These will be separated into two, that is, the soul and body of the new man, which have begun to desire to be one and the same [with each other]. And the three that are separated will be subject to the two, which are stronger under the governance of the newness of the Spirit.[148] Those who have preferred the love of one's household name instead of God's love[149] will be unworthy of inheriting the good to come.

25. Then the same course of teaching and understanding continues in what follows. After he commands us to forsake everything that is most dear in the world, he adds: *Whoever does not accept his cross and follow me, is not worthy of me.*[150] This is because those who are of Christ have crucified their body with its vices and desires.[151] We are unworthy of Christ if we do not accept his cross, in which we share in his suffering, death, burial, and resurrection.[152] We will not be victorious unless we have followed the Lord through this sacrament of faith in the newness of the Spirit.

26. *Whoever finds his life will lose it, and whoever has lost his life on my account will find it.*[153] In other words, through the power of the Word and separation from our old habits, we will obtain a benefit for our soul in death and the loss of prosperity.[154] It is necessary that we accept death for the newness of life while transfixing our vices to the Lord's cross. Against persecutors we must preserve the freedom of our glorious confession in contempt of the present age. So too, we must avoid profit that is destructive to the soul, knowing that the law in each soul is not abandoned and that with loss of a short life, we receive the benefit of immortality.

---

146. I.e., those whose bodies, souls, and will remain in the power of sin.
147. *libertas potestatis.*　　　148. Cf. Tertullian, *De bapt.* 4.5.
149. Mt 10.37.　　　　　　　　150. Mt 10.38.
151. Gal 5.24.　　　　　　　　152. Cf. *supra,* 3.1.
153. Mt 10.39.　　　　　　　　154. *salutem.*

27. *Whoever receives you, receives me, and whoever receives me, receives him who sent me.*[155] For everyone's sake the Lord makes a point with the force of his teaching and the application of his precepts. As he had indicated the danger for those who do not receive the apostles, by the witness of shaking the dust from their feet,[156] he stresses the merit of those who receive them as going beyond the benefit of an expected service. He also teaches us that he has the office of mediator,[157] so that when we have received him—and he having proceeded from God—God may be transfused[158] into us through him. And so, whoever receives the apostles, receives Christ. Whoever receives Christ, receives the Father because one receives none other in the apostles than Christ himself, and there is no other in Christ than God himself. It is through this blessed order[159] that by receiving the apostles we receive no other than God because Christ abides in them and God in Christ.[160]

28. *Whoever receives a prophet in the name of a prophet will receive a prophet's reward.*[161] Whoever receives a prophet, receives the one who dwells within the prophet, and he becomes worthy of a prophet's reward because he received the prophet in the name of a prophet.[162] Likewise, the one who receives a righteous person is given a similar reward. This one becomes righteous by honoring righteousness. Because righteousness is perfected[163] through faith,[164] this service obtains a reward. Given God's graciousness, there are many opportunities for striving for eternity. Whenever we receive the righteous person and prophet in an attitude of reverence, we receive the honor attributed to the righteous and the prophet.

155. Mt 10.40.

156. Cf. Mt 10.14.

157. 1 Tm 2.5; Heb 9.15.

158. *transfusus in nos sit.*

159. *ordinem gratiarum.*

160. An important and frequent christological point that Hilary emphasizes throughout the commentary. See *supra*, 3.1–5; 4.14; 5.15; 6.1; 8.2 and 6; 9.7–8; 10.27; *infra*, 12.11 and 17–18; 13.7; 14.2; 16.4–5, 7–8; 20.3; 23.6 and 8; 24.1; 27.4 and 8; 31.2–3. Cf. Tertullian, *De praescr. haer.* 21, which is the formula used for ascertaining the truth of doctrine.

161. Mt 10.41.

162. I.e., that a prophet is received solely on account of the fact that he is a prophet.

163. *consummatur.*

164. Rom 10.6.

29. *And whoever has given to drink a cup of cold water to one of the least of these,*[165] etc. The Lord taught that no deed done from a good conscience is in vain, and that the assurance of one's faith is not undermined by another's unbelief. Indeed, he foresees that many will glory in the mere name of apostleship, whereas their every action shows they are unworthy of the name. They deceive and lie constantly, and even if we have accorded to them our allegiance when it comes to religious convictions,[166] we are not cheated out of the reward of our own works and of hope. For even though these are the very least, that is, they are the greatest of sinners—there is nothing less than the least— nevertheless, the Lord insists we have a straightforward duty to them that is not in vain, even if a light responsibility, which he indicates by the name of *cold water.* It is not to the sins of a person, but to the name of "disciple" that honor has been bestowed. So too, the reproachful conduct of the one who deceives does not undermine the benefits of the other, since the Lord's reward is for the one who gives [a cup of cold water] by faith, not for the deceit of the one receiving it.

165. Mt 10.42. Hilary's reading, which follows most of the Old Latin versions, literally reads: "Whoever has given a drink (*potum*), a cup of cold water (*calicem aquae frigidae*), to one of the least of these ..." The awkwardness of the statement may partly explain other versions of the Latin Bible that read, "Whoever will have given (*potaverit*) to drink to one of the least of these a cup of cold water ..."

166. *sub religionis opinione.* It is unclear whether Hilary is obliquely referring to an actual group; cf. *infra,* 12.17–18.

# CHAPTER ELEVEN

*HEN JOHN HEARD in prison about the works of Christ, he sent his disciples to him asking, "Are you the one who was to come, or should we wait for another?"*[1] Because he was confined in prison, John was unaware of the Lord; such a great prophet did not know his God. As the forerunner[2] nonetheless, he announced the one who was to come; as the prophet, he acknowledged his [Christ's] existence; as the confessor,[3] he venerated his [Christ's] advent. How could there occur such an error in his knowledge, which was so varied and prodigious? If, however, we follow the Lord's testimony concerning John, we are not allowed to think this way. Clearly it is reasonable to believe that the glory of the Holy Spirit was not absent in John, who was held in prison, since it was the light of the Spirit's power which would minister to the apostles[4] when they were in prison.[5]

2. But a deeper understanding is revealed in these things which happened concerning John. As we perceive in John a grace expressed with the effectiveness of reality,[6] he also is the prophet that prophesies according to the manner[7] in which he was the embodiment of the Law.[8] For the Law announced Christ and preached the remission of sins, promising the Kingdom of heaven.[9] John completely fulfilled all of the works of

1. Mt 11.2–3.
2. *praeitor,* a neologism.
3. "Confessor" was a title given to those who were imprisoned for their confession of Christ and were regarded as possessing special insight about spiritual and doctrinal matters. See Cyprian, *Ep.* 39.2, 5; Tertullian, *Adv. Prax.* 1.
4. *apostolis,* in the sense of those who are heralds of the Gospel.
5. Acts 12.7.
6. *cum facti efficientia gratia . . . expressa.*
7. That of God's grace in him, to which he testified (Jn 1.17).
8. Cf. Mt 11.13.
9. Cf. Mt 11.12; Lk 24.44–47.

the Law. Now that the Law has become inactive, confined, so to speak, by the sins of the masses and chained as a result of the people's sins, John is restrained in chains and in prison so that Christ may not be understood by them. The Law,[10] therefore, points to the Gospel so that unbelief may consider[11] the truth of Christ's words in his deeds.

Whatever of the Law was bound through the deceit of sins is delivered when one learns the freedom of the Gospel.[12] For this reason, John was not seeking insight as a remedy for his own ignorance, but for that of his disciples, since he himself had preached about the One who was to come for the remission of sins.[13] So that they should know none other than the One whom John had preached, he sent his disciples to learn about his works. John knew that those works[14] would confer an authority on his words and that no other Christ should be expected than the One to whom his works bore witness.[15]

3. When the Lord had fully revealed himself by miracles, namely, giving sight to the blind, the ability to walk to the lame, healing to the lepers, hearing to the deaf, speech to the dumb, life to the dead, preaching to the poor,[16] he said: *Blessed is the one who has not been scandalized by me.*[17] Had Christ already done something that scandalized John? Not in the least. For John continued in the same course of his teaching and works. Yet the force of the preceding statement and its specific references must be considered: what is that good that is preached to the poor? What of those who have lost their lives, of those who will have accepted and followed their cross, of those who will become humble in spirit? It is for these that the Kingdom of heaven is prepared.[18] Since all these sufferings converged in

---

10. I.e., represented in John.　　　11. *contempletur.*

12. Cf. Rom 7.23; 8.2.

13. This is a common explanation for Hilary: John's seeming ignorance was in fact for the benefit of his disciples. See *infra*, 26.4; 31.7–8.

14. I.e., the Lord's.　　　15. Cf. Mt 24.4–5.

16. Mt 11.5.

17. Mt 11.6. The *scandalizatus* of the Latin versions is the perfect passive participle of the verb *scandalizare,* a loan-word from the Greek *skandalizein* ("to cause to stumble," "to give offense").

18. Or, "the Kingdom is prepared in heaven" (*regnum praeparatur in caelo*).

the Lord and since his coming cross was a scandal[19] to many people, he declared blessed those whose faith finds his cross, his death, and his burial to be no trial at all. And it shows that John was seeking a guarantee when the Lord said, "Blessed are those for whom there is no scandal on this matter." Because of his apprehension about Christ, John had sent his disciples to hear and to see him.

4. In no sense should this reference be directed to John, as if he had been in any manner scandalized by Christ. The Lord spoke to the crowd about John as his disciples were leaving: *What did you go out into the desert to see? A reed swayed by the wind?*[20] The *desert* ought to be regarded as the absence of the Holy Spirit, where there is no dwelling of God.[21] In the *reed* is shown an image of man, very great according to the glory of the world, so distinguished in the vanity of his life. Yet this man is nonetheless empty of the fruit of truth, because his focus was on the outside and nothing on the inside, being subject to every motion of the wind. The result is that he is necessarily affected by the blowing[22] of unclean spirits, incapable of achieving stability while being empty in the heart of his soul.[23] When the Lord says, therefore, *What did you go out into the desert to see? A reed swayed by the wind?* he means this: did you go out to see a man devoid of the knowledge of God, wandering around led by the wind of unclean spirits? This is said by way of a rebuke rather than as an affirmation, showing that he did not look at John as vain and unstable.

5. *What did you go out to see? A man dressed in fine clothes? Behold, those who are dressed in fine clothes are in kings' palaces.*[24] He indicates that the soul is clothed by the garment of the body,

19. Gal 5.11.

20. Mt 11.7b.

21. It was on account of this generally shared sentiment that the ascetics went out into the desert to face demons. See Athanasius, *Vita Antonii* 8 and 13.

22. *flatum.*

23. Doignon sees here a Ciceronian expression: *animi ... tanquam in veris medillisque* (*Tusc.* 4.24). *Sur Matt.* I.257, n.6.

24. Mt 11.8.

which envelops it,[25] and which is softened by luxury and lusts. Those who are dressed in fine clothes are in the kings' palaces. The word *kings*[26] is an appellation for the angels who transgressed; for these are the powers of the age, the authorities of the world.[27] Those who dressed in fine clothes are in kings' palaces, that is, those whose bodies have been softened and weakened[28] through luxury are the dwelling of demons, who choose a place similar to their intentions and works.

6. *But what did you go out to see? A prophet? I say to you, even more than a prophet,*[29] etc. The Lord reveals all glory attributed to John by saying the latter is more than a prophet because it was given to him alone both to prophesy and to see the Christ. How can one believe that he was ignorant of Christ, he who was sent by the power of the angel, who prepared the way of the one who is to come,[30] and of whom no greater prophet born among women has arisen?[31] There is the exception of the one who is less than John, that is, the one who is questioned,[32] the one on whom we do not stake our belief, the one whose works do not bear witness—this one is greater [than John] in the Kingdom of heaven.[33]

7. *From the days of John the Baptist until now, the Kingdom of heaven suffers violence, and those making violence attack it.*[34] As the nature of things demands, the more powerful exert violence, and the weaker are those on whom violence is exerted. We need to consider what is being attacked and what is suffering violence.

The Lord had remarked upon the unbelief of the disciples of John.[35] He had understood also the opinion of the crowd concerning John's pronouncement.[36] For he realized the im-

25. Cf. Tertullian, *De resurr.* 27.1.  26. *regibus.*
27. Cf. Eph 6.12.  28. *dissoluta.*
29. Mt 11.9.  30. Mt 11.10.
31. Mt 11.11.  32. Mt 11.7–9.
33. Cf. Mt 11.11b: "Yet he who is least in the kingdom of heaven is greater than he" (RSV).
34. Mt 11.12. There is great variation among the Old Latin MSS on this verse. A number of MSS that comprise the *Itala* version read, "The kingdom of heaven is pressed upon, and those who bring pressure attack it."
35. Mt 11.3.  36. Mt 16.14.

mense danger produced by the scandal of the cross to one's faith.[37] He commanded the apostles to go preferably to the lost sheep of Israel;[38] it was necessary that they be established in the Kingdom and be preserved in the family, the line of Abraham, of Isaac, and of Jacob. Yet all this preaching [to Israel] brought about effect to publicans and sinners.[39] It is from these that believers now come; from these now come apostles; from these now the Kingdom of heaven comes.

John, however, was not believed by the people; the works of Christ did not win authority; the cross was going to become a scandal. Now prophecy is ceased; now the Law is fulfilled; now all preaching is concluded; now the spirit of Elijah is sent ahead in the voice of John.[40] Christ is preached to some and acknowledged by others; he is born[41] in some and loved by others. His own people spew him out, while strangers receive him; his closest [friends] attack him, while his enemies embrace him. Those who are adopted seek his heritage, while his family rejects him. The children repudiate the Covenant,[42] while the servants acknowledge it.[43] And so it is that the Kingdom of heaven suffers violence. Those who seek to attack it do so because the glory pledged to Israel by the patriarchs, announced by the prophets, and offered by Christ, is now appropriated and seized by the faith of the pagans.

8. *To what likeness will I compare this generation? It is like children sitting in the marketplace and shouting to one another,*[44] and so on. This whole statement reproaches their unbelief, and from its tone flows a sentiment of rebuke expressed earlier.[45] As an insolent people, they had not learned from the different forms of proclamation. In other words, the Lord indicates that the "children" are the prophets[46] who rebuke the people—in the midst of the synagogue or the public gathering of the marketplace— for not having complied as a formal body with those who "sing"

---

37. Mt 16.22–23.
38. Mt 10.6.
39. Mt 9.11–13.
40. Mt 11.14.
41. *nascitur.*
42. *Testamentum.*
43. Cf. Rom 11.7–12.
44. Mt 11.16.
45. Mt 3.9–10.
46. Mt 11.16.

to them;[47] that is, for not having obeyed the prophets' words. The movement of the "dancers"[48] should be conformed to the rhythm[49] of the singers. Using simple expression, as if they were speaking for children, the prophets preached and initiated a profession[50] (of faith) in the playing of flutes unto God. This is found in the song of Moses, of Isaiah, of David, and the rest of the prophets.

Again, we see that John's preaching did not turn them to repentance of their sins and to sorrow and grief over past transgressions.[51] In their eyes the Law was regarded as a burden, difficult and cumbersome in its prescriptions concerning drink and food. On account of its difficulties they were obliged to sin against the Law,[52] claiming that their sin, rather, was announced by a demon.[53] They did not accept the preaching of the Gospel, its freedom of life in Christ, which eased the difficulties and burdens of the Law, although publicans and sinners have believed. The repetition of various kinds of warning were offered in vain; they were not justified by grace,[54] nor were they released from the Law.

9. *And Wisdom has been justified by her children,*[55] that is, those who fight against the Kingdom of heaven attack the very means of justifying their faith. They admit that the work of Wisdom is just, because she [Wisdom] has transferred her benefits from the obstinate and the treacherous to the faithful and the obedient. But it is useful at this point to consider the force[56] of the words: *And Wisdom has been justified,* which the Lord certainly spoke concerning himself. For he is himself Wisdom, not on

47. Mt 11.17.

48. Cf. Mt 11.17: "We piped to you, and you did not dance; we wailed, and you did not mourn" (RSV).

49. *modum.*

50. *ad confessionem.*

51. Mt 11.18.

52. Cf. Rom 7.7: "What then shall we say? That the law is sin? By no means! Yet, if it had not been for the law, I should not have known sin" (RSV).

53. Mt 11.18. John's call to repentance was rejected because he was said to have a demon.

54. Rom 3.24. See Introduction, 30–31.

55. Mt 11.19b.

56. *virtutem.*

account of his works, but because of his nature. For every thing contains potency,[57] and every activity is the realization of potency. The effect of power[58] and power are not the same, just as that which produces an effect is distinguished from that effect.

There are many who shun the apostolic dictum which says, "Christ is the power[59] and the wisdom of God."[60] They are in the habit of saying that the wisdom and power of God had appeared efficaciously in him when he came forth from the Virgin, such that the work of divine wisdom and power is understood in his nativity, and such that there is in him the acquisition of wisdom rather than wisdom by nature.[61]

Nothing of this sort should be understood from these words. He declares that he is Wisdom, showing that it is in him, not from him. The work of Wisdom is faith, love, hope, modesty, fasting, continence, humility, and compassion.[62] These are the results of nature and not nature itself. The [divine] reality itself does not consist in things which came into being and which it made. Why would the Apostle have called it the power of God and the wisdom of God if it is from Wisdom that Wisdom had been created?[63]

---

57. *potestatem.*

58. *opus virtutis.*

59. *virtutem.*

60. 1 Cor 1.24.

61. A reference to the "monarchical adoptionist" form of theology that was established in the west, judging from Hilary's remarks in *De synodis* 66–70, and in the condemnations of Euphrata of Cologne (345 or 346) and of Photinus of Sirmium (finally deposed, though unsuccessfully, in 351) on these grounds. See D. H. Williams, "Monarchianism and Photinus as the Persistent Heretical Face of the Fourth Century," *Harvard Theological Review* 99 (2006): 187–206. Hilary will later address the problems of adoptionist thought and its subordinationist implications in the commentary: *infra*, 12.17–18; 31.2. It is the application of adoptionist principles to the incarnate Son that represents the most troublesome theology for Hilary at this early stage of his career. See also Tertullian, *Adv. Prax.* 19.2 and 26.7.

62. Cf. Tertullian, *De pat.* 15.

63. Hilary's argument seems to be that Christ, the power and wisdom of God, is not a product or result of God's wisdom. Rather, he is revealed as God's own wisdom in his very nature. Like Tertullian (*Adv. Prax.* 6.1), Hilary interprets Prv 8.22 as a reference to the generation of the Son, minimizing the significance attached historically to a reference that calls the Son "created." The Vulgate ameliorates the theological problem by stating, *Dominus possedit me....*" Cf. Hilary, *De trin.* 12.35.

10. *Woe to Korazin and Bethsaida because if in Tyre and Sidon the miracles*[64] *had been performed that were performed in you,*[65] and so on. The curse of disobedience is contrasted with the blessing of obedience. It was necessary that the preaching come to the Jews first, although this privilege added to the spitefulness of their unbelief. They were refuted by the example of believers who, though they witnessed no extraordinary acts,[66] found salvation wholly on the basis of faith. In Bethsaida and Capernaum[67] those who were mute praised the Lord, the blind saw, the deaf heard, the lame walked around, the dead came to life, yet amazement at such events in no way stirred their will to the point of faith. Simply hearing of those events should have compelled them to fear and to faith. Not only Tyre and Sidon, but even Sodom and Gomorrah[68] made light of their sins perhaps because they would have been inclined to believe if the sight of such power had affected them.

11. *At that moment Jesus then said, "I confess you, Lord, Father of heaven and earth, because you have hidden these things from the wise and revealed them to little children."*[69] This trustworthy confession is added to his words spoken earlier. For even if the salvation of Israel had been probable,[70] there was still nothing other than joy for the Lord that the faith was preached hereafter to the pagans. The mysteries and power of heavenly words are hidden from the wise and revealed to little children;[71] not to little children of wicked intent, who are without understanding, but to *the wise* aware of their foolishness, rather than for their wisdom.[72] The Lord confirms the equity of this matter according to the judgment of the Father's will.[73] Those who refuse to become like a little child before God, will become foolish in their own wisdom.

---

64. *virtutes.*                          65. Mt 11.21.
66. *factorum admiratione.*              67. Mt 11.23.
68. Mt 11.23–24.
69. Mt 11.25. Hilary omits *et prudentibus,* which is in the Latin version, probably by oversight.
70. *optabilis* (lit., "desirable").     71. Mt 11.25.
72. 1 Cor 1.20. Cf. *De trin.* 2.12 and 3.8, used in reference to Homoian opponents.
73. Mt 11.25.

12. Let no one think there is anything in him [Christ] less than what there is in God. The Lord says that all things have been committed to him by the Father, that he is known to the Father alone, that the Father is known to him alone and to whomever the Lord wishes to reveal him.[74] He will reveal the Father's will to whoever asks. By this revelation he teaches that there is the same substance of both Father and Son within their mutual knowledge.[75] Whoever knows the Son will likewise know the Father in the Son because all things have been committed[76] to the Son by the Father. So too, there is nothing known to the Father alone that has not been committed to the Son. For what is of the Father is known only to the Son. In this mystery of mutual knowledge, we understand that there is nothing in the Son that is unknown to the Father.[77]

13. Finally, he calls to himself those who labor under the difficulties of the Law and those burdened with worldly sins. He promises to relieve their labor and their burden if only they take up his yoke.[78] In other words, they ought to accept the teaching of his commandments and come to him through the mystery of his cross, because he is humble and meek in heart and they will find rest in their souls. By establishing the appeal of his pleasant yoke and the attractions of a light burden,[79] he grants to believers knowledge of his goodness that he alone knows in the Father. And what is more pleasant than his yoke? What is lighter than his burden? By these we become worthy of approval, we abstain from wickedness, we desire to do good, we refuse to do evil, we love all people, we hate no one, we attain eternity. We are not infatuated[80] with the present times; we are unwilling to bring upon another the trouble which we ourselves would not wish to endure.[81]

74. Mt 11.27.
75. Tertullian makes a similar point in *Adv. Prax.* 22.8–11: in particular, the "mutual knowledge" of the Father and the Son establishes the identity of their substance since the Father and the Son are known to each other and are *unum* (*Sur Matt.* I.267, n.17).

76. *sunt tradita.*
78. Mt 11.28–29.
80. *capi.*

77. Cyprian, *Test.* 2.6.
79. Mt 11.30.
81. Cf. Mt 7.12; Lk 6.31.

# CHAPTER TWELVE

**A**T THAT TIME *Jesus went through the grain fields on the Sabbath; his disciples who were hungry began to pick the heads of grain and eat them.*[1] His entering the grain field, the day of the Sabbath, the hunger of the disciples, the plucking[2] of the grain heads, the allegation of the Pharisees, and the response of the Lord[3] have, as do the rest, an underlying explanation based on an interior cause.[4] For the full truth of the facts, as we have said, stems from the consequences of these events, and also provides the likeness of a future truth understood from this image.

2. From the beginning, we should consider the statement that begins thus: *At that time Jesus went through the grain fields.* It was at this time when he offered[5] thanks to God the Father for the salvation brought to the pagans so that we might connect the same idea both with what took place earlier and what was to follow. Let us briefly, therefore, touch on the remaining points: the field is the world, the Sabbath is rest, the crop is the production[6] of future believers for the harvest. Therefore, as he entered into the field on the Lord's Sabbath day of rest, so he proceeded into this world, to its crop, which he has sown into the human race.[7]

And because this hunger was a longing for the salvation of

---

1. Mt 12.1.

2. *praecerptio.* A neologism.

3. Mt 12.3–8.

4. *subiacentem interioris causae intelligentiam.* I.e., a principle of figurative or allegorical interpretation, leading to scriptural truth.

5. *confessus est.*

6. *profectus.*

7. Hilary is drawing on specific scriptural metaphors from the parable of the sower in Mt 13.

humanity, the disciples wanted to pluck heads of grain. In other words, the disciples hastened to fulfill the salvation of the saints. For grain [merely] as food does not benefit[8] a man, nor is eating the plucked heads of grain really useful. Rather, we have here the image of future events that describe the faith and the power of the words interposed [among these future events] brings clarity to the mystery of hunger and its fulfillment.[9]

3. The Pharisees, who thought they were in possession of the keys of heaven, accused the disciples of breaking the Law,[10] yet the Lord reminded them of the event in which a prophetic principle[11] was contained under the rubric of these facts: how David and those with him who were hungry had been satisfied with unlawful bread.[12] For if it were not allowed for them to do so, David would not have been believed to have done this without guilt. Instead David prophesies about these facts according to the Law with no sacrilege of guilt. As he and the others were satisfied by the shew bread,[13] so also Christ with the apostles ought to be satisfied with the salvation of the pagans, even though it seemed illegal to the Jews.

4. The Lord also reminded them of another prophecy so that they should understand that everything mentioned earlier about the Law had been fulfilled in him: the priests in the Temple broke the Sabbath without guilt.[14] By this he indicates that he is himself the temple in which, by means of the apostolic teaching, salvation is brought to the pagans, whereas the people of the Law lived in the lassitude of unbelief. Since he himself is greater than the Sabbath, the Gospel[15] is at work in Christ, who cannot be blamed for having violated the Law.

5. And in order to show that every one of these events that happened contains an image of a work to come, he added: *If you knew what this meant, "I desire mercy, not sacrifice," you would not*

---

8. *congruit.*
10. *illicita agere* (Mt 12.2).
12. Mt 12.3–4.
14. Mt 12.5; 1 Sm 21.6.

9. Cf. Is 55.1–3.
11. *prophetiae ratio.*
13. Ex 25.30; 35.13.
15. *evangelica fides.*

*have condemned the innocent.*[16] The work of our salvation is not in sacrifice but in mercy,[17] and, now that the Law has ceased, we are saved by the goodness of God. If they had understood the reality of this gift, they would never have condemned the innocent, that is, the apostles. On account of jealousy they were bound to be accused of having broken the Law, because it was through them that, once the ancient practice of sacrifices ceased, the reformation[18] of mercy came to the benefit of all people. The Pharisees should not have thought that the Lord of the Sabbath could be bound by the prescriptions of the Sabbath.[19] It was in the grain field that these words and deeds happened.

6. And after this, when the Lord entered a synagogue,[20] the Pharisees presented a man with a withered hand, asking him whether it was lawful to heal on the Sabbath.[21] They were seeking an opportunity to accuse him with his own response. He entrapped them instead by the example of a sheep that falls into a pit: whether those who are concerned with pulling it out on the Sabbath are guilty in doing so.[22] For it is better to heal a man, who is more valuable than a sheep,[23] and it is wrong-headed to think that the Sabbath can be violated in the service of saving humanity, since concern for pulling a sheep out of a pit does not violate the Sabbath.

7. Such healing is rightly attributed to the Lord. After their return from the grain field, where the apostles had already received the fruit of their harvest, he went to the synagogue in order to prepare there other workers for his harvest. Many of these would later stand together with the apostles.[24] These were healed, as was the man with the crippled hand.[25] The Pharisees did not have the means[26] of granting healing;[27] the man's hand ceased its function and service to the body that it had been able

---

16. Mt 12.7, quoting Hos 6.6.      17. Cf. Is 1.12–17.
18. *novitas.*                     19. Mt 12.8.
20. Mt 12.9.                       21. Mt 12.10.
22. Mt 12.11.                      23. Mt 12.12.
24. An allusion to Mt 12.15. Cf. Acts 1.12–15.
25. Mt 12.10.                      26. *substantiam.*
27. *salutis.*

to perform before it had withered. So the Lord told him to extend his hand, and it was restored just as sound as the other.[28] Complete healing is in the Word,[29] and the hand is returned to wholeness just as the other one. Here there is a likeness produced by the service of the apostles in their duty of offering salvation. The Lord taught that the Pharisees could hardly undertake the task of humanity's salvation as did the apostles. For the Pharisees to serve in the same way, their "hand" would have to be restored—if they would believe.

8. But the Lord's works incited jealousy among the Pharisees, who took counsel against him[30] because they regarded him with the body as a man, and did not understand him to be God in his works.[31] Because he knew their designs, he departed from them[32] that he might learn of their malicious plans from a distance. And large crowds followed him; plainly, he was standing in the company of the faithful as he left the unbelievers behind.

9. Those whom he healed he commanded to be quiet.[33] But did he order the silence of everyone he healed? Not at all, because the salvation rendered to each one was itself a witness to him. Yet by ordering secrecy, he was refusing the boastful glorification of himself. In doing so, he reveals an understanding about himself in the very act of warning them to be silent; a knowledge about himself is revealed by the restraint, since the need to be silent arises from the fact about which one must keep silent.[34]

---

28. Mt 12.13.

29. *Supra*, 8.6: *cui [Christo] subest totum posse quod loquitur.*

30. Mt 12.14.

31. A common christological complaint Hilary makes against contemporaries whom he considers to be heretical. See *infra*, 10.27, n.143.

32. Mt 12.15.

33. Mt 12.16.

34. *quia observantia silentii ex re quae sit silenda proficiscitur.* Cf. Mk 3.12; Lk 4.41.

10. Given the stress laid on keeping silent concerning him, the purpose of the [Lord's] words is fulfilled by Isaiah.[35] From this prophecy we, who are in the present, are reminded: that he was loved by God and in him the Father's will is well pleased, that the Spirit of God is upon him, that by him judgment for the pagans is declared, that the reed which has been bruised is not broken, and that the smoking wick is not extinguished.[36] In other words, the fragile and weak lives of the pagans have not been consumed, but rather preserved for salvation. Nor has the small flame which is only smoking on a wick been extinguished—the paltry spirit of Israel has not been withdrawn from the remnants of its former grace—because there is an opportunity in the time of repentance for recovering the entire light of the flame.[37] But that event is prescribed within a definite time frame: *until the time when he brings victory to judgment*,[38] that is, the power of death is destroyed at the return of his glory when he introduces his judgment on the pagans who will come to believe on his name by faith.

11. *At that time, they brought to him a man possessing a demon who was blind and mute*,[39] etc. There follows the healing needed for a blind and mute demoniac. It is with good reason that after he had spoken healing words to everyone in the crowd generally, a blind and deaf demoniac is then brought in from outside so that the same consistent pattern[40] might follow with no ambiguity. It is like this: the Pharisees accused the apostles of picking grain, that is, of plucking men from the world prematurely, [because] the apostles preached mercy over sacrifice.[41] The man with the withered hand presented in the synagogue is healed. But these things were not enough for converting Israel, since it was then that the Pharisees entered upon a plan of murder. In light of this situation, it was necessary that salvation would come to the pagans in the figure[42] of this one man, who, as the dwelling-

---

35. Mt 12.17–21 (Is 42.1–4).          36. Is 42.3.
37. Is 42.6–7.
38. Mt 12.20; Is 42.1b. The Old Latin version, which Hilary follows here, differs considerably from the Septuagint.
39. Mt 12.22.          40. *ordo*.
41. Mt 12.2, 7.
42. *forma*, i.e., allegorical figure.

place of a demon (both blind and mute), was being prepared to respond to God. For he acknowledged God in Christ, as he praised the works of Christ in his profession of God.

The crowd was amazed at the works that the Lord did,[43] though the jealousy of the Pharisees grew worse. In fact, because so many of his works surpassed human weakness, they avoided the embarrassment of confessing him by committing a greater wickedness of treachery. Because they were not able to attribute his works to a man, they refused to confess them of God, and claimed that all of his power against demons was from Beelzebub, the prince of demons.[44]

12. *Jesus, however, knowing their thoughts, said to them, "Every kingdom divided against itself will be dissolved."*[45] The Word of God is rich[46] and has been established to provide every kind of proof for various meanings. It exhibits from itself an abundance of examples. Whether it is understood in a simple fashion[47] or studied for the inner meaning,[48] it is necessary for every step of our progression.[49] Let us pass over those things that are commonly understood, and focus on interior causes.

13. *Every kingdom divided against itself will be dissolved.* In order to respond to that which had been said concerning Beelzebub, he answered them by turning their own response against themselves. Since the Law is from God and the promise of the kingdom of Israel is from the Law, so too, the birth and advent of Christ are from the Law. If the kingdom of the Law is divided against itself, it will necessarily be dissolved. Every authority is undermined by division, and the power of a kingdom that is separated against itself is overwhelmed; and thus Israel has lost the kingdom that came from the Law because the people of the Law oppose the fulfillment[50] of the Law in Christ.

---

43. Mt 12.23.                    44. Mt 12.24. Cf. *supra,* 5.15.
45. Mt 12.25.                    46. *dives.*
47. I.e., literal or narratival approach.
48. I.e, allegorical or figurative significance.
49. *ad omnem profectum.*
50. *adimpletionem.*

14. *But also a city or a house divided against itself will not stand.*[51]
There is the same underlying principle[52] for both the house
and the city as there is for the kingdom. Here the *city* indicates
Jerusalem, always glorious in its supremacy over the pagans.[53]
And yet when Jerusalem later inflamed itself against the Lord
by the anger of the people and put to flight his apostles along
with the multitude of believers, the city could not stand because of the division caused by those abandoning[54] her. As a
result of this division, it soon followed that the destruction of
Jerusalem was announced.[55]

15. *For if Satan drives out Satan, he is divided against himself.*[56]
On account of the malevolent words spoken earlier, when they
said he performed these deeds by Beelzebub, they condemn
him for the very sort of thing they had admitted. They did not
grasp how they themselves had confessed that Beelzebub is
divided. If Beelzebub is forced to divide himself, it would ensue that a demon drives out demons, and that the division is
against itself. We should conclude that there is a greater power
in the one who formed the division than in the ones divided.[57]
It follows that the one who is divided and compelled to act
against himself, his kingdom is already dissolved by such division. Even if Christ drives out demons by the power of Beelzebub, in whose name will his[58] sons, that is, the apostles drive
out demons?[59] Although the apostles are worthy to assert themselves as judges, it was Christ who acquired for them that power
against the demons. It was that power which the Pharisees denied he possessed. If the disciples accomplished their works in
Christ, and Christ accomplished his works by the Spirit of God,

51. Mt 12.25. Hilary has slightly reworded the verse. Cf. Mk 3.24–26; Lk
11.17–18.

52. *ratio.*

53. Cf. Rom 2.17–20.

54. *discedentium.*

55. Cf. Mt 23.37; Lk 13.34, 21.24.

56. Mt 12.26.

57. Presumably, that Satan is stronger than his demons.

58. Amending *filii eorum* to *filii eius.* Hilary reinterprets the passage (v.27)
to refer "sons" (or exorcists) of the Pharisees to the apostles. An *ad absurdum*
argument. How could the apostles have driven out demons in the home of
Christ if Christ drove out demons by Beelzebub?

59. Mt 12.27.

then the Kingdom of God is come,[60] assigned to the apostles by the office of the mediator.[61] But when Christ is accused of being enabled by Beelzebub, God is blasphemed in Christ, and thus an unpardonable[62] offense, an outrage, against God is effected by the Pharisees in the name of Beelzebub.

16. *How can anyone enter into a strong man's house and plunder his possessions?*[63] etc. He indicates that all the power of the devil was crushed by the Lord during the time of his initial temptation since no one may enter the strong man's house and plunder his possessions unless he has bound up the strong man. Then he can plunder his house, for whoever can accomplish that is surely stronger than the strong man. Satan was already bound at the moment when he had been so named by the Lord.[64] In fact, he was shackled when his own wickedness was named. Once he was bound in chains, the Lord was able to take away his possessions and his house. In other words, the Lord has led us, who were once his [Satan's] weapons and the army of his [Satan's] kingdom, back to his own rule. Now that he has conquered and bound up the strong man, he has provided for himself an unoccupied and useful house within us.

He shows, at the same time, that he is far from having derived any power from Satan, for whoever is not with him is against him and whoever does not gather with him, is scattered.[65] From this we may understand that it is a matter of great danger to suppose something evil about someone about whom it is said: *whoever is not with him, is against him, and whoever does not gather with him scatters.*[66]

17. *Every sin and blasphemy will be forgiven to men, but blasphemy of the Spirit will not be forgiven.*[67] With a very grave qualification, he condemns the view of the Pharisees and the perversion of those who also think like them. He promises pardon of all sins

60. Mt 12.28.
62. *inexpiabilis.*
64. Mt 4.10.
66. Ibid.

61. *Supra,* 10.27.
63. Mt 12.29.
65. Mt 12.30.

67. Mt 12.31. Some other Old Latin versions read, "whoever will have blasphemed against the Holy Spirit" (or "Spirit of God").

but refuses pardon for blasphemy of the Spirit. While other words and deeds are treated with a generous pardon, there is no mercy if it is denied that God is in Christ.[68] And in whatever way one sins without pardon, he is gracious to us and reminds us again that sins of every kind can be completely forgiven, though blasphemy against the Holy Spirit cannot be forgiven. For who is so completely beyond pardon as one who denies that Christ is of God, or repudiates that the substance of the Spirit of the Father resides in him?[69] Since Christ accomplishes every work by the Spirit of God,[70] and the Lord himself is the Kingdom of God, and God is reconciling the world to himself in him,[71] whatever sacrilege is directed against Christ is directed against God because God is in Christ and Christ is in God.[72]

18. *Either make the tree good and its fruit good, or make the tree evil and its fruit evil.*[73] This saying can be applied to the present as well as the future. In the present he refutes the Jews who, although they understand that the works of Christ are beyond human power, do not wish to confess that these are works of God. As for the future, he denounces the complete perversion of faith especially of those who, by divesting the Lord of the dignity and communion with the Father's substance,[74] have boiled over into various heretical allegiances. They choose neither to dwell among the pagans, who are pardoned for their ignorance,[75] nor do they turn to an acknowledgment of the truth.[76]

68. Throughout the commentary Hilary refers to the christological error *si Deus negetur in Christo* as the most serious mistake the reader of the Gospel can make when it comes to the identity of the Word incarnate. See *supra*, 10.27, n.143.

69. Mt 12.28. Here (as in the 3d century) Hilary uses *spiritus* as a reference to divinity.

70. Cf. *supra*, 4.14.

71. 2 Cor 5.19.

72. Doignon argues this passage is a close reprise of *Adv Marc.* 5.8.4: *In quo Christo consistere haberet tota substantia [dei]. Sur Matt.* I.285, n.9. Cf. *supra*, 10.27; *infra*, 24.1; 30.2.

73. Mt 12.33.

74. *dignitatem et communionem paternae substantiae.* Cf. *supra*, 8.8; *infra*, 26.5.

75. Acts 17.30–31; Eph 4.18.

76. Cf. Tertullian, *De praescr. haer.* 42, regarding the plight of heretics.

By "tree" the Lord refers to himself in his body since all fertility bears its fruit through the inner fecundity of his power.[77] A good tree inevitably produces good fruit, or the bad tree consistently produces bad fruit, because it is by its fruit that a tree is known.[78] A bad tree by nature cannot produce what is good, nor can the same tree have good branches if it is bad.[79] We should understand from this [analogy] that Christ either should be abandoned as useless, or retained as good by the usefulness of his good fruits. Either way, words spoken against the Son of Man are pardoned, but there is no pardon for blasphemy against the Spirit.

One might take a middle course by giving some deference to Christ while denying what is most important, that is, while worshiping him as God yet depriving him of communion with God: this is blasphemy against the Spirit.[80] You should not be so foolhardy as to undermine the name of God. Although you admire his great works, you dismiss[81] his nobility[82] because of a wicked intent and disposition; you were compelled to confess him [to be God] in name, but denied his communion with the Father's substance.[83] Even in this situation the Lord extends the

---

77. See Victorinus of Poetovio, *On the Apoc.* 21.20.

78. Lit., "will bear witness to itself"(*de se . . . testabitur*).

79. Hilary's point seems to be that the reader cannot interpret the passage literally since trees, on one hand, are made by God and are all good, but, on the other hand, cannot be morally good or bad.

80. Tertullian had already commented on this kind of oxymoron in *De carne Chr.* 15.4 (CCSL 2.901–2): *haeretici credendo non credunt.* So too, Marcion accepted Christ as Son who came from God with all the divine properties, and yet this was not the Christ of God the Creator with the properties of that God (*Adv. Marc.* 3.3). See *Sur Matt.* I.286, n.13.

81. *decerpas.*

82. *generositatem.*

83. This passage is cited as an allusion to Arian doctrine by Hanson, *The Search,* 468; Burns, *The Christology of Hilary of Poitiers' Commentary on Matthew,* 16–22; and Smulders, *La doctrine trinitaire de saint Hilaire de Poitiers,* 39, n.102. Smulders specifically sees an allusion to Arius's teaching as reported in *Contra Arianos* 1.5: *generositatem eius quam confiteri es coactus in nomine.* For an alternative view see Williams, "Defining Orthodoxy in Hilary of Poitiers' *Commentarium in Matthaeum,*" *Journal of Early Christian Studies* 9 (2001): 151–71. There seems to be no evidence in Hilary's statements that necessitates a reference to "Arians." Moreover, whomever Hilary is describing, they make the same confession of faith as he does, but do not mean it as the same thing. For the terminology of *substantiae communio,* see Tertullian, *De resurr.* 52.11; Novatian, *De trin.* 31.20.

gift of his goodness, saying that it is inevitable that a bad tree be characterized by bad fruit and a good tree by good fruit. Because pardon has been granted to the evil tree according to the mystery of God's indulgence[84]—every sin should be forgiven—there is eternal fruit in a good confession. So we should not fall into a middle position between two concepts in which we dare not establish evil and yet do not want to profess the good,[85] by resigning ourselves to an implacable line[86] of thought that has corrupted itself.

19. The Lord taught that all our perverted thinking stems from vices of our nature by saying that it is only from an evil treasury that evil can be produced.[87] And he says that a reason for all our idle, careless, and useless words must be rendered to God, for it is by the words of our confession that we must either stand condemned or be justified. We will receive the appropriate kind of graciousness in the future judgment based on the conviction we have maintained about the Lord of heavenly glory.[88]

20. He was then asked to show a sign,[89] to which he responded that there will be given the sign of Jonah.[90] Just as Jonah was enclosed for three days and three nights in the belly of the sea-monster,[91] so shall he lie within the depths of the earth for the same amount of time.[92] But he shows that there will be greater faith among the pagans.[93] For once Jonah preached to the people of Nineveh, they came to repentance, and by their confession of repentance they obtained pardon from God.[94] Even the queen of the south—here presumed to be a model of the Church[95]—who admired the wisdom of Solomon, came

---

84. *sub secreto indulgentiae Dei.*

85. Doignon points to parallel concepts in Cicero's *De nat. deor.* 1.117 and 2.10. *Sur Matt.* I.287, n.16.

86. *iudicio.*  
88. Mt 12.37.  
90. Mt 12.39.  
92. Mt 12.40.  
94. Mt 12.42.

87. Mt 12.35.  
89. Mt 12.38.  
91. *ceti.*  
93. Mt 12.41.

95. Given the context of believing pagans, among whom was the "queen of the south" (or "Sheba," 1 Kgs 10.1–10), it is unclear why Hilary thought she was an *exemplum* of the Church.

from the ends of the earth to hear that wisdom which she had so admired. This comparison, therefore, serves to heighten their [the scribes' and the Pharisees'] jealousy while the faith of the pagans allows no excuse for the Jews. Whereas the Jews have believed in the prophets, that is, in Jonah and Solomon, the Jews do not believe in Christ, who is greater than Jonah and Solomon.[96] And for this reason pagans will judge unbelieving Jews at the resurrection because the fear of God was found among those to whom the Law had not been preached. Those unbelievers who are of the Law are more unworthy of pardon than those who have been ignorant of the Law but in whom a greater faith is found.

21. *When an unclean spirit comes out of a man, it wanders through arid places seeking rest and will not find it,*[97] etc. As we continue within the reading, the Lord indicates from the beginning of his opening words that he is proceeding from the previous idea;[98] in fact, he is beginning from a conjunction of terms. The underlying principle, however, of all the comparisons being proposed must be treated.

When the unclean spirit departs from a man, it goes about in arid and waterless places in which no spring[99] of life flows. Because it will not find rest, it then will say to itself that it ought to return to the house from which it left, which it will find unoccupied, swept clean with a broom and put in order.[100] And it will take with it seven spirits more wicked than itself, and, entering, they will live there, and the latter situation of that man will be worse than in the beginning. The Lord has concluded, saying: *So it will be for this wicked generation.*[101]

22. We cannot, therefore, doubt that all this is supposed to be directed at the personality[102] of this people,[103] though it is

---

96. Mt 12.42b.
97. Mt 12.43. There is much textual variation among some of the earlier MSS concerning this text's wording, which uses *ambulat, loca arida,* and *inveniet.*

98. *Supra,* 12.19.
99. *fons.*
100. Mt 12.44.
101. Mt 12.45.
102. *personam.*
103. I.e., *the wicked generation.*

necessary to consider in what way each point is taken up with
its specific circumstances and events. We saw earlier that the
faith of the pagans was justified under the rubric of the Ninevites and the queen of the south.[104] But long before this, after
many serious sins were committed against God, the Law was
given to the Jews. Their sins were contained in the books of
Moses.[105] Even after so many instances of divine power were displayed, such as when Egypt was struck with the ten plagues,[106]
or the column of cloud and light assisted them by day and by
night,[107] or the way to the Red Sea was shown to them,[108] or the
springs of water poured out from split rocks,[109] or the manna
was provided to those who hungered,[110] or finally, how the
people were living in the life and manner of the angels during
the period of forty years.[111] They afterwards worshiped beasts
and rocks, dancing [before them] with choirs and songs, and
called gods the things that they made of metal.[112] It was the
Law, through its later intervention, acting like a kind of powerful guardian, that threw out the unclean spirit that was settled
in the hearts of this people.[113] Once they left that place, they
wandered around among the deserted and arid nations, and
abandoned their ancient home in order that they might rest in
a place untroubled in those days unto the day of judgment.

23. In contrast [to this people], God's grace was bestowed
on the pagans who have since come to the living fountain flow-
ing in baptismal waters.[114] There is no place, however, for the
pagans to live with these others,[115] nor is there now rest for the

104. Mt 12.41–42.                    105. I.e., the Pentateuch.
106. Ex 7–12.                         107. Ex 13.21.
108. Ex 13.20.                        109. Ex 17.6–7.
110. Ex 16.14–21.                    111. Ps 78.25.
112. Ex 32.1–4. Cf. Tertullian, *Adv. Iud.* 3.13.

113. Attributing to demons the Jews' disobedience of God's revelation
finds an antecedent in the second-century Christian apologists who accused
demons of misleading pagan philosophers and causing them to distort the
truth about God and creation that they had. See Justin, *Apol.* 14, 18, 56; Mi-
nucius Felix, *Oct.* 27; Cyprian, *De idol.* 7. But Hilary is the only writer to cite
demonic influence as a reason for Israel's sins.

114. *aquae lavacrum.*
115. Those who are the subject of 12.22.

latter. They imagine and believe that it is best to return to the house from which they left.[116] Once this house is cleansed by the Law and put in order by the proclamation of the prophets and prepared for Christ's coming, it is found unoccupied. The protection of the Law is withdrawn (because everything had to do with the Law until the time of John),[117] and Christ was not received as a dwelling-place.[118] And so the house is emptied by its occupant and deserted by its guardians. Nevertheless, it has been cleansed and put in order for the occupant, who is coming with compassion for those who lived there before.[119]

As a result, seven more wicked spirits[120] are accepted because such was the number of the gifts of grace destined to be with Christ in whom the manifold wisdom of God is arranged in a sevenfold glory.[121] As much as there was a possession of sin, so great a future grace was to be possessed. Nonetheless, *the final condition of that man will be worse than the first,*[122] since the unclean spirit has left him out of fear of the Law, though it will soon return to them as divine retribution for having repudiated grace.[123]

24. And while he was saying all these things in the power of the Father's majesty, it was told to him that outside his mother and brothers awaited him.[124] Extending his hand toward the disciples, he responded that they are his brothers and his mother,[125] and whoever follows the will of the Father, that person is his brother, and his sister, and his mother.[126] As a benefit to all people, he establishes himself as that model[127] of action

---

116. Mt 12.44.                117. Mt 11.13.
118. *ad habitandum.*

119. Namely, the believing pagans. In 12.7 the apostles are said to have the service of salvation, and in 10.14 the number of believing pagans must be filled first before Israel is saved.

120. Throughout the Bible, seven is the number used to symbolize completion and fulfillment (e.g., Gn 8.4; Ex 21.2; Jos 6.4, 15; Ps 119.164; Mt 15.34–37; Mk 8.8; Acts 6.3) as well as the summation of divine judgment (Dn 9.25; Rv 1.6; 8.1; 16.17).

121. Cf. Tertullian, *Adv. Iud.* 9.27.          122. Mt 12.45b. Cf. Lk 11.26.
123. *Supra,* 12.21.                            124. Mt 12.47.
125. Mt 12.49.                                  126. Mt 12.50.
127. *formam.*

and thought as it pertains to the rights and title of all his relatives,[128] not merely by the virtue of birth, but for the one who follows in the communion of the Church.

We must not think that he felt disdain for his mother, whose experience of suffering produced in him a feeling[129] of the greatest solicitude. There is also a figurative reason[130] disclosed in this event: his mother and brothers stood outside although they, as others did, had the opportunity[131] of at least coming to him. Because he came to his own people and his own did not recognize him,[132] in his mother and brothers are prefigured the synagogue and the Israelites, who refrained from approaching and entering.[133]

128. *nomen.* That is, being considered Christ's brother or mother.
129. *adfectum. Infra,* 31.2–3.           130. *typica ratio.*
131. *potestatem.*                               132. Jn 1.11.
133. To Jesus on the inside (v.46).

## CHAPTER THIRTEEN

 *HAT DAY Jesus went out and sat down beside the sea, and crowds gathered around him such that he got into a boat.*[1] There is an underlying principle for the reason that the Lord sat in the boat and the crowd stood outside. He necessarily spoke in parables[2] and indicates by this genre that those who are located outside of the Church[3] can find no understanding of the divine word. The ship presents a type of the Church, within which the Word of life is situated and preached. Those who lie outside in barren and fruitless places, like the desert, cannot understand. It is redundant,[4] however, to explain the parables when the Lord has already clarified the issues.[5]

2. *Whoever has, it will be given to him, and it will be in abundance; but whoever does not have, even what he has will be taken away from him.*[6] Faith perceives the mysteries of the Kingdom. For those who have faith, their [understanding] will increase, and its growth in progressive steps will be abundant. But for those who do not, even what they have will be taken away from them. In other words, the Lord declares that a loss of the Law is from a lack of faith. Jews without faith have also lost the Law which they had. And so the faith of the Gospel[7] possesses the perfect

1. Mt 13.1–2. Some versions of the Old Latin combine verses 1 and 2, as Hilary does here, into one sentence. There are differences in the wording among the versions, and Hilary's text does not precisely follow any one of them.

2. Mt 13.3.

3. Cf. Cyprian, *De unit. eccl.* 6: "Whoever is separated from the Church … is separated from the promises of the Church." For Latin text, see Maurice Bévenot, ed., *De Lapsis, and De Ecclesiae Catholicae Unitate* (Oxford: Clarendon Press, 1971), 66.

4. *otiosum.*

5. Mt 13.3–9, 13–15, 18–30, 36–43. In other words, he is not going to comment on this part of this text.

6. Mt 13.12.

7. *fides evangelica.*

gift, because it enriches those who have received its new fruits, just as it has taken away the resources of the ancient authority from those who turned away.[8]

3. *But blessed are your eyes which see and your ears which hear.*[9] He teaches about the blessed[10] era of the apostles, whose eyes and ears were enabled to see and hear the salvation of God. That which the prophets and righteous men longed to see and hear[11] was reserved for the apostles in the fullness of appointed times and with the joy of expectation.[12]

4. *The Kingdom of heaven is like a mustard seed.*[13] The Lord compared himself to a mustard seed, which is the most pungent and smallest of all seeds and whose internal force and power[14] is increased by tribulations and pressures. This seed is planted in the field; that is, it is taken by the people and given over to death, just as if planting the seed in a field was the burying of a body.[15] The seed grows up beyond the height of all other plants and surpasses all the glory of the prophets.[16] As in the case of a plant that has languished, so the preaching of the prophets was given to ailing Israel, whereas the birds of heaven dwell on the branches of the tree reaching from the earth into the heights, which we understand to be the apostles, who derived [their] power from Christ, whose "branches" cover the world.[17] It is to these that pagans will "fly" in the hope of life, just as birds to tree branches, where the pagans rest from the storms of the sky, that is, from the wind and blowing of the devil's vexations.

---

8. *substantiae.*
10. *beatitudinem.*
12. Mt 13.17a.

9. Mt 13.16.
11. Cf. Eph 1.10; Gal 3.23–27.
13. Mt 13.31.

14. *virtus ac potestas.* Doignon (*Sur Matt.* I.298, n.5) points out that *virtus ac potestas* already possesses a thematic status based on Lk 22.31, developed by Cyprian, *Epp.* 11.5 and 58.1, which applied the *virtus* of the martyr in the context of "pressures" and "tribulations."

15. Hilary's use of the seed as a type of Christ and his sufferings is apparent.

16. Cf. Mt 13.32.

17. The same image is used by Cyprian, *De unit. eccl.* 5, concerning the diffusion of the Church in the whole world.

5. *The Kingdom of heaven is like yeast that a woman took and mixed into three measures of flour until it worked completely through the batch.*[18] Yeast is from flour because it returns to the mixture from which it originated the vigor that it took. The Lord compared himself to the yeast that the woman took. In other words, the synagogue leads to the judgment of death by accusing the Gospels of having destroyed the Law and the prophets. The yeast, however, is recovered in three equal measures of flour: namely, of the Law, the prophets, and the Gospels; all is made into one.[19] That which the Law has established, and which the prophets have announced, is realized when we "mix" in the Gospels.[20] All together they share the same vigor and purpose in the Spirit of God so that nothing will be found separated from the other because the yeast worked its way through the batch in equal measure.

6. I recall, however, that there are many others who have thought the three measures of flour must be a reference to the mystery of faith, that is, the unity of Father, Son, and Holy Spirit, or to the calling of the three peoples from Shem, Ham, and Japheth.[21] But I do not know whether the reasoning in this latter example is warranted since, although the calling of all peoples is done equitably, Christ is not hidden in them. He is, rather, revealed to them. Given such a multitude of unbelievers, the yeast could not have entirely permeated the whole. The Father and the Son and the Holy Spirit, however, do not require the yeast from an outside source; all things are one in Christ.[22]

7. *Again, the Kingdom of heaven is like a treasure hidden,*[23] and the rest. Through the likeness of a treasure in a field, he shows

18. Mt 13.33. Hilary seems to have jumped over the parable of the sower and the mustard seed entirely.
19. *coopertum omnia unum.*
20. The unity of the Law, the prophets, and the Gospels is a longstanding apologetic theme against Gnostic and Marcionite views as expressed in Irenaeus, *Adv. haer.* 4.9.1–3; Tertullian, *Adv. Marc.* 4.1.1–3; 4.11.11.
21. See Tertullian, *De orat.* (Trinity) 25.2; *De bapt.* (Trinity) 6.2; *De nat.* (the three races) 1.8.11.
22. *in Christo omnia unum sint.*        23. Mt 13.44.

how the riches of our hope are located in himself, since God has been found in a man.[24] The price of this is that all the resources of the world should be sold so that [we may give] clothing, food, and drink to the needy in order that we might gain the eternal riches of the heavenly treasury.[25] But we should consider that the treasure that was found had been hidden, and what was found could have been carried off in secret during the time it was hidden. There would be no need to buy something that has already been snatched away. There must be a reason for explaining both the events and the words. For the treasure has been hidden because it was necessary that the field be purchased. The treasure in the field, as we said, is understood to be Christ in the flesh, who is found at no cost.[26] On this point the preaching of the Gospels is clear, but the opportunity[27] of using and of possessing this treasure along with the field cannot be had without cost because the heavenly riches may not be possessed except by eschewing the world.

8. Concerning the pearl,[28] there is the same principle at work. But in this case, we have an account about a merchant, who was steeped in the Law for a long time. After long and hard labor he has accrued knowledge of the pearl and abandons those things which he had obtained under the burden of the Law.[29] For a long time he had done business, but once he found such a pearl, he desired it. Since he was willing to pay the price for this singular gem, we may say that it was obtained only through the sacrifice of his previous labor.

9. *Again, the Kingdom of heaven is like a net which was let down in the sea,*[30] etc. With good reason did the Lord compare his preaching to a net. Once it is let down[31] into the world, without any damage to the world, it gathers together, as into a net, those living in the world, because it sinks into the sea and is brought up from the depths in order to capture[32] everything

---

24. See *supra,* 10.27, n.143.   25. Cf. Mt 25.35–36.
26. Cf. Col 2.3; Rom 3.24.      27. *potestas.*
28. Mt 13.45.                   29. Mt 13.46.
30. Mt 13.47.                   31. Lit., "comes" (*veniens*).
32. *clausos.*

moving in that element and to pull up what has been caught. Thus the Lord's preaching leads us up from the world to the light of the true sun.[33] By the selection of those who are good[34] and the rejection of those who are bad, it shows us the scrutiny of a future judgment.

33. See *Sur Matt.* I.303, n.13. This expression is found in Cyprian, *De orat. Dom.* 35, referring to Christ in glory.

34. Following the reading *bonorum* instead of *honorum* in Doignon's text (Perrin, 146).

# CHAPTER FOURTEEN

"ᴀᴠᴇ ʏᴏᴜ *understood all these things?" And they said to him: "Yes." And he said to them, "Therefore, every scribe who has been instructed in the Kingdom of heaven,"*[1] etc. The Lord spoke not to the crowd but to the disciples and provided a proper explanation to those who understood the parables. He makes a comparison between them and himself in the guise of the master of a house,[2] because they accepted instruction from the Lord's treasury of new and old things. Given their knowledge, he calls those "scribes" who understood these things, new and old, which were presented in the Gospels and in the Law; they understood that there is the one master of the house for one and the same treasure.

2. *And it happened that when Jesus had finished these parables, he moved from there and came to his home country,*[3] and the rest. The Lord was dishonored by his own [people]. Although they admired the wisdom of his teaching and the power of his acts, their unbelief prevented them from accepting the truth of his claim. They did not believe that God was doing these things in a man.[4] In fact, they identified his father, his mother, and his brothers and were contemptuous of his father's trade.[5] Plainly he was the son of a carpenter who hammers on iron with fire, he who smelts all the power of this world by his judgment, and who gives form to matter all for the benefit of humanity. In other words, he is the one who molds the formless matter of our bodies so that our members may perform different functions and do every work that leads toward eternal life.[6]

1. Mt 13.51–52.    2. *sub patris familiae nomine.*
3. Mt 13.53–54a. Some Old Latin versions combine these two verses into one as Hilary does here.
4. A frequent characteristic of unbelief for Hilary; see *supra*, 3.5; 10.27; 12.18.
5. Mt 13.55, interpreted in light of Jn 6.42; 7.15.
6. The analogy here is that of a craftsman who fashions from raw materials

All of them were scandalized by these things.[7] Though he performed many magnificent deeds among them, they were troubled[8] about his corporeality.[9] The Lord responded that a prophet is dishonored in his homeland,[10] just as he would be despised in Judaea to the point of being condemned to the cross.[11] He refrained from doing any works of divine power, because of their incredulity and because the power of God belongs only to the faithful.

3. *At that time, Herod the tetrarch heard reports about Jesus,*[12] etc. We have often stated that we should use all diligence in the reading of the Gospels because, in the events that are recounted, there is often a principle of deeper understanding underlying them.[13] The narration of all the events occurs in its order,[14] and an image of the underlying cause is prefigured in these events, as is understood in the case of Herod and John.[15]

Now Herod was the leader of the people and by the right of his authority announced his marriage to Herodias, the spouse of his brother Philip.[16] This Herodias had a daughter, and when her dancing pleased Herod on his birthday,[17] she received a promise from him that she could have whatever reward she wished. The girl, prompted by her mother, requested that the head of John,[18] who had been held for a long time in prison, be brought to her and offered on a plate. Although Herod was saddened, he fulfilled his promise, and the girl then presented the reward to her mother.[19] Then John's disciples, after having buried him, went to Jesus.[20]

4. When the Lord heard about these things, he withdrew in a boat to a deserted place.[21] The crowds followed him and he

---

(such as iron) useful implements for human life, as God shapes, hammers out, and smelts humanity for temporal and eternal benefits.

7. Mt 13.57.

8. I.e., that a human being could do such things.

9. *contemplatione.*      10. Mt 13.57b.

11. *ad cruces sententiam.*      12. Mt 14.1.

13. *interioris intelligentiae ratio reperiatur.*

14. I.e., a literal reading of the account.

15. Mt 14.3–12.      16. Mt 14.4.

17. Mt 14.6.      18. Ibid.

19. Mt 14.9.      20. Mt 14.12.

21. Mt 14.13.

had compassion because of their troubles,[22] though the apostles argued that they should be sent away into the villages in order to buy food.[23] In response the Lord said that there was no need for them to return [to their village], instructing that food be given to them.[24] But the apostles objected that they had only five loaves of bread and two fish.[25] He ordered them to bring these items to him[26] and for the crowd to spread out on the grass. And he blessed what was brought[27] to him, and he broke the bread intended for the crowd to eat, giving it to his disciples for distribution.[28] After everyone was satisfied, there were twelve basketfuls left over even though five thousand men had been filled, besides a number of women and children.[29]

5. Then he instructed the disciples to board a boat and cross to the other side ahead of him.[30] Once the crowd was dismissed, he went up alone into a mountain to pray and was alone until evening.[31] Meanwhile the boat, in the midst of the sea, was being rocked by an opposing headwind and buffeted by the waves.[32] At the time of the fourth watch, the Lord came walking upon the sea. Seeing him, the disciples were thrown into panic. Believing foolishly that they saw a ghost, they cried out with fear.[33] Then the Lord spoke and told them to remain calm.[34] And Peter, one of the group, responded and asked that he might come to the Lord on the [surface of the] water.[35] Upon getting out of the boat and having progressed a short bit, Peter grew afraid of the increasing wind, and he began to sink.[36] Catching hold of him, the Lord rebuked him for his little faith.[37] When they entered into the boat, the Lord quieted the wind and sea and returned calm to the boat.[38]

22. Mt 14.14. Cf. Mt 9.36.
23. Mt 14.15.                              24. Mt 14.16.
25. Mt 14.17.                              26. Mt 14.18.
27. *oblata benedixit.*                    28. Mt 14.18b.
29. Mt 14.21.                              30. Mt 14.22.
31. Mt 14.23.                              32. Mt 14.24.
33. Mt 14.26.                              34. *constantes esse.* Mt 14.27.
35. Mt 14.28.                              36. Mt 14.30.
37. Mt 14.31.
38. See Doignon, *Hilaire de Poitiers,* 235–41, on this section of Hilary's interpretation in *In Matt.* 14.

6. These are the events as we have related them. But besides all these persons, consequences, causes, numbers, and measures, whatever occurred was according to its natural tendency; that is, everything operated from its own nature.[39] Everything happened outwardly[40] as an example for forming our views with a greater reverence. No matter how varied were the circumstances, one and the same understanding came about as the result. It is necessary for our interpretation[41] to be recorded with the actual[42] account.

7. John, as we have often expressed, represented a pattern of the Law, because the Law predicted Christ, and John (who proceeded from the Law) foretold that Christ came from the Law. Then there is Herod, chief of the people, and as chief of the people he assumed their name and embraced all their causes. John had warned Herod that he should not marry his brother's wife.[43]

There are and have been two peoples: one of the circumcision and the other of the pagans. The Law warned Israel, however, not to join itself to the works and unbelief of the pagans. Indeed, unbelief is associated with the pagans, being connected to them as if by the bond of conjugal love.[44] Nonetheless, these two peoples are brothers of the human race, emerging from the same father.[45] Because the truth [was told to Herod] in the form of a severe rebuke,[46] John, just like the Law, was kept in prison.

On Herod's birthday, the daughter of Herodias danced; that is, [she used] the enticements of the flesh. Just as lustfulness was generated from Israel's unbelief and many pleasures,[47] so were Herodias's seductive movements. In Israel's case, the

---

39. The sea and the wind.
40. As it happened literally according to the account.
41. *sermo.*                                    42. *ad originem.*
43. *ne fratris sui uxorem sibi iungeret.*
44. Pagan entertainment, theater, or sporting competitions often depicted immoral or sadistic behavior. See K. M. Coleman, "Fatal Charades: Roman Executions Staged as Mythological Enactments," *The Journal of Roman Studies* 80 (1990): 44–73.
45. *parente.*
46. John rebuking Herod for having broken the moral truth of the Law.
47. A likely reference to Israel dancing before the golden calf; Ex 32.6.

people surrendered themselves completely for sale by an oath.[48] On account of sin and worldly desire they sold their gifts of eternal life. Now prompted by her mother, that is, by unbelief, the daughter of Herodias requested that the head of John—the glory of the Law—be delivered to her. By the authority of its divine commandments, the Law accused Israel of incest.[49]

8. Herod indicated earlier that he wanted to kill John, though he was restrained from doing so out of fear of the people who regarded John as a prophet.[50] But now that John's head was demanded, especially since he was bound by the scruple[51] of having given an oath, why would Herod be grieved?[52] It is clearly contradictory that he wanted it[53] before, but did not want it now. His present concerns do not correspond to the wishes expressed earlier. There is, however, a pattern[54] in the facts of the previous events. In these matters, there is an outline[55] of a sequential order established here.

When sensuality originates from unbelief, the glory of the Law is mitigated.[56] While the people were cognizant of the Law's goodness, they closed their eyes to their [own] sensual conditions, though not without any worry about their own peril. They knew that they should not have forsaken the glory of such commandments, but they submitted to sin, as if compelled by an oath. Once they were corrupted and overcome, even afflicted, by fear and the example of their present leaders, they yielded to the seductions of pleasure.

Amidst the continued revelries of this licentious company, John's head was brought in on a platter (in the absence of the Law, the pleasure of the flesh and worldly indulgence were exalted), which the daughter offered to her mother. And thus shameful Israel, with its pleasures and the unbelief of its lineage,[57] surrendered the glory of the Law to that of the pagans. Now that the era of the Law was ended,[58] buried along with

---

48. *sacramento.* Ex 32.1–6; 1 Cor 10.7–8.
49. John's condemnation of Herod for taking his brother's wife Herodias.
50. Mt 14.5.　　　　　　　　　　　　51. *religione.*
52. Mt 14.9.　　　　　　　　　　　　53. John's death.
54. *ordo.*　　　　　　　　　　　　　55. *species.*
56. *occupavit.*　　　　　　　　　　57. *familiae.*
58. *finitis igitur legis temporibus.*

John, his disciples reported these events to the Lord,[59] coming, as it were, from the Law to the Gospels.

9. Once the Law had ended, the Word of God[60] entered the Church upon boarding the ship and withdrew to a deserted area.[61] Obviously, having abandoned his dialogue with Israel, he crosses over to the hearts of those who are devoid of divine knowledge.[62] Upon hearing the Lord, the crowd follows him on foot out of the city into the deserted places, as those do who withdraw from the Synagogue into the Church. Seeing the crowd, he takes pity and heals each person of his weakness and infirmity.[63] In other words, he cleanses their minds and bodies, which were held captive by the lethargy of unbelief. This was done in preparation for understanding the new preaching.[64]

10. And when the disciples were sending the crowd away into the nearby villages to buy food, the Lord responded, *They do not need to go away.*[65] He wanted to show that those whom he healed had no need of the food of teaching that is for sale,[66] nor was it necessary for them to return to Judaea in order to buy food. Instead, he ordered the apostles to give them something to eat. Was the Lord ignorant of the fact that he had nothing to give? Did he, who perceived the inner thoughts of the human mind,[67] not know about the amount of food in the possession of the apostles? But there is a figurative reason[68] that deserves to be explained.

The apostles were not yet permitted to make and serve heavenly bread that leads to the food of eternal life.[69] Their response

---

59. Mt 14.12.
60. *Dei Verbum.* Following traditional "Logos theology," Hilary accepted the view that the pre-incarnate Word was responsible for the creation of the world, the appearances of God in the OT, including the giving of the Law to Moses, and the gift of prophecy to the prophets.
61. Mt 14.13.                              62. *vacua divinae cognitionis.*
63. Mt 14.14.                              64. Cf. Cyprian, *Test.* 1.9; 15.
65. Mt 14.16.
66. I.e., this imagery is in keeping with Hilary's emphasis on the Gospel as gift and as that which no labor can earn.
67. Mt 12.25.
68. *typica ratio.* Cf. 2.1; 8.4; 13.24; 14.10; 17.8; 19.1; 33.3.
69. Jn 3.14–15.

to the Lord directs us toward a model[70] of spiritual understanding. For they responded that they had only five loaves of bread and two fish.[71] As for the five loaves, the apostles were upholding the five books of the Law; as for the two fish, they were being nourished by the preaching of the prophets and of John. For there was life in the works of the Law just as there was in the bread. Likewise, the preaching of John and the prophets fostered the hope of human life by the power of water.[72] The apostles presented the loaves and fish first because they remained in this mode of life.[73] The preaching of the Gospels is shown to have progressed from these beginning stages[74] until it grew into a great abundance of power.[75]

11. Once he received the loaves and fish, the Lord looked up to heaven, blessed and broke them,[76] giving thanks to the Father that he was changed into the food of the Gospel following the era of the Law and the prophets. Then he told the people to sit down on the grass. These people are supported not only by lying on the ground but by the Law; each one is borne up by the fruit of his works no less than by the grass of the ground. Bread is also given to the apostles because through them the gifts of divine grace were to be offered.

After the people were fed and filled by the five loaves and the two fish, and were satisfied,[77] there was so much bread and fish left over that it filled twelve baskets.[78] So the multitude was satisfied by the Word of God coming from the teaching of the Law and the prophets, while an overabundance of divine power through the serving of eternal food (which abounded in the twelve apostles) was preserved for the pagan peoples.[79] The same number of those who ate[80] is found among those who

70. *ordinem.*                              71. Mt 14.17.
72. *in virtute aquae.* That is, the waters of John's baptism for repentance.
73. *in his adhuc erant.*
74. *his originibus.*
75. Cf. Tertullian, *De praescr. haer.* 20.4–6.
76. Mt 14.19.
77. Lit., "after those sitting down were satisfied" (*saturatis accumbentibus*).
78. Mt 14.20.
79. Cf. Victorinus of Poetovio, *Fab. Mundi* 10, for the significance of twelve.
80. Mt 14.21.

would be future believers. It is contained in the book of Acts[81] how out of the countless number of people in Israel, five thousand men believed.[82]

The wonder produced at these miraculous events stands in relation to the proportion of its underlying purpose. From the broken bread and fish gathered after the people were satisfied, the amount collected corresponds to the destined number of the people who believe,[83] those who would be filled by the heavenly grace of the apostles. The measures taken[84] comply with the number, and the number complies with the measures taken. An underlying principle closely adheres to and continues[85] within the means of divine power for fulfillment of what happens next.

12. The realization of these facts surpasses human understanding. Although these are the very ideals which have been conceived by the mind, the idea[86] is not explained. In such matters, however, the subtlety of meaning becomes foggy, and our perception of reality is dulled because of our difficulty in fully comprehending the invisible. When he had taken the five loaves, the Lord looked up to heaven, professing the honor of him from whom he was.[87] It was not necessary that he look upon the Father with eyes of flesh, but he did so for the benefit of those who were present that they might know from whom he had received the capacity[88] for such power.[89]

Then he gave bread to his disciples. Multiplying five loaves does not amount to much, but pieces came from other pieces, and it escaped the notice of those breaking off the pieces that

81. *libro Praxeos.* Hilary's Latin represents a transliteration of the Greek title Πράξεις, unlike the Latin Vulgate's *Actus apostolorum.*

82. Acts 4.4.

83. The number converted in Acts 4.

84. *modus.*

85. *et intra fines suos ratio conclusa ad consequentis effectus . . .*

86. *sermo.*

87. A very literal translation is given here so as not to obscure Hilary's theology. Here and elsewhere (16.4; 31.3) it appears that Hilary is not familiar with the doctrine of the Son's eternal generation.

88. *effectum.*

89. *virtutis tantae.* This is yet another way Hilary stresses his position that the Son, in the flesh, was not constrained by the frailties of the flesh as it concerned the divine power. See Introduction, 29–30.

they, in fact, continued taking these pieces.[90] In that instance matter came into being; I do not know whether it was on tables, or in the hands of those taking it, or in the mouth of those eating.[91] There is no surprise that the resources flowed forth.

In the case of the wine, it is comprised of grapes, and from the grapes wine is poured out, just as all the resources of the world flow forth every year in an endless rhythm. With this enormous profusion of bread, we see how the Author of this universe speeded up[92] the [usual] means of deploying matter in such stages. The activity of what is invisible is administered by the works of what is visible,[93] showing how the Lord of the heavenly mysteries[94] acts within the mystery of present time. This power of the one who acts surpasses all of nature, as his use of power exceeds our understanding of the facts. Only our wonder at his authority[95] remains. [From this event] there follows a proper ordering[96] of its causes and actions.

13. *After this, Jesus ordered the disciples to board the boat while he himself dismissed the crowd, and once the crowd was dismissed, he ascended a mountain to pray, and he was alone when evening came.*[97] The underlying reason for these events should be distinguished from the time in which they occurred. That he is alone in the evening shows the solitary nature of his Passion, since the others had scattered in fear. Then he orders the disciples to board a boat and to cross over to the other side, while he himself dismisses the crowd. Once they were dismissed, he ascends up the mountain; he gives a directive to be within the Church and across the sea. In other words, he orders that [the disciples] be carried across the world until that time when he returns at his glorious advent.[98] He will bestow salvation on all people, the

90. *praefracta*, a neologism; cf. *infra*, 15.6.
91. Cf. Doignon, *Hilaire de Poitiers*, 357; *Sur Matt* II.27, n.17.
92. *adderetur.*                          93. Tertullian, *Apol.* 17.2.
94. *arcanorum caelestium.*               95. *admiratio potestatis.*
96. *ordo.*
97. Mt 14.22–23. Hilary is conflating two verses into one either on purpose for expediency's sake, or because he neglected the middle of v.22 and the "there" at the end of v.23. While there is much variation in wording, no extant version of the *Itala* reads in this way.
98. This is a difficult passage both conceptually and linguistically to follow. While we have the precedents of the boat representing the Church and the

remnant of Israel,[99] and forgive their sins. Once they are for-given, or rather admitted to the heavenly Kingdom, he gives thanks to God the Father standing in his glory and majesty.

14. As these events were happening, the disciples were being buffeted by the wind and waves,[100] by all the agitations of the world, and by the opposition of the unclean spirit. In the fourth watch of the night, the Lord came, for it was at that point that he returned to an errant and foundering Church.[101] In fact, *in the fourth watch of the night*[102] is an appropriate number that repre-sents his concern. The first watch is that of the Law, the second of the prophets, the third of his bodily advent, so the fourth is in his glorious return.[103] But will he find the Church exhausted and buffeted about by the spirit of Antichrist[104] and by all the world's troubles?[105] For he will come especially to these who are anxious and in anguish. Because it is typical of the Antichrist to harass by using every new kind of temptation, they will panic at the Lord's coming, fearful of the false and insidious images of things which deceive the eyes.[106] But the good Lord will immedi-ately speak to them, drive away their fear, and say, *It is I*,[107] ban-ishing their fear of a certain shipwreck with faith at his coming.

15. Out of all those who were on board, Peter dares to re-spond and asks that he be told to come on the water to the Lord.[108] This indicates the state of his will at the time of the

---

sea representing the world, Hilary seems to have conjoined these images to an eschatological interpretation within a figurative exegesis.

99. Cf. Hab 2.18; Rom 11.5 (the Gentiles and believing Jews).

100. Mt 14.24.　　　　　　　　　　101. *Supra*, 8.1.

102. Mt 14.25.

103. Cf. Tertullian, *Apol.* 21.15; *Adv. Marc.* 3.7, 6–8, for Christ's second ad-vent.

104. The word *antichristus* has a broader meaning than the devil or wicked spiritual agent. See 1 Jn 2.18; 4.3; 2 Jn 7 (false teacher). Or the Antichrist can be one who directly opposes the truth of the Christian faith, such as a hereti-cal Christian emperor. Hilary will refer to Constantius II with this very term in *In Constantium*.

105. Cf. Lk 8.18.

106. I.e., the world's troubles, inspired by the spirit of Antichrist, repre-sented by the wind and waves threatening the boat (Church).

107. *Ego sum.* Mt 14.27, an allusion to Ex 3.14.

108. Mt 14.28.

Passion. Peter alone, turning away from the others, forsakes the world just as he did the waves of the sea, and sets out to follow the Lord's steps. Possessing a power sufficient for scorning death, he accompanies the Lord, but his fear shows his timidity in the face of a future temptation. For, although he had dared to walk out [on the water],[109] he began to sink,[110] compelled by the fragility of the flesh and the fear of death, even in the desperation of having to deny him.[111] But he cries out and asks the Lord to save him. That cry is Peter's sigh of repentance. He then returned to his profession [of confidence] and found grace at the time of his denial since the Lord had not yet suffered. It was only later that Christ would suffer for the redemption of all people.[112]

16. There was a reason that the Lord did not grant to Peter's fearfulness the ability[113] of reaching him. He instead extended his hand, and caught him and held him up:[114] Peter was not yet worthy of approaching his Lord (he tried to draw near). We see also a typological pattern[115] has been observed in this situation.

The fact that the Lord walked upon the upheavals and storms of the world shows that no one is able to participate in his Passion. He alone is going to suffer for all, and it is he who forgives the sins of all.[116] Whatever is granted to the whole world is granted by the one who admits no associate. If he himself was the redemption of the entire world, he could also preserve Peter—before he was redeemed—for that faith of redemption, even as to the point of becoming a martyr of Christ.[117]

17. And we must consider that Peter's faith preceded that of the others. While the others remain in ignorance, he is the first

---

109. Mt 14.29.

110. Mt 14.30.

111. Peter's loss of faith here is the type of his denial of Christ in Mt 26.69–75.

112. The point seems to be that Peter's first denial is easily overcome because he was solely in the presence of the Lord. This is unlike Peter's later denial when he was alone and the Lord was on trial as the world's Redeemer.

113. *virtutem.*                    114. Mt 14.31.

115. *typicus ordo.*                116. Gal 1.4.

117. Peter is a *martyr designatus* in Tertullian, *Ad Mart.* 1.1.

to respond: *You are the Son of the living God.*[118] He is the first to have rejected the Lord's Passion, thinking it was evil.[119] He is the first to promise that he would go to his death and that he would not deny [the Lord].[120] He is first to forbid that his feet be washed.[121] He also drew his sword against those who were apprehending the Lord.[122]

18. Once the Lord boarded the boat, the wind and sea became calm,[123] which indicates the peace and tranquility of the Church eternal after his return in glory. And because he will come manifested to all, the entire world will rightly be amazed and declare: *Truly, he is the Son of God.*[124] For then the confession of all humanity will be both unqualified and public. Now the Son of God [will appear] no longer in the humility of the body but in his heavenly glory, having restored peace to the Church.

19. *When they had crossed over, they came to the territory of Gennesaret, and when the men of that place recognized him, they worshiped him.*[125] After the gathering and satisfying of five thousand men, many things happened in the interval, which have delayed us from eagerly mentioning an underlying principle, although our meaning in this passage is the same. Since the era of the Law had ended and the five thousand men of Israel had been gathered into the Church,[126] those who believed now went out to meet the Lord, being saved from the Law through faith. They brought to the Lord those infirm and sick among them.[127] Those who were presented wanted to touch the edge of his garment so that they would be healed through faith.[128] But just as the edges are made manifest from the whole garment, so the power of the Holy Spirit came from our Lord Jesus Christ. That power was given to the apostles, who also came from the same body, as it were, and it granted healing to those who touched it.

---

118. Mt 16.16. Hilary omits *Christus,* which is in the Old Latin version.
119. Mt 16.22.                          120. Mt 16.35.
121. Jn 13.8.
122. Cf. Mt 26.51. Hilary assumes that the unnamed companion was Peter.
123. Mt 14.32.                          124. Mt 14.33.
125. Mt 14.34–35.                       126. Acts 4.4.
127. Mt 14.35.                          128. Mt 14.36.

# CHAPTER FIFTEEN

*HEN SINCE the scribes and Pharisees from Jerusalem*[1] *approached him saying,*[2] etc. The reason for the words and deeds in the following events is clear: in light of the reports that had been related to the Lord, he responded by saying every plant that is not planted by his Father must be eradicated.[3] In other words, human tradition should be uprooted when it comes transgressing the precepts of the Law. The Pharisees and scribes are themselves blind guides who do not see the way of eternal life, which they promise.[4] Blind men and the blind guides all together fall into a pit.[5]

2. *And leaving from there, Jesus withdrew into the regions of Tyre and Sidon. And behold, a Canaanite woman who came from that vicinity cried out,*[6] and the rest. Different types of healing produce different effects depending on the situation, but the action and word [of healing] infer a pattern[7] comparable to what happened earlier. The Lord refuted the unbelief of the Pharisees, reproaching their blind guidance and their superstitious human traditions. Then he came to the regions of Tyre and Sidon, where a

1. A number of MSS omit "from Jerusalem."
2. Mt 15.1.
3. Mt 15.13. There is clearly a jump from v.1 to vv.13–14, which is nowhere accounted for, except in the *capitula* (chapter summaries). See *Cap.* 15 in Appendix II, *infra*. If we accept the *capitulum* as an accurate description of Chapter 15, we would suspect that some of the original text has dropped out. There is, however, no evidence in the extant MSS to support such a view. Nonetheless, the section makes little sense as it stands, and it seems unlikely that Hilary would have penned such a disjointed paragraph. This is supported by the next section, which alludes to "action and words *ex superioribus*" that would have been discussed in the previous section.
4. Cf. Mt 15.8.
5. Mt 15.14.
6. Mt 15.21–22. Jesus' explanation of the parable (vv.15–20) is bypassed.
7. *ordinem*.

Canaanite woman from that place shouted out and begged help for her daughter, while confessing the Lord as the Son of David. The Lord said nothing, but the disciples implored him to do something for her.[8] He responded that he was sent to the lost sheep of the house of Israel.[9] Prostrating herself, she entreated his help,[10] yet the Lord said it is not right to throw the children's bread to dogs.[11] She replied in turn that it is customary for little dogs to eat the crumbs that fall from their master's table.[12] At that point the Lord highly praised her faith, and in that hour the health of the little girl was restored.[13]

3. In order to follow the underlying principle operating within[14] these events which took place, we must consider the force of the words presented in the person of the Canaanite woman.[15] A certain confidence[16] that the number of proselytes has been and still is within the people of Israel, those who passed from paganism into the works of the Law.[17] Once they left their former way of life, they were incorporated—like those in a household—in an unfamiliar religion[18] and placed under the dominion of Law. The Canaanites have lived on the land that is now Judaea.[19] They were either absorbed by war, or dispersed throughout local regions, or subjected to slavery as a conquered people.[20] The result is that they bear only their name, possessing no ancestral land. This people, now mixed with Jews, came from the pagans. Because some of those among the crowd who believed were undoubtedly proselytes, this Canaanite woman should rightly be considered as a model[21] of the proselytes because she left her

8. Mt 15.22.
9. Mt 15.24.
10. Mt 15.25.
11. Mt 15.26.
12. Mt 15.27.
13. Mt 15.28.
14. Lit., "interior" (*interior*).
15. That is, she is the vehicle by which we are able to understand the inner or spiritual meaning of the passage.
16. *fides*.
17. *Sur Matt.* II.36, n.2. Cf. Tertullian's definition of a proselyte in *Adv. Iud.* 2.2.
18. A number of important MSS read "region" rather than "religion," which fits the context just as well.
19. Pss 104.11; 134.11–12 (LXX numbering).
20. For these three conditions, see Dt 7.1; Gn 10.18; Jos 17.13.
21. *formam*.

territory, that is, one who transferred her identity from the pagans to another people.[22] She who pleads for her daughter is evidently pleading for the people of the pagans. Since she knew the Lord is from the Law, she called him the Son of David. For it is contained in the Law that "a sprout" comes "from the root of Jesse" and that the Son of David is King of an eternal and heavenly Kingdom.[23]

4. This one who confessed Christ as Lord and Son of David is not herself in need of healing, but pleads on behalf of her daughter, that is, for the pagans who have been weighed down by the domination of unclean spirits. The Lord says nothing, reserving by his maintenance of silence the privileges of salvation for Israel. And the disciples, feeling pity for her, join in the supplication.[24]

He who comprises the mystery[25] of the Father's will[26] responds that he has been sent to the lost sheep of Israel, making it absolutely clear that the daughter of the Canaanite woman represents a figure[27] of the Church. She sought what was offered to others,[28] not because salvation should be denied to the pagans, but the Lord had come for his own in his own land. He was waiting for the first-fruits of faith from those among whom he had been born.[29] The others would later be saved by the apostolic preaching. For this reason he said: *It is not right to take the children's bread and give it to the dogs.*[30] Honor has been accorded to Israel. God's affection for Israel is augmented by his jealousy for it; next to Israel the pagans received the name "dog." But the Canaanite woman, already saved by faith,[31] responded with a certainty of

22. That is, Gentile proselytes in that region.

23. Is 11.1; Jer 23.5.

24. This sympathetic reaction on the part of the disciples is not supported by v.23. Hilary read, *accendentes discipuli eius rogabant eum,* without noticing that the disciples urged Jesus to send her away (*"Dimitte eam"*) because of her continual crying after them.

25. *arcanum.*  26. Cf. Eph 1.9.
27. *typum.*  28. I.e., Jews.
29. Cf. Jer 2.3.  30. Mt 15.26.

31. The use of *salus* as both "healing" and "salvation" is quite common in Hilary's commentary, for the ultimate healing is the salvation of the person. *Salus* was also a summary term for the way Hilary referred to justification. It is no accident that the Canaanite woman who sought healing for her daughter

inward mysteries[32] by saying that little dogs feed on the crumbs fallen from the table. The reproach of the name "dog" was thereby softened under its guise as an affectionate nickname.[33]

5. So we understand that the Lord's silence had to do with a consideration of timing, not from a conflict of his will. He then said, *O woman, your faith is great*,[34] namely, that she who was already certain of her own salvation was no less confident (being associated with the pagans) of a time when believers will be freed, just as her daughter, from all domination of unclean spirits. An assurance of these events is provided in what followed.

Immediately after the pagans were prefigured in the daughter of the Canaanite woman, those beset by various kinds of illnesses were brought by the crowds to the Lord.[35] Both unbelievers and the sick were instructed by believers[36] to worship and prostrate themselves.[37] These were healed, and all functions of mind and body were restored for perceiving, comprehending, praising, and following God.[38]

6. *After Jesus called the disciples together, he said, "I have compassion on this crowd because it is already three days that they have remained with me,"*[39] and the rest. This course of action[40] preserves a pattern,[41] as does a comparable principle which follows from his words. For we remember how a figure of the Church was established in the daughter of the Canaanite woman, and we recounted how the healing of the people who were following him represented the pagan "illness." Now we must carefully examine the words and deeds of the Lord in order to see if we should regard the things that follow with the same significance[42] of understanding as the preceding matters.

<hr />

is "already saved by faith." See Thomas Buffer, *"Salus" in St. Hilary of Poitiers* (Rome: Pontificia Universitas Gregoriana, 2002), 29.

32. Recalls 1 Tm 3.9.
33. *catelli* ("little dogs," "puppies") instead of *canes*.
34. Mt 15.28.                              35. Mt 15.29–30.
36. Presumably, the disciples.
37. Probably suggested by v. 30b: "they put them at his feet" (RSV).
38. Mt 15.31. Cf. correspondence to the infirmities listed in Mt 15.30–31.
39. Mt 15.32.                              40. Feeding of the four thousand.
41. *ordinem*.                             42. *auctoritatem*.

The Lord had compassion on the crowd, which had remained with him for three days. He did not want to dismiss [them] in a state of fasting lest they fall down for lack of sustinence on their way. But the disciples reasoned that they did not have enough bread to fill and satisfy them.[43] The Lord inquired how many loaves they had. They responded that there were seven loaves and a few fish.[44] The Lord ordered the crowds to sit down on the ground,[45] and, taking the bread and fish, he gave thanks and broke them, and he gave the pieces to the disciples for them to distribute.[46] The pieces of the seven loaves and few fish filled four thousand men.[47] Even after everyone was satisfied, the left-over pieces of bread filled seven baskets.[48]

7. Many things suggested here are new. The disciples had compassion on five thousand men fasting for a single day[49] (wanting to send them away to their villages in order to buy food), whereas the disciples say nothing after three whole days.[50] In the earlier account, the crowd sat on the grass,[51] taking their place on the ground. There, five loaves are presented; here, it is seven loaves. There, it is two fish; here, it is an indefinite number though a few are indicated. There, it is five thousand men; here, it is four thousand. There, twelve baskets are filled; here, it is seven baskets.[52] And I think that the response to the earlier situation and everything that has been suggested was conformed to the identity of the people. Let us now try to find a suitable underlying principle for the event and its purpose. However much these facts correspond to the believing Jews, they apply also to people of the pagans.

8. There is the same pattern in the word of the Lord as that which abides in the reception of grace. Those who come to baptism first confess that they believe in the Son of God and in

43. Mt 15.33.  44. Mt 15.34.
45. Mt 15.35.  46. Mt 15.36.
47. Mt 15.38.  48. Mt 15.37.
49. Mt 14.14.  50. Mt 15.32.
51. Mt 14.19.

52. Different kinds of baskets are named. Hilary points out that in the account of the feeding of the five thousand, the baskets are *cophini,* whereas in the story of the four thousand, the baskets are *sportae.*

his Passion and Resurrection, and by this sign[53] of profession, the faith is given back.[54] So that this verbal promise[55] may follow the truth of these events, they spend the entire time of the Lord's Passion in fasting,[56] united to the Lord in a kind of fellowship of shared suffering. Either through the promise of the covenant or in the act of fasting, the whole time of the Lord's Passion is passed with the Lord.

9. The Lord, having compassion on those who possessed this hope and fellowship, said that they had been[57] with him for three days. Lest exhaustion should ruin their course of life in the world, that is, the completion of their path, he wished to feed them with his food and to undergird their strength for the accomplishing of the entire journey by the power of his bread, despite the fact that the disciples were complaining there was no bread in this desert.[58] Surely in the previous events they had learned the lesson that nothing is impossible with God.[59] But the significance of the events presents the occasion for a principle of an interior understanding.[60] The apostles were quite eager for the salvation of Israel, as the epistles of the most blessed Paul teach.[61] And with this same expectation, now in the gathering of the pagans, both their complaint about the lack of bread as well as their silence about the crowd's fasting[62] are introduced.

53. *sacramento.*

54. *redditur.* A possible reference to the process of catechetical preparation. The bishop imparted (*tradere*) to the catechumens the faith in credal form for memorization so that they may give it back (*reddere*) as a profession of their faith at the time of baptism. Some scholars argue that this pre-baptismal liturgy was not developed until later in the fourth century. See Doignon, *Sur Matt.* II.44, n.15, who denies that this is any echo of a baptismal liturgy. There is no evidence that disallows the use of catechetical vocabulary of this kind prior to the witnesses of the rites as seen in Ambrose's *Expositio* and Augustine's *Sermons* 212–15.

55. I.e., the profession of faith.

56. Possibly a reference to the period of fasting and prayer during Holy Week.

57. Lit., "were with him" (*secum esse*, the infinitive being concurrent with the indicative verb).

58. Mt 14.15.

59. That is, in the earlier feeding of the five thousand. Cf. Lk 1.37.

60. *rationem interioris intelligentiae.*

61. Rom 9.2–5.                    62. *Supra,* 15.7.

10. Seven loaves were presented. For the pagans salvation does not come by the Law and the prophets. Rather, they are given life through the grace of the Spirit, whose gift is seven-fold as Isaiah informs us.[63] And so there is salvation for the pagans through faith of the Spirit. It is they who sit down on the ground;[64] they were not subject to works of the Law before sitting down. Seeing that the origin of their sins is integral to their bodies,[65] they are called to the gift of the sevenfold Spirit.

An indefinite number of fish signifies the distribution and functions of the different gifts and charisms,[66] by which the faith of the pagans is filled with a diversity of graces. That the seven baskets are filled indicates an overflowing and multiplied abundance of the sevenfold Spirit, who abounds in what he freely bestows. Once satisfied, we are always richly and deeply filled [by the Spirit].[67]

That the four thousand men gathered together[68] indicates that there was an innumerable multitude from the four parts of the earth. As an image of the future, the people who are enumerated in so many thousands of members complete the many thousands of those who will believe when they gather to-gether from the four parts [of the earth] to partake of the gift of heavenly food. Once the crowd has been satisfied and filled, it is dismissed.[69] Because the Lord remains with us all the days of our lives, he boards the ship with the company of believers, that is, the Church.

---

63. Is 11.2.

64. Cf. Mt 14.19. The overall argument is that the reason for two accounts of feeding (the five thousand and then the four thousand) is that the first was for Jews and the second was for pagans. Together, the two events show the progression of the Gospel from the house of Israel to the Gentiles, in resem-blance to Paul's theology.

65. *peccatorum et corporum suorum origini inhaerentes.* Cf. Rom 15.8–9 (RSV): "For I tell you that Christ became a servant to the circumcised to show God's truthfulness, in order to confirm the promises given to the patriarchs, and in order that the Gentiles might glorify God for his mercy. As it is written, 'Therefore I will praise thee among the Gentiles, and sing to thy name'"; 15.18b–19a (RSV): "For I will not venture to speak of anything except what Christ has wrought through me to win obedience from the Gentiles, by word and deed, by the power of signs and wonders, by the power of the Holy Spirit."

66. *charismatum.*  67. Cf. Cyprian, *Epp.* 63.8; 69.14.

68. Mt 15.38.  69. Mt 15.39.

# CHAPTER SIXTEEN

ND THE *Pharisees and Sadducees came to him, testing him, and they asked him to show them a sign from heaven.*[1] The Pharisees and Sadducees present were arrogant because of their confidence in the Law. Disdaining his powerful works of faith, they sought a sign to be shown to them from heaven. When they looked upon the humility of the flesh and the body of Christ, they refused to accept teaching from these works which he accomplished as a human being.[2]

With ridicule for their arrogance and foolishness, the Lord responds that they were accustomed to interpreting many omens from the nature of the heavens; that is, when they predicted a clear or cloudy sky on the basis of a red sky at dawn or in the evening.[3] Yet they are ignorant of the signs of the times,[4] since all the Law and the prophets indicate the proofs of his coming from the miraculous works that he does. In whatever way the redness of the sky in the morning or in the evening betokens the certainty of a storm, so the proofs of his power and works should no less reveal a knowledge that clarifies the time at hand.

2. The Lord offers them an earthly sign derived from heaven by saying that the sign of Jonah has to be given.[5] He does this to secure their acknowledgment of his bodily humility. The Lord compares himself to this sign of Jonah, who, in the preaching of repentance to Nineveh, had anticipated an image identical to the realization of the Lord's future Passion.[6] After Jonah had

---

1. Mt 16.1.
2. *sub hominis habitu.* A common form of spiritual and theological myopia according to Hilary; *supra,* 3.1; 5.15; 8.6; 13.8; 14.2.
3. Mt 16.3.                                          4. *Infra,* Mt 24.35–45.
5. Mt 16.4.
6. Cf. Tertullian, *De pudicitia* 10.4, on how Jonah suffered as a figurative example of the Lord's Passion.

been thrown from the ship on account of fierce winds and swallowed by a sea monster,[7] he had come forth alive after three days, not being crushed by the monster. Nor was he chewed as one chews food, but contrary to the nature of the human body, he escaped, intact and not injured, back to the open air[8] as a powerful prefiguration of the Lord.[9] The Lord shows that the sign of his power has plainly been established, while preaching the remission of sins in him through repentance.[10] It was necessary that he be rejected from Jerusalem and the synagogue by the domination of the unclean spirits, and be delivered over to Pilate's authority, that is, to the judgment of the world. He then had to be swallowed by death, just as the monster does in its own environment.[11] After three days he emerges alive and incorruptible, no longer encumbered by the condition of humanity, which he had assumed. The qualities of his humanity, which he had assumed from his virginal conception, were full of divine powers; he wanted these to be acknowledged and understood as his own, because of both the sign of the prophet and the example of a man.

3. *And leaving them, he went away.*[12] It is not like what we read in the other passages: "After the crowd was dismissed, he went out."[13] Because the error of unbelief possessed the souls of the arrogant, it is written not that he dismissed them, but that he left them.

*And after he had come across the lake, his disciples had forgotten to take bread. Jesus said to them, "Beware of the yeast of the Pharisees and the Sadducees."*[14] There is complete and total obscurity when it comes to the "yeast" of the Pharisees and the Sadducees. That the apostles are ordered to keep themselves from it

7. *ceto.*                                   8. *in auras superas.*

9. Following Tertullian's *De cast.* 10.4 and the general tendency in early church art and literature to see Jonah's emergence from the whale as *typicus* of Christ. Cf. Mt 12.38–40; Cyprian, *Test.* 2.25. See Y.-M. Duval, *Le Livre de Jonas dans la littérature chrétienne grecque et latinae* (Paris, 1973), 217ff.

10. Eph 1.14.                               11. The sea.

12. Mt 16.4b.                               13. Cf. Mt 14.23; 15.39.

14. Mt 16.5–6. There is variety of differences in the Latin MSS for this verse. Some read, "When his disciples had come across the lake," and others, "into the region that was across the lake."

meant they were being warned not to mingle with the teaching of the Jews,[15] because the works of the Law had been established for the prompting[16] of one's faith and as a foreshadowing[17] of events to follow. This truth was supposed to affect their times and lives, and in no way should they imagine that there is a hope of a similar truth lying beyond [what they have received].[18] The point of such teaching was to prevent the teaching of the Pharisees, ignorant of Christ, from corrupting the realization of the Gospel's truth.

4. *Jesus came into the area of Caesarea Philippi, and he asked his disciples,*[19] and so on. In the course of his words and works, he presented to his disciples a complete self-awareness,[20] and laid down a certain pattern and reason for how he should be understood. For this is the true and inviolable faith: that from the eternal God—who, because he has always had a Son, always has the right and title of Father; if the Son had not always been [a Son], the Father would not always have been a Father[21]— God the Son had proceeded, to whom belongs eternity from

15. Mt 16.12.                           16. *effectum.*

17. *praeformationem.*

18. A refrain commonly associated with Irenaeus's refutation of the gnostic contention that there existed other and deeper truths beyond what had come down through the apostles. See *Adv. haer.* 1.8.1 and 3.1.1.

19. Mt 16.13.

20. *cognitionem suam.*

21. Tertullian, *Adv. Prax.* 10.4–5: *Quae enim me faciunt si habuero, tunc ero pater si filium habeam, filius vero si patrem. Porro si ipse ero quid eorum, iam non habeo quod ipse ero, nec patrem quia ipse ero pater, nec filium quia ipse ero filius. In quantum autem alterum ex his habere me oportet, alterum esse, in tantum, si utrumque fuero, alterum non ero, dum alterum non habeo. Si enim ipse ero filius qui et pater, iam non habeo filium sed ipse sum filius. Non habendo autem filium dum ipse sum filius, quomodo pater ero? Habere enim filium debeo ut pater sim: non sum ergo filius, quia patrem non habeo qui facit filium. Aeque si ipse sum pater qui et filius, iam non habeo patrem sed ipse sum pater. Non habendo autem patrem dum ipse sum pater, quomodo filius ero? Habere enim patrem debeo ut filius sim: non ergo ero pater* (ed. Kroymann and Evans, CCSL 2.1169). It is clear that Tertullian's Father-Son language is in the context of his refutation of Monarchian modalism. Hilary may well have been drawing on the terminology, but it was not for the same polemical purpose. Tertullian's point is to show that the Father-Son relation demonstrates that the Father cannot also be the Son, and vice versa. Hilary draws on this argument, but for his own purpose against any form of adoptionism or subordinationism that would separate the divinity of the Father and Son.

his eternal Father.[22] It was the will of the Father to beget[23] the Son, the Father's power and authority being present in the one born.[24] The Son of God, therefore, is God from God, one [God] in two,[25] for he received the *theotēta*[26] (what the Latins call "deity") of his eternal parent, from whom he proceeded by his birth. He received that which he was, and is born the Word, which was always in the Father. The Son is both eternal and born because there is nothing born in him other than what is eternal.[27]

22. *parentis.* This is not the doctrine of eternal generation that Hilary will later espouse in *De trinitate* 2.15; 3.6; *et passim,* but is more similar to the view of Novatian (*De trin.* 31.16) in that the Son receives his eternal nature from the eternality of the Father. See John McDermott, "Hilary of Poitiers: The Infinite Nature of God," *Vig. Chr.* 27 (1973): 178–79 ("He is not eternal because his birth is eternal, but because by his birth he comes into full possession of the eternal divinity"), and P. Smulders, *La doctrine trinitaire,* 78–79: "L'éternité du Fils consiste en ce qu'il est éternel par celui qui l'a engendré, c'est-à-dire du fait que lui a été communiquée la nature éternelle du Père. Ainsi donc, même ici, le Fils ne semble pas éternel par sa propre personnalité, mais parce que le Père lui a donné une nature qui, en lui-même, est éternelle."

23. *Nasci autem eum voluntas eius fuit.* Like Latin theologians, Hilary will use *nascor, nasci, natus* in a completely immaterial way to mean the Son's divine begetting. Hilary never uses *innascibilitas* (state of being unborn) in reference to the Son as he later will do in *De trin.* (1.34; 9.31), and which is also used for the eternity of God the Father (*De trin.* 9.6; 7.21; 9.54; 10.6).

The concept that the Son is begotten or born according to the will of the Father had its origin in anti-gnostic polemical theology. Whereas the gnostics' Unknown God emanated the aeons by virtue of its innate fertility, the catholic response was that the Son, as proceeding from God, had always been within the Father's purpose and will. To say otherwise would annul the argument that the prophetic promises of the Old Testament speak of Christ as part of God's design. See Tertullian, *Adv. Prax.* 7.9; 8.4; 10.3; *Adv. Hermog.* 20.

24. *cuius in virtute ac potestate inerat ut nasceretur.* Very similar to Novatian, *De trin.* 31.4: "He is born, in that he is born of the Father who is without a beginning. When the Father willed it, he (the Son) proceeded from the Father; and He who was in the Father came forth from the Father ..." (*quia nascitur, et per Patrem quodammodo (quamvis originem habet qua nascitur) vicinus in nativitate, dum ex eo Patre qui originem solus non habet, nascitur. Hic ergo quando Pater voluit, processit ex Patre, et qui in Patre fuit, processit ex Patre*); PL 3:949C–950A.

25. *unus in utroque.* Although Hilary will never call the Son the "second one," as does Tertullian, *Adv. Prax.* 7–8, or Novatian, *De trin.* 31.

26. Col 2.9—a scriptural term. Cf. *infra,* 26.5.

27. Cf. Novatian, *De trin.* 31.16: *dum qui ex illo nascitur merito ex eo venit qui originem non habet, principium probans illud esse ex quo ipse est, etiam si Deus est qui natus est, unum tamen Deum ostendit, quem hic qui natus est, esse sine origine comprobavit* (PL 3:980B).

5. Accordingly, the whole confession is that he had assumed a body and was made man; just as eternity received a body of our nature, so we should acknowledge that the nature of our body was able to assume the power of eternity. Since this point is the most important[28] for [our] faith,[29] he asked the disciples what men were saying about who he was, and added the term "Son of Man."[30] The reason for maintaining this confession is that we may remember that he is both the Son of God and the Son of Man.[31] The one without the other offers no hope for our salvation.

6. Once the various opinions that others held about him were disclosed,[32] Jesus then inquired what they themselves thought concerning him.[33] Peter responded: *You are the Christ, the Son of the living God.*[34] Peter was aware of the implication of the question when the Lord had said: *Who do men say that I am, the Son of Man?*[35] Of course, his bodily manifestation showed he was a son of man. By adding, "Who do they say that I am?" Jesus indicated it was essential to consider another element beyond the obvious fact that he was a son of man. What answer did he seek from those thinking about him? It is not, we may suppose, that which he confessed about himself. Rather, it was hidden from anyone who sought it so that the faith of believers was obliged to delve into what he was.[36]

---

28. Lit., "highest good." For Latin, see n.29.

29. *summum in fide ista bonum est.*

30. Mt 16.13.

31. See Hilary, *De trin.* 9.14; 11.13; 10.21. Augustine will elaborate on this point in *De trin.* 1.3, 14; 1.22, 24.

32. Mt 16.14.

33. Mt 16.15.

34. Mt 16.16. R. P. C. Hanson, *The Search*, 844, claims that Hilary interprets Mt 16.16–17 in a way that deliberately excluded the Monarchian refusal to acknowledge the distinct existence of the divine persons.

35. Mt 16.13. As one would expect, this form of Jesus' statement squares with the Old Latin version (*Itala*, 114), contrary to the Vulgate, which incorporates *Filium hominis* into the question: *quem dicunt homines esse Filium hominis* ("Who do men say is the Son of Man?").

36. Cf. Tertullian, *De praescr. haer.* 10.2.

7. Clearly Peter's confession received an appropriate reward because he had seen the Son of God in the man.[37] He is blessed and exalted for having directed his view beyond human eyes, regarding not only that which was from flesh and blood, but perceiving the Son of God through the revelation of the heavenly Father. And he was judged worthy to be the first one to recognize that what was in Christ was of God. O happy is the foundation of the Church on account of the announcement of his new name.[38] Worthy is the rock upon which the Church is built, against which the laws of hell[39] and the gates of Tartarus and all the prisons of death are broken. O blessed porter of heaven, by whose decree the keys of eternity's entrance are handed over, and whose earthly judgment with heavenly authority has already been decreed. Whatever has been bound or loosed on earth acquires the status of the very same decree in heaven.[40]

8. He also commanded his disciples not to tell anyone that he himself is the Christ,[41] since it was necessary that others bear witness to his Spirit,[42] namely, the Law and the prophets. Otherwise, the testimony of the Resurrection is peculiar to the apostles. As the beatitude of those who know Christ in the Spirit[43] has shown, there is the opposite danger for those who deny his humility and Passion.[44]

9. Once he began to teach, [he said] it was necessary for him to go to Jerusalem, to suffer there many things at the hands of the elders of the people and from the scribes and chief priests,

37. Mt 16.17.
38. Mt 16.18. That is, Peter's new name.
39. *infernas.*　　　　　　　　40. Mt 16.19.
41. Mt 16.20.
42. That is, to his divinity. *Spiritus* often functioned in Latin theology as a term for expressing the Word by the name of Spirit. Cf. Irenaeus's concept of one God, which involves the Father and his two hands, Word and Spirit. *Adv. haer.* 4.20.1.
43. Mt 7.21–23. Tertullian, *Adv. Prax.* 26.4: *Hic Spiritus Dei idem erit sermo. . . . Spiritum quoque intellegimus in mentione sermonis, ita et hic sermonem quoque agnoscimus in nomine Spiritus* (ed. Kroymann and Evans, CCSL 2.1196–97).
44. *Supra,* 3.5; 12.18; 24.1; cf. Tertullian, *De carne Christi* 5.6–8.

to be killed, and, after three days, to rise again.[45] Peter, seizing him, said: *"Let it be far from you, Lord; that will not take place."* But *the Lord, turning around, said to Peter: "Get behind me, Satan, you are a stumbling block[46] to me."*[47] Just as the gift of God is to know Christ as God in the Spirit, so the work of the devil is to deny Christ in the man.[48] There is the same danger in denying that that body is without God or denying that he was God without a [true] body.[49] If the body of this flesh is nullified by God in the eternity of his Spirit, so is the reason for human salvation, which is Christ in a body that he assumed from humanity.

10. After the announcement of his Passion, the devil seizes the opportunity—until the moment when he had withdrawn from Peter—because it seemed completely unbelievable to the apostles that God should suffer in Christ.[50] By grasping this occasion of human unbelief, the devil instills in Peter the conviction of such a viewpoint.[51] In short, Peter rejected the Passion when he said, "Far be it,"[52] a word which conjures an execration of detestable things. But the Lord, knowing that it was inspired by diabolical means,[53] said to Peter: *Get behind me;*[54] that is, Peter should follow him in the precedent of his Passion. The Lord likewise turned against the one who had made this suggestion[55] when he added: *Satan, you are a stumbling block to me.*[56] It is not right to think that the name of Satan and the offense of a stumbling block should be imputed to Peter after [he made] so many affirmations of [God's] gifts, blessing, and power. Nonetheless, because all unbelief is the work of the devil,[57] the Lord—troubled at Peter's response—rejected the instigator[58] of that unbelief by reproaching his name [Satan].

45. Mt 16.21.
47. Mt 16.22–23.
49. Cf. Novatian, *De trin.* 11.57–59.
46. *scandalum.*
48. *Supra,* 3.1–5.
50. This is the sentiment of the Jews, according to Tertullian (*Adv. Iud.* 10.1), and for Peter to make this statement shows he is "a man of the Law" (*Adv. Marc.* 4.11.1).
51. Cf. *supra,* 3.1.
53. *diabolicae artis.*
52. *Absit:* lit., "May it not happen."
54. Mt 16.23.
55. "the one who had made this suggestion": i.e., the devil.
56. Mt 16.23: *scandalum mihi es* (*supra,* 4.7).
57. Cf. Tertullian, *De anima* 3.2; *De fuga* 2.1.
58. *auctorem.*

11. *Then Jesus said to his disciples, "If anyone wants to come after me, let him deny himself,"*[59] and the rest. O blessed loss and happy sacrifice! The Lord wants us to grow rich through the loss of soul and body,[60] encouraging us to become as he is. Because he was established in the form of God,[61] being humbled and made obedient unto death, he received the first place of God's complete authority.[62] We must, therefore, follow him by taking up the cross and accompany him, if not in the circumstances of his Passion, then in our will.[63] For what do we gain by possessing the world and total domination over earthly power and clinging to worldly riches, if we lose our soul and embrace death? What will we give in exchange for our soul, once it has been given up?[64] For Christ will come with the angels, rendering to each one what he has deserved.[65] What should we offer for our life?[66] I believe that treasures prepared for future purchase of earthly riches, that the ambitious titles of our dignity and glory, that ancient images of our cherished nobility—all these things must be denied so that we may live in the abundance of better things. We must follow Christ by our contempt of everything. Our gain of eternal spiritual benefits necessarily entails the loss of earthly ones.

59. Mt 16.24.

60. That is, of the whole self.

61. *in figura dei.*

62. Phil 2.6–7.

63. Cf. Cyprian, *Ep.* 12.1, who makes a distinction between the will of the martyr and the consummation of his sufferings.

64. Mt 16.26.

65. Mt 16.27.

66. I.e., eternal life; Rom 5.17.

# CHAPTER SEVENTEEN

*RULY, I SAY to you that some of those standing here will not taste death, until they see the Son of Man coming in his Kingdom.*[1] The Lord teaches us that deeds and words, speech and action, in equal proportion guide us in the faith of our hope.[2] For the heavy burden of human weakness has been imposed on us so that when we began to sense an awareness of life by experiencing it, we would put aside the benefits and deny bodily pleasures. The hope is that we might not become what we had begun to be. Since we have the beginning of this awareness from the inclination of our will,[3] we follow an ambiguous and uncertain hope during these present times in which we are attracted to joyful pleasures. By the authority of certain and clear examples, contrary to using force and right of judgment, he taught that the loss of present gain is desirable, an indubitable gain of things yet to come.[4]

After the Lord had warned[5] them that they had to take up the cross, lose their lives, and exchange the loss of the world for eternal life, he turned to the disciples and said that there would be some among them who were not going to taste death until they beheld the Son of Man in the glory of his Kingdom.[6] As the Lord tasted death in his circumstances, he showed the faithful how the drink of death has its limits.[7] And so his words are followed by deeds.

---

1. Mt 16.28.
2. Regarding the double-sided proof of faithfulness, see also Tertullian, *Adv. Marc.* 3.17.5.
3. *ex adfectu voluntatis.*
4. Cf. Tertullian, *De paen.* 7.8.
5. Hilary picks up the Gospel narrative again (Mt 16.24–28).
6. Mt 16.28.
7. *tenuem quamdam.*

2. After six days, Peter, James, and John were taken apart from the others and brought to the top of a mountain.[8] As they were looking on, the Lord was transfigured and resplendent in all the brilliance of his garments.[9] In this manner there is preserved an underlying principle,[10] a number, and an example.[11] It was after six days that the Lord was shown in his glory by his clothing; that is, the honor of the heavenly Kingdom is prefigured in the unfolding of six thousand years.[12] By the three disciples who were taken apart is shown the future election of the people who were to come from a threefold origin: Shem, Ham, and Japheth.[13] That Moses and Elijah, out of the entire company of saints, were standing by,[14] shows Christ in his Kingdom standing among the Law and the prophets, with whom he will judge Israel, in whose testimonies he was foretold. So too, the reason that Moses was visibly standing by was to teach that the glory of the resurrection was designated for human bodies. As the Lord became brighter than snow or the sun,[15] he was conspicuous with a splendor that exceeds even our view of the heavenly lights. But to Peter, who offered to make there three tabernacles, he did not respond at all; for it was not yet the time that the Lord should be found in his glory.

3. While Peter was still speaking, a bright cloud overshadowed them, and they were encompassed by the spirit of divine power.[16] A voice called out from the cloud: *This is my Son, whom I love, with whom I am well pleased; listen to him,*[17] so that the Lord himself should be the proper author[18] of such teachings. After the sacrifice of the world, after willingly going to the cross, after the death of the body, the Lord reaffirmed the glory of his heavenly Kingdom by the resurrection from the dead as our

8. Mt 17.1.                    9. Mt 17.2.

10. *ratio.*

11. *ratio* (a plan), *numerus* (numerology), and *exemplum* (lesson to be learned).

12. This is the number of the world's duration according to tradition reflected in Cyprian, *Exhort. ad Mart.*, praef. 2; Lactantius, *Inst.* 7.14. See *Sur Matt.* II.63, n.6.

13. *Supra*, 8.4.                    14. Mt 17.3.

15. Mt 17.2.                    16. *divinae virtutis spiritu.*

17. Mt 17.5. There are some minor variations among the MSS for this verse, which Hilary is loosely paraphrasing.

18. *auctorem.*

model to follow.[19] At that point, they were terrified and fell to the ground. He raised them up, and they looked only upon him[20] standing in between Moses and Elijah.[21] Serving as a figure[22] of things to come and as a confirmation[23] of the present, Moses and Elijah stood on the mountain.

The Lord commanded the disciples to be silent about the events they had seen until he should rise from the dead.[24] Indeed, this was a reward reserved for the faith of those who honor the Lord's sole authority with the utmost seriousness. For he realized their inability[25] to hear the voice,[26] such that they should then be witnesses of spiritual events when they were filled with the Holy Spirit.[27]

4. Still apprehensive [in light of what had just happened], the disciples inquired about the times of Elijah.[28] He responded that Elijah will come and restore all things.[29] In other words, Elijah is going to recall the rest of Israel, whom he will have gathered, to knowledge of God. The Lord also indicated that it is in the power and spirit of Elijah that John had come, against whom hostility and bitterness had been exercised.[30] By declaring the Lord's advent, John was the forerunner of his Passion by the example of suffering and troubles inflicted on him.

5. *And when he had come to the crowd, a man approached him, having fallen on his knees, saying, "Lord, have pity on my son."*[31] As the Lord turned to the crowd, the father, kneeling, presented his child, a demoniac, who often threw himself into water and into fire. The disciples were unable to bring healing.[32] After the crowd was scolded and the demon rebuked, the boy was made whole.[33]

19. There is no indication in Hilary's treatment of 17.5 of an awareness of a Sabellian interpretation such as that which he later attacked in *De trin.* 2.23.

20. In contrast to Jesus' baptism, where, besides the Father's voice, there was the manifestation of the Holy Spirit.

21. Mt 17.8.
22. *formam.*
23. *ad facti fidem.*
24. Mt 17.9.
25. *infirmos.*
26. Mt 17.5.
27. Cf. Acts 1.8.
28. Mt 17.10.
29. Mt 17.11.
30. Mt 17.12–13.
31. Mt 17.15a.
32. Mt 17.15–16.
33. Mt 17.17–18.

6. Though the apostles believed, their faith was not yet perfect. While the Lord was delayed on the mountain, they themselves were sitting with the crowd, and a kind of torpor had weakened their faith. This is why he said to them: *Unbelieving and perverse generation, how long will I be with you?*[34] In his absence, their ancient habit of unbelief had stolen upon them. He taught them that they can obtain no healing, just as if, during the time intervening between the Gospels and the second coming, they abandoned their faith as though the Lord were absent.

7. When the disciples finally asked him why they were not able to drive out the demon,[35] he responded that their lack of faith had rendered them unable to do so. If they had faith like that of a mustard seed, they would have been able to command this mountain with effectual power to move from one place to another.[36] But by this time he had come down the mountain and was speaking among the crowd. He declared that he himself was like the smallest of all seeds, the mustard seed, referring to the devil as a "mountain" because evil spirits and heavenly powers are found on its heights.[37] He must be ejected and hurled into the depths of the sea, even to the bottom of hell;[38] this will be done through those who pray and fast for this result.[39]

8. We will also find by observing this pattern[40] that the persons of the Pharisees and the scribes are indicated under the name of the "disciples." The Law offered healing for the people, just as it did for the [Pharisees and the] disciples, and just as the father wanted for his son[41] in the Lord's absence. Under

34. Mt 17.17. Hilary is assuming that Jesus' remark was directed to the disciples as well as the crowd.

35. Mt 17.19.                                      36. Mt 17.20.

37. For instances where the mountain heights are said to be the habitation of false gods and evil spirits, see Dt 12.2–2; Is 36.7; Ezek 6.13; Mt 4.8.

38. *inferni.* Cf. *infra,* 17.33; also expressed as "gehenna," 4.21; 10.17; or *aeternus ignis,* 4.17; 5.12; 24.1; *flammae aeterni ignis,* 22.5.

39. Whereas the better Greek MSS have omitted v.21, the Old Latin preserves it, which Hilary follows here: "But this kind does not go out except by prayer and fasting."

40. *ordinem.*                                      41. Mt 17.15–16.

the domination of their sins, these perished at one time by the fire of judgment,[42] and at another time were plunged into water for their daily sins.[43] These things, however, brought no help at all because, as Moses was delayed on the mountain with the Lord, their unbelief was realized.[44]

In order to fulfill a figurative purpose,[45] the disciples are surprised that they could not drive out the demon since all authority had been granted them not only for driving out demons but also for raising the dead.[46] But because the Law was no longer going to apply to them, the Lord said: *Unbelieving and perverse generation*—it does not seem that he spoke this to those whom he had sanctified[47]—*"how long, he said, will I be with you?"*[48] Those who did not have faith were going to lose the very Law which they possessed. If they had maintained faith in him, even if it was a mere mustard seed,[49] the burden of their sins and the heavy weight of their unbelief would have been cast off by the power of the Word, just like the mountain thrown into the sea.[50] They would have been transferred to the ways of the Gentiles and of the age.

9. *As they were going about in Galilee, Jesus said, "It will happen that the Son of Man will be delivered into the hands of man."*[51] A sadness follows the acknowledgment of his Passion;[52] the sacrament of the cross, which he would have to bear, had not yet been revealed by the power of the Resurrection.

10. *And when Jesus had come to Capernaum, those who were collecting the two-drachma tax approached Peter.*[53] The Lord was asked

---

42. Cf. Dt 32.22; Jas 15.14; Lam 4.11.
43. *in aquam diurnarum sordium.* Cf. Lv 14–15; Nm 19, purification rites for leprosy and bodily discharges.

44. Ex 32.1–6.
46. Cf. Mt 10.8.
48. Mt 17.17.
50. Mt 17.21; Lk 17.6.

45. *typica ratio.*
47. I.e., the disciples.
49. I.e., the smallest of all seeds.
51. Mt 17.22.

52. Mt 17.23. The sadness was that of the disciples. Hilary denies that Christ ever experienced a sadness that would have introduced a weakness to his divine nature.

53. Mt 17.24. Most of the Old Latin texts do not include Jesus in the verse and read rather, "And when they had come…"

to pay the two drachmas. It was intended for those devoted to serving the Temple, which the Law had established for the redemption of body and soul for all of Israel.[54] But the Law, as we know, is a shadow of things to come.[55] God did not desire an amount of money for crimes committed of body and soul as if so paltry a sum for one's redemption should be accepted. Instead, the Lord desired that we offer ourselves to Christ, in whom we are inscribed,[56] acknowledged, and sealed in his name.[57] Christ is the true Temple of God,[58] so that the offering of two drachmas was intended as a witness to the Son of God.

11. After a period of silence, the Lord anticipated Peter with the question: *What do you think, Simon? From whom do kings of the earth accept tribute or taxes?*[59] etc. Is there doubt that the sons of kings are not subject to tribute? or that the royal heirs are free from servitude? This question raises [the need for] a deeper meaning.[60]

Two drachmas are demanded from the people [of the Law] whereas the Law was summed up in a faith which was revealed through Christ.[61] According to the custom of the Law, this same two drachmas were requested of Christ as from a man. But in order to show that he is not subjected to the Law and that the glory of the Father's majesty is witnessed in him, he offered an example of earthly privileges: that the sons of kings are not bound by the tax and tribute.[62] For Christ is the Redeemer of our soul and body, not forced to seek anything for his own redemption. Since it is proper for the son of the king to be beyond the common lot of the others, he made a stumbling block[63] by dissolving [the tax law]. But as it is, he is free from the Law's obligation.

---

54. *Sur Matt.* II.71, n.14. The duality implied by the double drachma is that of the man, soul and body, according to a *topos* already apparent in *supra*, 10.18. Cf. Tertullian, *De paen.* 3.4; *Adv. Marc.* 4.37.

55. Col 2.17; Heb 8.5.

56. *inscriptos*. 2 Cor 3.2–3.

57. This is a reference to baptism, in which one makes profession and receives the *signaculum*.

58. 1 Cor 3.16; 6.19.

60. *sermo interius intendit.*

62. Mt 17.26.

59. Mt 17.25.

61. Gal 3.23.

63. *scandalum.*

12. The Lord then established the significance of the Law and constancy of the Gospel's liberty under the guise[64] of present circumstances so that it would be readily understood how the two drachmas are prefigured in the Law. He orders Peter to go to the sea, put down his fishing line, and look into the mouth of the first fish he catches, and offer the small silver coin that he found both for himself and for the Lord.[65] The Lord was asked for a two-drachma coin, that is, two denarii; why did Peter have to offer a four-drachma coin? Peter was then told to check the first fish of many which were visible on the surface. Is it in keeping with the nature of fish that it should be found near the shore by accident with a silver coin in its mouth rather than [swallowed and] lodged in its viscera? A deeper[66] reason, therefore, underlies the presentation of these events.

13. As one destined for the task of preaching and as fisher of men, Peter let down his line of teaching in the world, where once people taste its sweet food, they are found floundering and thrashing about in it.[67] On this fishing-line the Lord attached that first blessed martyr,[68] who contained in his mouth a fourfold-denarius.[69] In the unity of the number of Gospels, he preached the glory of God and the Lord,[70] looking unto Christ in his Passion. Stephen was the first to ascend, and it was Stephen who contained in his mouth a silver coin, in which also were held two drachmas, equivalent to the two denarii of the new preaching.[71] The Law prefigured this [new preaching], which contained a shadow of this truth, just like an image of

---

64. *effectu.*

65. The coin or *stater* was the value of four drachmas. See 1 Kgs 9.8 (Vulgate) and Mt 17.27.

66. Lit., "interior" (*interior*).

67. I.e., in the net.

68. Stephen, Acts 7. Cf. Cyprian, *De pat.*16.

69. *quadrigeminum denarium*, representing the four Gospels.

70. In Acts 7.55, Stephen "gazed into heaven and saw the glory of God and Jesus standing at the right hand of God" (RSV). Cf. Ps 110.1.

71. Despite this tortuous exegesis, Doignon thinks that the two parties in Hilary's mind are the Gospels and apostles in light of Tertullian, *Adv. Prax.* 15.1: "I find in both the Gospels and the apostolic writings a visible and an invisible God"; see Latin edition of Kroymann and Evans, CCSL 2.1178.

his body. This redemption of soul and body was indicated when he said: *Give it for me and for you.*[72] It was not so much about the two-drachma, but about the silver coin that had to be offered for Christ and for the preaching of Christ.

72. Mt 17.27; i.e., the coin found in the fish's mouth.

# CHAPTER EIGHTEEN

*N THAT DAY, the disciples came to Jesus, saying, "Who do you think is the greatest in the Kingdom of heaven?"*[1] and the rest. The Lord teaches that no one enters the Kingdom of heaven unless he returns to the nature of childhood.[2] This means that the sins of our body and soul should be revoked in childlike simplicity. He declares that children believe everyone because they trust what they hear.[3] They follow their father, they love their mother, they do not know how to wish evil on their neighbor, they are indifferent to the desire for riches, they are not arrogant, they do not hate, they do not lie, they believe what is said to them, and they accept as true what they hear. Once we have assumed all these attitudes, both in our habit and will, we are shown the accessible way to heaven. We must, therefore, return to the simplicity of childhood. Once we have embraced it, we will bear a resemblance[4] to the Lord's humility.[5]

2. If anyone receives such a one in the name of Christ,[6] he will obtain the reward which Christ received: *But whoever will have caused one of these little ones to stumble* (that is, whoever introduces a stumbling block[7] of temptation), *it is better for him to hang around his neck a millstone turned by an ass and be drowned*[8] *in the depths of the sea.*[9] There is a good reason why so important and so many comparisons are drawn here: the millstone, the ass turning it, the one who is supposed to be plunged into the sea with it, and how this is advantageous for him.

1. Mt 18.1.
2. Mt 18.3.
3. Cf. Rom 10.17.
4. *speciem humilitatis dominicae.*
5. Mt 18.4.
6. Mt 18.5.
7. *offendiculum.*
8. A few Latin versions read "pitched headlong."
9. Mt 18.6.

By general consensus, whatever is advantageous is always useful. But what is useful about being drowned with an ass's millstone hung around one's neck? So harsh a death strikes us as a punishment. I do not see how it is useful to seek that which is a great evil.[10] We ought to investigate, therefore, into how to understand this matter.

The turning of a millstone is labor for the blind. Mules are led around in a circle with their eyes enclosed. We often find the name "ass" to be synonymous with the pagans[11] because the pagans do not know what they are doing. In activities of their lives, they are imprisoned by the ignorance of their blind labor as they go about the activities of their lives. For the Jews, the path of knowledge has been revealed by the Law. But if they cause the apostles of Christ to stumble,[12] it would be better that they be drowned in the sea having an ass's millstone shackled around their neck. In other words, the Jews are handicapped[13] by the ignorance of the world, weighed down by pagan activities. Even so, it was more tolerable for the latter not to know Christ than for the former not to have received the prophets.

3. *Woe unto this world because of those who make stumbling blocks. Such stumbling blocks are bound to come, but woe to that man by whom the stumbling comes.*[14] The humility of Christ's Passion is a stumbling block to the world.[15] Human ignorance is contained especially in this statement: that it will not accept the Lord of eternal glory in light of the ugliness[16] of the cross. What else in the world is as dangerous as not receiving Christ? By this reference to "man,"[17] the Jewish people are designated as the author

10. It appears initially that Hilary has misunderstood this passage. He reads the words *expedit ei* ("useful for him") to mean that it is preferable to have a millstone hung around his neck. His subsequent exposition, however, indicates he has grasped the comparative phrase.

11. In contrast to Fortunatianus of Aquileia, *Commentarii in Evangelia* (fragment) 2, who associates the ass with the synagogue, and its colt with the "new people" or the Christians (CCSL 9.368).

12. *scandalizarent.*                    13. *demorarentur.*

14. Mt 18.7.

15. Rom 9.32b, "They have stumbled over the stumbling-stone" (RSV).

16. *deformitate.*

17. Mt 18.7b.

of this stumbling. All the world is jeopardized by their denial of Christ in his Passion, whose suffering the Law and the prophets have declared. But it is also inevitable that stumbling will come, he says, because the entirety of the Passion's humility had to be fulfilled in him so that the sacrament of eternity could be restored to us.

4. Earlier[18] we established that the cutting-off of a hand or a foot discloses the names of our most vital[19] bodily members.[20] It signifies that the bloodline of Israel's race ought to be abandoned,[21] which is represented by a kind of removing one's members, because it is through them that the stumbling block is made evident to the world.[22]

5. *See that you do not look down on one of these little ones who believes in me.*[23] He has forged a tightly linked chain of mutual love[24] for those especially who truly have believed in the Lord. For the angels of little children look upon God every day,[25] because the Son of Man comes to save that which was lost.[26] The Son of Man saves, the angels see God, and the angels of the small children protect them.[27] It is absolutely important[28] that the angels assist the prayers of the faithful,[29] for the angels offer prayers to God every day for those who are saved through Christ.[30] It is dangerous to look down upon the one whose wish-

18. *Supra,* 4.21.                          19. Lit., "closest" (*propinquitatum*).

20. Mt 18.8.

21. And it is only through "the bloodline of Israel's race" that Christ came into the world; *supra,* 1.1.

22. Because Hilary has already discussed the meaning and implications of a similar passage in 4.21, he offers a short explanation here.

23. Mt 18.10.

24. The expression is based on Cicero's *vincula amoris artissima* (*Sur Matt.* II.79, n.9).

25. See *Shepherd of Hermas,* Similitude 9.29, about the natural innocence of children and their relation to the Kingdom of God.

26. Mt 18.11. Old Latin versions include this verse, which is omitted by many of the earliest Greek MSS.

27. Cf. Clement of Alexandria, *Eclogae propheticae* 41.1, on the guardian angel protecting small children who have been exposed.

28. *auctoritas.*

29. Tertullian, *De orat.* 16.6. Cf. Lk 1.11–13; Rv 8.3–4.

30. Heb 1.14.

es and petitions are conveyed to the eternal and invisible God by the devoted service and ministry of the angels.

6. In order to show that there is great rejoicing in heaven at the rendering of humanity's salvation, the Lord posed a comparative example of one who left his ninety-nine sheep in the mountains and sought for the one that had strayed.[31] When it is found, he will have more joy than he had while happily watching over the ninety-nine others.[32] The one sheep should be understood as a man, and by a single man we are supposed to comprehend that the Lord is speaking of all mankind. The entire race of humanity strayed by the error of the one Adam.[33] The ninety-nine who did not stray should be reckoned as the multitude of the heavenly angels, who are happy and have the care of human salvation.[34] Christ is the one who seeks the man; the ninety-nine that are left are the multitude of heavenly glory. The man who strayed is led back into the body of the Lord with greatest rejoicing. For good reason this number is in the form of a letter which was added to [the name of] Abraham and completed in [the name of] Sarah.[35] [The name] Abraham is derived from [the name] Abram, and Sarah from Sara. We are all in the one man, Abraham,[36] and we are all together, those in whom the number of the heavenly Church will be accomplished.[37] For that reason, every creature waits for the revelation of the sons of God, sighing and grieving[38] that the number added in the form of the

31. Mt 18.12.

32. Mt 18.13.

33. The word "Adam" means "man" in Hebrew.

34. Cf. Lk 15.6–7; *Shepherd of Hermas*, Mandate 5.1; Novatian, *De trin.* 20; *Apocalypse of Paul* 9.

35. Gn 17.5, 15. The "a" added: from Abram to Abraham (Ἀβραμ to Ἀβρααμ in the LXX), and the "r" added; from Sarah to Sarrah (Σάρα to Σάρρα).

36. The theme of justification, much emphasized by Hilary, has its covenantal and prophetic roots in Abraham (Gn 12.3; Gal 3.6–9). The number "one" finds a parallel between the one sheep that is found (salvation received) and the changing of a single letter in Abram's name (salvation promised).

37. Sarrah is a type of the Church in Cyprian, *Test.*. 1.20. On the unity of the heavenly Church, see Tertullian, *De bapt.* 15.1. With the addition of one letter to her name (a *rho* in Greek), she becomes the type of the heavenly Church.

38. Rom 8.19–22.

*alpha* to Abraham and completed in the *rho* to Sarah (Sarrah)[39] may be fulfilled by the growth of believers in the heavenly establishment.

7. *If your brother sins against you, go and correct him,*[40] and the rest. The Lord has set down for us how the order of love should be followed, which he had established in the preservation of Israel.[41] He commands that the brother who sins should be corrected and admonished only by the one against whom he had sinned.[42] For the Lord corrected the people of the Jews, who were sacrificing to other gods, by the advent of his majesty and by the terror of his powerful presence. Even when this same people were separated by the mountain, they were not able to endure the advent of God's approach.[43] So he commands one or two persons to be brought before the disobedient person, so that in the mouth of two witnesses the word and truth may be established with certainty.[44] The Law and the prophets and John were sent to insolent Israel, and by these witnesses there was a consensus that Israel should cease to sin. On the third occasion, that is, of the Lord's coming, let the brother be warned in the assembly of the church's examiners. If these admonitions are in vain, let him be disregarded as one having the worthlessness of a tax-collector or a pagan.[45]

8. In order to impress a tremendous fear upon everyone present, the Lord commissioned the immovable judgment of apostolic severity, with the result that whomever they have bound on earth (that is, those intertwined within the entanglements of their sins, whom they have abandoned), and whomever they have loosed (namely, whomever they have accepted for salvation

---

39. As in the LXX, the *alpha* added: from Abram to Abraham (Ἀβραμ to Ἀβρααμ); and the *rho* added: from Sarah to Sarrah (Σάρα to Σάρρα). Doignon notes that the *rho* would have signified "one hundred" and therefore totality to Hilary's readers; see *Sur Matt.* II.80–81, n.13.

40. Mt 18.15.                    41. Cf. Rom 11.1a.
42. Mt 18.15b.                   43. Ex 19.16–25.
44. Mt 18.16. Presumably, the point here is that as God alone approached the people in Ex 19, so the offending brother should be approached by one brother (or two).
45. Mt 18.17.

with a declaration of pardon), these will be loosed or bound in heaven[46] by the agreement of the apostolic sentence.[47]

9. So greatly has the Lord desired peaceful harmony among men that he declares everything will be done which is deservedly sought from God in an accord of unity.[48] Where two or three have been gathered together in like spirit and[49] will, he promises that he will be there in their midst.[50] For peace and love themselves have made their home and settlement among those of a good and peaceful will.

10. When Peter asked whether he should forgive a brother who sins against him seven times,[51] the Lord responded: *Not seven times, but seventy-seven times.*[52] In every way we are instructed to be like him in humility and beauty. As a means of softening and lessening the sting from our confused actions,[53] he encourages us by the example of his readiness to forgive by granting pardon through faith to everyone who sins. Since our sinful nature does not deserve his mercy, complete pardon comes from the Lord, who offers mercy even when those who sinned against him returned to their [former] profession.

Whereas the punishment meted-out to Cain was fixed at sevenfold,[54] his was a sin against a man. Against his brother Abel, Cain sinned against him to the point of his brother's death. But in the case of Lamech, the punishment was fixed at seventy times seven.[55] In this instance,[56] I do believe, the punishment against the instigators of the Lord's Passion has been established. At the same time, the Lord grants pardon for this crime by the confession of those who believe.[57] Through the gift of

---

46. Mt 18.18.
47. As in the examples of Ananias and Sapphira (Acts 5), and Simon (Acts 8.19–24).
48. Mt 18.19.
49. Reading *ac* (PL 10:1002A) instead of *se* in Doignon (*Sur Matt.* II.84).
50. Mt 18.20.                    51. Mt 18.21.
52. Mt 18.22.
53. *turbidorum motuum nostrorum aculeis.*
54. Gn 4.15.                    55. Gn 4.24.
56. I.e., the Gospel's instructions about forgiveness.
57. An echo of Tertullian, *De orat.* 7.1 (CCSL 1.261): "the one who seeks

baptism, he endows with the grace of salvation those who were his detractors and persecutors.[58] He therefore shows how much more fitting it is for us to offer pardon without measure and without number, not keeping count of how many times we forgive. Rather, we should cease from being angry at those [who] sin against us, considering how many times the occasion has arisen for anger to be directed at us! At any rate, being persistent in offering pardon teaches that there is no occasion at all in which it is right for us to be angry, since God bestows his pardon for all of our faults[59] according to his mercy rather than our merit. Nor is it right that we set a limit to the number of pardons that we allow, as if from a legal prescription, since God has given us his favor through the boundless grace of the Gospel.

11. In fact, he has also provided us with a comparative example[60] that pertains to the notion of perfect goodness:[61] here a master remitted all the debt to his servant who did not have the means to repay it. The same servant extorted from his fellow-servant a paltry amount owed to him. Because of this willful offense, the first servant lost the benefit of his master's munificence and his freedom. The reason for this comparison is evident and wholly explained by the Lord himself.[62]

---

pardon is making a confession of his sin." This chapter continues its discussion of Mt 18.20–21 with reference to the vengeance enacted on Cain and Lamech (Gn 4.15, 24).

58. Cf. Cyprian, *Test.* 1.24; *De opera et eleemosynis* 2; *Epp.* 64.5; 70.1; 73.4; 73.7; 73.18.

59. *peccaminum*, a neologism (Kinnavey, 4).

60. Mt 18.23–34, the parable of the merciful king.

61. *bonitatis*, a term Hilary uses to refer to the attributes and qualities of God; cf. *supra*, 4.2; *infra*, 22.7; 28.1; and in *De trin.* 1.3, *et passim*.

62. The emphasis on the *ab ipso Domino omnis exposita est* reflects Hilary's idea that, because the parable is self-evident, there is no need to look for a deeper meaning in Jesus' words.

# CHAPTER NINETEEN

ND IT *happened that, after Jesus had said these words,*[1] *he passed through Galilee and came to the region of Judaea,*[2] etc. He healed Galileans in the region of Judaea. For he had not been able to tire[3] from the crowds of the sick or bringing aid to the infirm within the land of Galilee.[4] But we must also see that a figurative reason was involved given the particular[5] places where the Lord pardoned the sins of the pagans—a pardon that had been prepared for Judaea.

2. *Then the Pharisees came in order to test him saying, "Is a man permitted to divorce his wife for any reason whatsoever?"*[6] To this question concerning disavowing a wife, the Lord responded that it was written elsewhere in Genesis about these present circumstances. In that passage[7] the whole matter about Adam is explained. Here the Lord shows that everything was spoken by him who fashioned the man and made the woman.[8] But we, following apostolic authority, which has declared that this is a great mystery and that it is received in Christ and in the Church,[9] will leave this passage untouched just as it is.[10] We advise the reader, nevertheless, that however often one looks

---

1. MSS for this verse vary mostly between *sermones istos* and *verba ista*.

2. Mt 19.1.

3. Hilary's Latin here sounds awkward but leaves its meaning open. It does suggest again that the divine nature of Christ did not tire from doing miraculous deeds because the divine does not suffer from human frailties.

4. Mt 19.2.

5. Lit., "privileged" or "special right" (*privilegiis*).

6. Mt 19.3.  7. Gn 1.27; 2.24.

8. Mt 19.4–5.  9. Eph 5.32.

10. I.e., Paul offered an explanation for interpreting "one flesh"; Hilary finds this explanation also sufficient for Mt 19.4–5. No clearer example of the patristic approach to the Bible's intertextuality for interpretation may be found. *Supra,* 13.1.

into the same question,[11] we must carefully pay attention to the power of the words of the Lord's response,[12] and the words that the disciples used.[13]

Consider the view of the apostle Paul in this matter, both in his silence[14] and in his occasional treatment of it in other places.[15] In word and heart, we should be like the eunuchs.[16] The Lord observes that this state is given to one by nature; in another, it is a necessity;[17] for a third, it is by volition. It is nature for the one who is born that way, it is necessity for the one who has become that way, and it is by volition of the one who has determined to become a eunuch in hope of the Kingdom of God.[18] The Lord declared we ought to resemble this latter state if we are able.

3. *Then they brought to him little children*[19] *that he might place his hands on them and pray for them. But the disciples forbade them,*[20] and the rest. It is strange[21] that the disciples had forbidden small children to come to Christ, who were brought to him so that he might lay his hands on them and pray for them. The substance of the Gospel,[22] as we have said, is accomplished between a realization of the present and the future, in the very middle of both. And it provides a suitable context[23] to show how an image from the past[24] corresponds to these events which took place. In reality, little children had been brought forward, but they were in reality prohibited. But these children also prefigure[25] the pagans to whom salvation was rendered through the

11. *quaestione,* here referring to the legitimacy of divorce and remarriage.
12. Mt 19.8–9.              13. Mt 19.10.
14. 1 Cor 7.10–11.            15. 1 Cor 7.12–40.
16. *Nobis circa eunuchos sermo sit et voluntas.* In other words, the renunciation of marriage.
17. One thinks of Origen (d. 253), who, according to Eusebius of Caesarea (*HE* 6.8.2), castrated himself lest there be any hint of scandal between him and his female pupils (!).
18. Mt 19.12.
19. *infantes.* Just as many MSS read *pueri* ("youths" or "young children").
20. Mt 19.13.
21. *novum.*             22. *res evangelica.*
23. *rationem.*
24. Lit., "of the future" (*futuri*). As found throughout the Old Testament.
25. *forma* or "figure."

hearing of faith.[26] Because of the objective that Israel should be saved first of all,[27] the children were prohibited by the disciples from approaching. Of course the notion that they should be prohibited conflicts with the apostles' graciousness.[28] The point of prohibiting the little children was the fulfillment of a type.[29] The Lord said that they should not be prohibited because for such is the Kingdom of heaven.[30] Now the gift and the offering of the Holy Spirit through the laying-on of hands and prayer[31] are bestowed on the pagans because the works of the Law are ended.

4. *And behold, a man came up to him and said to him, "Teacher, what good should I do so that I may have eternal life?"*[32] and the rest. After the preceding passage where the little children were prohibited and it was said that for such is the Kingdom of heaven, it is fitting that there follows the young man seeking what good works he needed for eternal life. This young man also asked a question[33] in a haughty manner and was, in turn, disappointed.[34]

All these things that were written did occur and were done as reported.[35] But we have taught that whatever happens according to God's [plan] prefigures, by means of present realities, what is to follow. In the heavenly Scriptures every word was always carefully chosen[36] so that the events which happened completely agree with what is going to take place. This young man prefigures the Jewish people, who are arrogant in their use of the Law and who, apart from the precepts of Moses,

26. Rom 10.17.

27. Cf. Rom 1.16; 2.10; 9.3–5.

28. Lit., "readiness to forgive" (*placabilitati*). See Tertullian, *De praescr. haer.* 20.8, remarking that the role of apostolicity was to bring peace.

29. *typicam consummationem.* That is, they served as a symbol. Cf. *supra*, 7.9; 12.24; 14.16; 17.8; 19.1; *et passim*.

30. Mt 19.14.

31. Cf. Acts 8.14–17.

32. Mt 19.16. Some of the Old Latin MSS begin with the greeting "Good Teacher."

33. Like the Pharisees earlier (19.7).

34. Mt 19.22.

35. That is, the narrative should be taken literally or as historical events.

36. *temperatum.*

await for no hope at all from Christ. It is to them that the Lord bore witness[37] to the severity of future judgment when he says in response: *Why do you call me good?*[38] While it is necessary for him to punish impiety and iniquity, he refrains from the term "good,"[39] reserving this term for God the Father alone.[40] It is he [the Father] who, by delivering the right of judgment to him [Christ], removed from himself the utterance of this severe [retort];[41] not because Christ was not himself good,[42] but because it was appropriate that, as the future judge, he took severe measures against the young man.[43]

5. This young man, possessing an arrogance from the Law and anxious about his salvation, is sent back to the Law so that he would understand that, in this very Law in which he boasted,[44] he had performed no works of righteousness at all.[45]

---

37. *protestatus est.*          38. Mt 19.17.
39. *bonitatis.*
40. Hilary registers no awareness of Arius's letter, which stated outright that the Father is alone good, as Hilary will later quote in *De trin.* 4.12 (Arius's letter): "We confess one God, alone unmade, alone eternal, alone unoriginate, alone possessing immortality, alone good, alone mighty, Creator, Ordainer, and Disposer of all things" (see Latin ed. of Smulders, SC 448.32); cf. 9.2. Moreover, when Hilary treats the same passage in *De trin.*, he is much more circumspect about its subordinationist interpretations. See *De trin* 1.29: "The infidels (*inpiis*) ... are accustomed to bring forward the expressed words of the Lord, 'Why do you call me good? There is no one good except the one God.' When the man claimed that he is good, the Lord bore witness that no one except God is good, and he is good [though] apart from God's goodness, and he is not in reality he who is One" (Smulders ed., SC 443.254); 4.8: "Then [they say] that he [Father] alone is wise, while nothing remains of the Son's wisdom ... Then that he [the Father] is alone good, while there is no goodness in the Son because it was said by him, 'There is no one good except the one God'" (Smulders ed., SC 448.24); 9.15: "For types of each utterance can be safely discerned since the sole faith may be professed that he is Word and flesh, that is, God and man, Jesus Christ. The heretics believe it is necessary to deny that our Lord Jesus Christ was by nature God because he said, 'Why do you call me good? No one is good except the one God'" (Smulders ed., SC 462.44).
41. Lit., "the function of severity" (*officio severitatis*). See n.34.
42. This remark is easily understood in light of Tertullian's refutation of the division posed by the Marcionites between the Father and Son in terms of one God of judgment and another as good God (*Adv. Marc.* 1.6.1). Tertullian argues that God is judge and good (*Adv. Marc.* 2.23.3). *Sur Matt.* II.95, n.14.
43. The emphasis is not merely on the Son's equality of goodness, but that his judgment of the young man is good because it was derived from the Father.
44. Mt 19.20.          45. Rom 9.31–32.

In fact, the Lord responded to him in the words of the Law.[46]
But the youth, just like his arrogant and boastful people,[47]
put confidence in the Law, although nothing happened from
his compliance with it. He had been commanded not to murder,[48] yet he killed the prophets; he had been commanded not
to commit adultery, yet he introduced corruption of the faith
and adultery into the Law, and worshiped strange gods; he had
been commanded not to steal, yet (before Christ could restore
him to the freedom of believing by faith) he broke the teachings of the Law by committing theft; he had been commanded
not to bear false testimony, yet he denied that Christ was raised
from the dead; he was commanded to honor his father and
mother,[49] yet he has separated himself from the family of God
the Father and from the Mother Church.[50] He was instructed to
love his neighbor just as himself, yet he persecuted Christ (who
assumed our common body and, in that bodily state, became
a neighbor to each one of us) as far as the punishment of the
cross. The young man was, therefore, told to return to the Law
after renouncing and forsaking all his sins.

6. But the young man responded that he had done all
these things from the time of his youth and now sought what
remained for him to do.[51] As we said, he had not done those
things to which he was directed earlier, but boasting in them,
he spoke as if he had accomplished them. The Lord responded
that he should sell all of his goods and give them to the poor,
and then he would be perfect and have treasure in heaven.[52]
This statement, in response to the youth, is a most beautiful
and especially useful teaching for us to forsake the world,
because the loss of earthly substance is the gain of heavenly
wealth. By being commanded to sell his goods and give them to
the poor, he is being told to forsake his confidence in the Law
and to exchange it in a happy trade. We should remember that
there is a shadow of the truth in this exchange which should

46. Mt 19.18–19.                    47. Rom 2.17–24.
48. Mt 19.18.                       49. Mt 19.19.
50. Cf. Cyprian, *De unit. eccl.* 6; *De lapsis* 9.
51. Mt 19.20.                       52. Mt 19.21.

be divided among the poor, that is, to the pagans in the body of the truth itself.[53] No one is able to realize this fact except for the one who begins to follow Christ.

7. But once the young man heard these things, he went away sad,[54] for he had a great deal of confidence in the Law on account of his wealth.[55] In this situation there is also a plausible figurative reason[56] being observed: though the text identified this one as a youth, he himself said earlier that from the entire period of his youth he had observed the teaching in the Law. Adolescence occurs within one's youth, and the later stage[s] of life cannot be circumscribed[57] within this earlier period.[58] Because the young man had observed the Law since his youth, it shows that a long time has already passed for the people [who remained] in the works of the Law.

8. Seeing the young man's disappointment at this point, the Lord responded that it was difficult for a rich man to come into the Kingdom of heaven.[59] As we said,[60] the rich man—or Israel —boasts in the confidence of the Law.[61] Entry into heaven is difficult for a vain people[62] who cling to the ancient riches [of the Law] in their ostentation under the name of Abraham.

9. In fact, the Lord adds further that a camel can more easily pass through the opening of a needle than for a rich man

53. Or "of himself," *sub ipsius veritatis corpore*, perhaps implying the Incarnation.

54. Mt 19.22.

55. While Hilary's remark *ex lege* is obscure, he seems to be linking the young man's confidence in the Law and in his wealth, neither of which could bring him the salvation he sought.

56. *typicae efficientiae ratio.*

57. *contineri.*

58. Doignon points out the classical division of life stages fixed by Varro and reported by Maurus Servius Honoratus, *Commentary on the Aeneid of Vergil*, 5.295: *infantia, pueritia, adulescentia, iuventus,* and *senectus.* Hilary is simply observing, in literalist fashion, that the terminology of 19.16–22, in which an *adulescens* could be said to observe the Law as a *iuvenis*, is seemingly contradictory and must have a particular purpose. *Sur Matt.* II.97, n.19.

59. Mt 19.23.                          60. *Supra*, 19.6.

61. Cf. Ps 49.6.                       62. *inanis prosapiae.*

to enter the Kingdom of heaven.[63] To possess things is not a crime; rather, the issue is about how one is supposed to preserve his possessions. How are we supposed to share, and how are we supposed to hold things in common[64] if we do not relinquish those material things to be shared and to be held in common? It is, therefore, a worse crime to possess things for their own sake[65] than [merely] to possess things. But it is a dangerous matter to want riches when innocence is violated by the heavy burden of being occupied with accumulating wealth. On the contrary, serving God is not pursuing the things of the world without [also sharing in] the sins of this world. For this reason it is difficult for a rich man to enter the Kingdom of heaven.

Because many people can use their possessions justly, an underlying principle is preserved according to the word of the Lord: it is not that no one at all is able to enter the Kingdom of heaven. We must, rather, understand how few will enter because of hardships involved in this matter. And while this point presents a simple explanation for our understanding, we should observe the ordering of a deeper purpose[66] in this very issue.

10. The arrogant young man, as we said, plunged into disappointment and sorrow when he was told to give up the Law. So too the cross and the Passion are a stumbling block to this people, because there is no salvation in the cross or Passion for them. He boasts in the Law[67] and despises the pagans as co-heirs,[68] refusing to cross over to the freedom of the Gospel. This is why it is difficult for him to enter the Kingdom of heaven. For there were few (compared to the multitude of pagans) among them [the Jews] who were going to believe. It was difficult to bend the will of those who have been hardened by the Law to the preaching of the Gospel's humility.

11. A camel will more easily pass through the opening of a needle, although a camel cannot fit through the opening of a

---

63. Mt 19.24.
64. Acts 2.44.
65. *illud ipsum.*
66. *interioris causae.*
67. Rom 2.23.
68. Gal 3.29.

needle, nor can a huge unsightly beast be fit into the narrowest passage of the smallest hole. But in the beginning of our book,[69] we have suggested that the pagans are signified by the camel under the guise of John's [the Baptist's] clothing. This animal obeys the words spoken to it, is controlled by fear, endures times of want, and, with a certain amount of teaching, yields to burdens placed upon it. By way of comparison, the barbarity of the pagans is becoming tamed[70] to obey heavenly instruction.[71] They are entering the very narrow way of the Kingdom of heaven,[72] namely, the "needle," which is the preaching of the new Word.[73] By this needle the wounds of the body are mended, the tears of clothing are woven anew, and death itself is stung.[74] This is the way of the new preaching; the infirmity of the pagans will enter it more easily than the opulence of the rich man, that is, one who boasts in the Law.

69. *Supra,* 2.2.

70. Lit., "softened" (*emollitur*).

71. Cf. Novatian, *De cib. Iud.* 3: "So it is in the animals: according to law, a certain mirror of human life was established" (see PL 3:986C).

72. Cf. Mt 7.13–14.

73. *verbi novi,* i.e., the Gospel.

74. 1 Cor 15.55.

## CHAPTER TWENTY

FTER THEY HEARD these things, the disciples were astonished and troubled, saying that no one can be saved.[1] The Lord responded that what is impossible with men is possible with God.[2] They in turn said to the Lord that they had left everything in order to be with him.[3] The Lord promised them that when he sits upon his throne in majesty, they will sit upon twelve thrones and will judge the same number of the tribes of Israel.[4] For anyone who leaves everything for his name's sake, there are reserved benefits one hundredfold. The many who are last will be first, and those who are first will be last.[5]

2. There are many things that disallow us from accepting the words of the Gospel in a simple sense. Because some facts have been inserted into the text that contradict each other according to the nature of human common sense,[6] we are urged to seek the underlying principle of its heavenly meaning.

The apostles say that they had left everything in order to follow Christ. Why then did they become troubled and fearful by claiming that no one can be saved? If they themselves could have done anything, others should have been able to do it as well. Furthermore, if they could have done some [good work], why would they be fearful at all? In the Lord's response, he added this point: that with man it is impossible; with God it is possible.[7] Would not the things impossible with men be those

---

1. Mt 19.25.       2. Mt 19.26.
3. Mt 19.27. Peter says this.       4. Mt 19.28.
5. Mt 19.29.
6. Hilary is not referring to heretical interpolations, but observing that Scripture contains contradictory or senseless statements if read in the literal sense. Since the unveiling of Scripture is by God's design, we are compelled to look for its spiritual or "heavenly" meaning.
7. Mt 19.26.

same things which the apostles nevertheless boasted they had done and which the Lord acknowledged they had done? And finally, were most of them going to leave everything for the blessedness of martyrdom?[8] Or is it possible for God to need anything?[9] Is there anything that remains lost that God has to find, culminating in some action that he alone is committed to take? All of this is for spiritual consideration.[10]

3. The apostles heard in a spiritual sense that no one can be saved by the Law, even though they themselves were still in the Law. They strongly embraced a love of and favor for the Law. Due to the fact that they had not yet inwardly been convicted by the truth of the Gospel's mystery, they were afraid no one could be saved without the Law. At that time they also based their salvation entirely on the Law. But with brief and clear reasoning, the Lord freed them from their ignorance and fear saying: *This is impossible with man but it is possible with God.*[11] Would it not seem just as ineffective[12] for the Jews to wait for salvation through the agency of a man more than from the Law,[13] as it would be for them to disregard their legislation, their covenant, their adoption, and their heredity[14] because of the scandal of the cross?[15] But what is more possible for the power of God than to save by faith,[16] to regenerate through water,[17] to conquer through the cross,[18] to adopt us on account of the Gospel,[19] to raise to life what was dead through the resurrection?[20]

---

8. *usque ad martyrii beatitudinem.* Cf. Tertullian, *De praescr. haer.* 36.3.

9. Cf. Acts 17.25: "... nor is he served by human hands, as though he needed anything, since he himself gives to all men life and breath and everything" (RSV).

10. *hic sermo est spiritalis.*

11. Mt 19.26. Hilary has omitted the *omnia* ("all things") which appears in the Old Latin; see *supra,* 20.1.

12. *sine effectu.*          13. Moses.

14. See Rom 9.4.

15. Cf. Gal 5.11: "But if I, brethren, still preach circumcision, why am I still persecuted? In that case the stumbling-block of the cross has been removed" (RSV).

16. Rom 3.27–28; 5.1.          17. I.e., baptism.

18. Cf. Rom 3.25–26.          19. Rom 8.14–15.

20. See Rom 6.3–4 for the paradigm Hilary is using for his last sentence.

4. After hearing these words,[21] the apostles immediately believe and profess that they have left everything.[22] No less does the Lord immediately reward their obedience, clarifying every difficulty of their earlier question when he says: *You who have followed me in regeneration will judge the twelve tribes of Israel.*[23] For they followed him in the washing of baptism,[24] in the sanctification of faith, in the adoption of heredity, in the resurrection from the dead. Such is the regeneration that the apostles have followed, which the Law cannot produce, but it united the apostles (as they sit upon twelve thrones in judgment of the twelve tribes of Israel) with the glory of the twelve patriarchs.[25] To others who likewise follow him in contempt of the world, a hundredfold benefit is promised.[26] This hundredfold benefit is fulfilled by the finding of the hundredth sheep resulting in heavenly joy.[27] This hundredfold benefit is the richness of a perfect land which will be provided; an honor has now been destined for the Church in the name of Sarrah,[28] which is merited by the sacrifice of the Law and by the faith of the Gospel. Thus those who are last will be made first, because those who are first will become last.[29]

5. *The Kingdom of God is like the master of the house*[30] *who went out early in the morning to hire workers,*[31] etc. The construction of the whole parable[32] is clear in itself though we need to distinguish the persons mentioned as well as determine its circumstances. The master of the house should be understood as our Lord Jesus Christ, who, having concern for the entire human race, calls people in every age to respect[33] the Law.[34] We un-

21. Mt 19.26.                    22. Mt 19.27. Cf. Rom 10.17.

23. Mt 19.28. Hilary seems to have compressed the wording of the verse in order to stress its highlights.

24. *lavacro baptismi,* which seems to be a pleonasm.

25. Cf. Acts 7.8; Victorinus of Poetovio, *Comm. in Apoc.* 7, who describes the twenty-four elders of Rv 5.14 as the twelve apostles and the twelve patriarchs.

26. Mt 19.29.

27. Drawing on Lk 15.3–7.

28. Sarah is a type of the Church; see *supra,* 18.6. Rom 4.18–24.

29. Mt 19.30; 20.16.                    30. *homini patri familias.*

31. Mt 20.1.                    32. *comparatio omnis.*

33. *ad culturam legis.*

34. Compare Tertullian, *Adv. Iud.* 2.2, who speaks of a universal law that

derstand the vineyard is supposed to signify the practice of the Law, which is obedience. The denarius[35] indicates the reward of that obedience. We have already treated the matter of the denarius at an earlier point.[36] But concerning the vineyard, we will establish the reason at a more suitable point in what follows.[37] The marketplace,[38] just like the world, suggests that our state of affairs has to be accepted as it is. It is always and generally agitated by crowds of people where there are disputes of deceitful and harmful practices and problems stemming from different sorts of interests.

6. In the first hour, signified by the morning,[39] we should recognize the covenant established with Noah, then with Abraham at the third hour,[40] with Moses at the sixth hour,[41] and at the ninth hour with David and the prophets.[42] If we count the number of covenants established for humanity through individuals, so there are enumerated in the marketplace those who went out.[43] At the eleventh hour[44] the Lord shows the time of his advent in the body. His birth from Mary, which had been determined to take place during the present age out of all ages, pertains to that eleventh hour of the day. In fact, when one divides all 6,000[45] years by the number 500, the time of his birth in the flesh is computed according to a counting of the whole divided by elevens.[46]

---

God gave to all nations, starting with Adam, and that later took the form of the Mosaic Law.

35. Mt 20.2.

36. *Supra,* 17.13.

37. *Supra,* 22.1.

38. Mt 20.3.

39. Mt 20.1.

40. Mt 20.3.

41. Mt 20.5.

42. A somewhat similar scheme is elaborated by Victorinus of Poetovio, *De fab. mundi* 3, for the concept of seven epochs in covenantal history according to the seven ages of human history. See Lactantius, *De divinarum institutione* 7.14, on the six ages of the world (6,000 years) corresponding to the days of its creation.

43. That is, into the vineyard.

44. Mt 20.9. The eleventh hour or 5:00 PM.

45. The six ages, or 6,000 years, since creation.

46. See Hippolytus, Frag. from *De Daniel* 2.4–6. Christ is said to have been born after 5,500 years of human history, leaving 500, which will complete the designated 6,000 years before the end of the age. Hilary is drawing on this calculation as a given. Hippolytus states, "Christ appeared in the world, bear-

7. Then there is the distinctive word spoken at the eleventh hour to the various workers. To the first ones as well as to the others, it is said: *Go into the vineyard*[47] (although the remuneration was set at a denarius for the first ones while the others had the promised hope of a just payment).[48] It is also said to the last workers: *Why are you standing here?*[49] This is because, although the Law had been given to Israel, benevolence[50] toward the pagans was not excluded from the Law.

They responded: *No one has hired us.*[51] It was necessary that the Gospel be preached throughout the whole world, and that the pagans be saved by the justification of faith.[52] It is they who are sent into the vineyard. And when it began to get late, the workers of the evening hour[53] were the first to obtain the payment as determined by a whole day's work. Payment is not the same thing as a gift[54] because it is owed for work rendered, whereas God has freely granted his grace to everyone by the justification of faith.[55] But much like the arrogance of the rebellious people at that time under Moses, there was grumbling now on the part of the workers.[56] On this occasion there was jealousy over a remuneration freely given because the same wage was rendered to workers who did not experience the difficulties of long labor and did not have to endure the blazing heat (which is associated with the devil under the designation of "summer"). But again, what with man is impossible, is possible with God.[57] As a reward for the Law's excellence and

---

ing the imperishable ark, his own body. At a time which was the fifth and half, John declares: 'Now it was the sixth hour' (Jn 19.14), intimating by that one-half of the day. But a day with the Lord is 1000 years, and the half of that, therefore, is 500 years. For it was fitting that He should appear earlier, for the burden of the Law still endured, nor yet when the sixth day was fulfilled, but on the fifth and half" (ANF 5.179).

47. Mt 20.4, 7.                          48. Mt 20.4.
49. Mt 20.6.                             50. *voluntas*. Cf. Rom. 4.11–12.
51. Mt 20.7.

52. This passage in the Gospel is the high point of Hilary's proof that justification is unmerited and so comes by faith. *Supra,* 5.7; 8.6; 11.8, 10; 12.22; *et passim.*

53. That is, the workers hired last.

54. Lit., "not derived from a gift" (*ex dono nulla est*).

55. Rom 3.24.                            56. Mt 20.11.
57. Lk 1.37.

blameless preservation, God bestows the gift of grace by faith on those who believe, whether they are first or last.

8. *And as Jesus was going up to Jerusalem, he took the twelve disciples aside and said to them: "Behold, we are going up to Jerusalem,"*[58] etc. At this point the Lord explains the mystery[59] of the cross to the apostles who were ready to listen without stumbling.[60] In the end no sadness followed these words.[61] In fact, they were strengthened by his earlier words that by faith in the cross, the last will be the first.[62] For the rich, that is, for those who are confident in the Law, and scandalized by the same cross, the way of the Kingdom of heaven will be impassable.

9. *Then the mother of the sons of Zebedee came to him with her sons,*[63] and the rest. We should understand that this request was no small thing that the mother of the sons of Zebedee asked of the Lord. Didn't her sons know what she was seeking? But this happened so that the events prophesied in the past would be realized.[64]

The apostles had already come to faith on the basis of the Law, which prepared them to believe in the Gospel. The mother of the sons of Zebedee should be understood as the Law because the Law, confident of its privileged status,[65] was an advocate for those whose faith was drawn only from the Law. When she heard earlier that the first shall be last, and the last shall be first,[66] she asked that her sons be preferred in the Lord's Kingdom so that one may sit at his right hand and the other on his left.[67] The Lord responded that she did not know what she was asking[68] (for his earlier words had left no doubt concerning the glory of the apostles and that they were going to be judges).[69] In the midst of the discussion, the Lord asked whether they were

---

58. Mt 20.17–18.     59. *sacramentum.*
60. *scandalo.* As they stumbled earlier, in Mt 16 (*supra*, 16.10).
61. *Supra*, 17.9.     62. Mt 20.16.
63. Mt 20.20.
64. That a spiritual understanding of what was spoken should be unfolded.
65. To sit on God's right and left hands.
66. Mt 19.30.     67. Mt 20.21.
68. Mt 20.22.     69. Mt 19.28.

able to drink his cup.[70] He certainly was not speaking of the type of commonly used cup since there is no effort in drinking from it. Rather, he was asking about the sacramental cup of his Passion.[71] For those who already attained the freedom and resolve of a martyr,[72] it is promised that they will drink of this cup. Extolling their faith, the Lord says that they are able to suffer with him in martyrdom, but to sit at his left or right had been prepared for others by God the Father.[73]

10. As far as we know, that honor[74] has indeed been reserved for others,[75] although the apostles will not be prevented from sharing in it, seeing how they will sit on the throne of the twelve patriarchs and judge Israel.[76] And to the degree that we are allowed to investigate the [text of the] Gospels, [we believe] Moses and Elijah will sit in the Kingdom of heaven. Because the Lord promised that some of the apostles, before they tasted death, were going to see the Son of Man coming in his Kingdom,[77] he took along Peter, James, and John. He appeared to them on the mountain in his glorious raiment in the company of Moses and Elijah.[78] We understand that these are the same two prophets who preceded his advent, of whom the Revelation of John says they must be killed by the Antichrist.[79] There exist, however, varied and sundry opinions concerning whether the second of the two was Enoch or Jeremiah, since he was supposed to die just as Elijah.[80] But we are not able by our own opinion to tamper with the certainty of the truth which the Lord has revealed by the three preceding witnesses.[81] Nor

70. Mt 20.22.

71. Lit., "cup of his mystery of passion" (*calice sacramenti passionis*).

72. Cf. *supra*, 10.21; Tertullian, *Ad mart.* 2, contrasting the darkness and shackles of the prison with the martyr who bears light and is made free by God. See *Ad mart.* 6 for the resolve of the martyr.

73. Mt 20.23.

74. Of sitting at his left or right hand.

75. I.e., the martyrs.          76. See Rv 18.20; 21.14.

77. Mt 16.28.          78. Mt 17.2–3.

79. Rv 11.3–7.

80. Mt 16.14. Cf. Tertullian, *De anima* 50.5, who claims the two prophets are Elijah and Enoch, whereas Victorinus is willing to identify only one of the two as Elijah, *In Apoc.* 11.3.

81. Mt 17.4.

should we think that any others are going to come than those who have been seen coming in the promise of faith. Although it is unnecessary to speculate beyond the Gospel's truth,[82] if anyone should focus attention on the matter of Moses' death and burial,[83] or if one has obtained knowledge of secret scriptures according to the authority of an apostle,[84] he will understand that everything has been dealt with [in Scripture], just as Moses was made visible.[85] And so these things[86] are spoken for the purpose of our instruction.

11. Furthermore, the mother asked the Lord about her two sons so that a reason of spiritual understanding might be fulfilled. For these are the two callings of Israel: one, of the disciples of John; and the other, of the Pharisees by means of the apostles.[87] We read earlier how, after the passion of John, his disciples went over to the Lord.[88] It is for this purpose that supplication is made for two of them: they are a double calling[89] that believed in the Gospel of Christ.

Afterwards, the [other] ten disciples were troubled by the incident of the two brothers,[90] though there was no regret[91] on the part of the two disciples. The reason[92] for this does not mean that there was regret on the disciples' part because of the insult of the other two. Of course, the ten disciples could have felt sorry for themselves, since the Lord's refusal in the case of the two disciples seemed to be a refusal to them all. But a typological pattern[93] has been presented here.

82. Cf. Tertullian, *De praescr. haer.* 14.3: "To know nothing against the rule [of faith] is to know everything."

83. I.e., both manner and burial are not disclosed in Scripture.

84. "Secret scriptures" is a reference to those texts commonly accepted by gnostics as authoritative since they bear the name of an apostle, e.g., *Gospel of Thomas, Apocryphon of John.* See Irenaeus's argument about the illegitimacy of secret or previously unknown apostolic texts: *Adv. haer.* 3.11.9; 3.14.1.

85. Ex 34.33–34; cf. Tertullian, *De resurr.* 55.10.

86. I.e., the mother's inquiry in 20.9.

87. Probably an allusion to Paul, who was a Pharisee (Phil 3.5; Acts 23.6).

88. Mt 14.1–2.

89. The connection between the two sons and the two groups of disciples is not clear. Indeed, the entire section reveals a forced exegesis around the significance of the number two. See *infra*, 20.13.

90. Mt 20.24.

91. Lit., "sadness" (*maestitia*).

92. *ratio.*

93. *typicus ordo.*

The apostles were confident concerning themselves; they were troubled about the two others because they too desired these two callings,[94] which moved beyond the Law to the fellowship of this glory. Thus the passage directs us to an underlying principle, for both the present and the future. It was written not for their own sake, nor for the ten disciples, nor for the two who were anxious, but that the annoyance of the ten disciples over the other two would be suited to the matter of a present purpose.

12. Wishing to show us the significance[95] of this prefiguration as well as the presumption of those who would come from the Law and presume upon the prerogative of Israel's name, the Lord teaches that they should not exercise their pre-eminence[96] as the pagans do.[97] The glory of the greatest honor is shown by ministers and servants,[98] not by those who have been served. Such is found by the example of the patriarchs and the prophets who served, by the example of the apostles who ministered, and also by the example of the Lord, who yielded his life for the redemption of our salvation.[99]

In light of the glory of this humility, he instructs them by means of a meal or a banquet, reminding them not to recline at the more eminent places of the table, lest someone who is more distinguished come along and they suffer the insult of being humiliated by the master of the meal asking them to give up their place.[100] If they recline at a modest place at the table to begin with, they might be moved up to the prominence of a more elevated place[101] when more lowly guests come along. And thus it is not right to presume upon any honor, but to merit it by one's works of humility.[102]

---

94. Mt 20.21.

95. *proprietatem.*

96. *principatum.*

97. Mt 20.25.

98. Mt 20.26–27.

99. Mt 20.28.

100. Hilary is glossing the Matthean text with the parable from Lk 14.8–11.

101. There is a slight paronomasia in Hilary's phrasing of *accedet* ("move up") with *decedet* ("give up") of the previous sentence.

102. Cf. Cyprian, *Test.* 3.5, which presents a catena of Gospel passages (mainly from Matthew and Luke) on the necessity of humility and shunning the behavior of the proud, who "love the first place of reclining at feasts" (Mt 23.6–8). ANF 5.534.

13. *And as they were leaving Jericho, a large crowd followed him, and behold, two blind men who were sitting along the road heard that Jesus was passing by,*[103] etc. We saw earlier in the figure of the two sons of Zebedee how the people of Israel, who had originated from the seed of Shem, were being treated.[104] It is appropriate that the two blind men who were sitting along the road are two peoples of the pagans originating from Ham and Japheth, who observed[105] the Lord's route of departure and asked that their sight be restored.[106] Then the crowd ridiculed them because of their cries and harshly told them to be silent. This was not because the crowd regarded silence itself as a sign of respect,[107] but because they heard bitterly from blind men what they denied, namely, that the Lord is the Son of David.[108] When the minds of the blind were illumined, God in man was proclaimed. So it was true what the Lord said: "For judgment I have come into this world that they who see may not see, and they who are blind may see."[109]

Although they were hindered by the people of the Law, *they cried even more,*[110] bearing witness to the fervor of their faith ever more strenuously. The Lord took pity and asked them what they wanted.[111] They asked that their eyes be opened. Having pity, he touched their eyes and restored their vision which is the knowledge of God. In order that a figure[112] of the pagans called to believe find fulfillment and receive the knowledge of heavenly grace, those who had been blind saw the Lord and followed him.[113]

---

103. Mt 20.29–30a. Hilary typically joins the two verses into one with a conjunction.

104. *Supra*, 8.4; 20.11.

105. Rather humorously Hilary says that the two blind men "observed" (*observant*) the Lord's movements.

106. Mt 20.33.

107. *silentium causa honoris.*

108. Mt 20.30.

109. Jn 9.39.

110. Mt 20.31.

111. Mt 20.32.

112. *typus.*

113. Mt 20.34.

# CHAPTER TWENTY-ONE

**T**HEN JESUS *sent two of his disciples saying, "Go to the village which is ahead of you,"*[1] etc. Two disciples are sent to the village in order to loosen a donkey tied up with her colt and lead them to the Lord.[2] If anyone should ask why they are doing this, the disciples are supposed to respond that they are necessary to the Lord and must be brought immediately.[3]

Considering the earlier passage in which we remember that the double calling of Israel was signified in the two sons of Zebedee,[4] it is now appropriate that two disciples are appointed to untie the donkey and the colt because a double calling[5] was extended to the pagans. They were and are from the Samaritans, who formerly originated by separating from the Law,[6] though still by custom they had continued to observe it.[7] They were also a wild and ferocious pagan people.[8] Two disciples are sent, therefore, to untie those who have been bound and held captive, shackled by the chains of error and ignorance.

The two are sent from outside Jerusalem because it is from outside of the city that these two callings are realized. In contrast, the mother of the sons of Zebedee sought the Lord within Jerusalem because there is a dual calling that comes from the Law. Israel is saved through the apostles and through John,[9] but Samaria has also believed through Philip;[10] however, Cor-

---

1. Mt 21.1b–2.      2. Mt 21.2.
3. Mt 21.3.
4. *Supra,* 20.11. Cf. Tertullian, *Adv. Marc.* 3.13.9; *Adv. Iud.* 9.13.
5. *duplex ... vocatio.*
6. Ezra 4.10. Peoples from various nations were settled on formerly Jewish lands. See Mt 10.5.
7. Jn 4.20–22.
8. 2 Kgs 17.29–34. Child sacrifice was still being practiced by the Samaritans even as they adhered to the Mosaic Law.
9. *Supra,* 20.11.
10. Acts 8.5–8.

nelius, the firstfruits of the pagans, was led to Christ through Peter.[11]

The disciples are instructed to respond, to anyone who asks, that the two animals are needed by the Lord and that they must be released immediately.[12] This means that preachers of the Gospel faith should be sent back to their own nations. Thus the prophecy was fulfilled which was announced: the Lord is going to enter Jerusalem, mounted on a donkey and a young colt.[13]

What was prophesied finds its fulfillment in what happened. A donkey, so to speak, is untied from the village and presented [to the Lord]. This means that Samaria, oppressed by hostile and foreign domination, is unloosed by the apostles and returned to her Lord.[14] The Lord then mounted the colt, which was young, defiant, obdurate (all these are the sins of ignorance that dominate the pagans), and untamed in spirit, yet it is made a vehicle for God.[15]

2. This entire image comprises a pattern of the future, and its prefiguring is anticipated by metaphorical[16] expressions and by the situation of present events. In the advent of his glory, the Lord undertakes to rein in the pagans. By restraining their impulses (just like riding the colt), he will be preached by the entire body of his company of patriarchs, prophets, and apostles.[17] With their vestments, the patriarchs spread[18] their glory before the Lord (for it is by their generations, by their names,

---

11. Acts 10.34–48.                      12. Mt 21.3.

13. Mt 21.4–5. See Zec 9.9.

14. In the Matthean commentary of Fortunatianus of Aquileia, the donkey is said to represent the synagogue, whereas the colt is the people who believe, that is, the *futurum Christianum* (2.44; CCSL 9.369).

15. *vectio Deo.*

16. *parabolica,* a neologism (see Hilary, *De trin.* 9.70).

17. Cf. Fortunatianus, 2.53–56. The spreading of brambles before the Lord and shouting of "Hosanna" are said to signify "the preceding fathers [OT saints] who preached before him [the Lord], the apostles and others following them" (CCSL 9.369). See also Victorinus, *In Apoc.* 4.10, which identifies the crowd as two peoples: one of the patriarchs and the other of the prophets, who cast all their palms of victory under the feet of Christ.

18. Hilary makes repeated use of the verb *substerno* ("prostrate") in this section; it is found twice in his version of the Latin text, Mt 21.8, to show that each of the three groups of patriarchs, prophets, and apostles have strewn their "garments" before the Lord for their own purposes.

and by their persecutions that the Lord has been prophesied). By yielding to him the ornamentation of their dignity, they prostrate themselves before his seat.[19] They teach that all their glory had been devoted to the preparation of the Lord's advent. For this reason the prophets also spread their garments on the path of the one who is coming.[20] In this way they predicted how the pagans were going to carry[21] God. Each one of the prophets set his love of the world aside, offering himself to death and to stoning.[22] They cast off their bodies in this way, presented as the first step on so great a road.

After the apostles spread their garments, they scattered branches cut from trees. There is nothing in this act that is done out of a regard for human obligation. Indeed, the branches would entangle the way of one coming and confuse the route of anyone looking hurriedly for an entry. The entire prophetic reason, however, is explained, and a figure[23] of the future is preserved. There are the branches of the pagans, which are unfruitful; that is, the fruit of the pagans is a kind of unbelief which is spread by the apostles on the Lord's route. Yet the pagans are made righteous by the entry of the Savior, and he is come for their sakes. Using these barren branches, a very great honor[24] is offered to God as he comes along the road.

3. *The crowd that went ahead of him and those that followed shouted, "Hosanna, to the Son of David. Blessed is he who comes in the name of the Lord."*[25] Yet how is it that the crowd could praise so highly the one who had to be crucified, and how did he earn their hatred when he was favored earlier? Even their words of praise expressed the power[26] of redemption in him, for "Hosanna" in Hebrew indicates the redemption of the house of David.[27] They proclaimed that he was the Son of David in whom they recognized the lineage of the eternal Kingdom.[28] They lat-

19. Mt 21.7; Rv 4.10.
20. Mt 21.8.
21. *vecturarum.*
22. Heb 11.36–37.
23. *forma.*
24. *gratissimum … officium.*
25. Mt 21.9.
26. *potestatem.*
27. Doignon, *Sur Matt.* II.127, n.7. Jerome treats the etymology of the term, but see J. Daniélou's "Hilaire et ses sources juives," in *Hilaire et son temps* (Paris, 1969), 143–47.
28. Cf. 2 Sm 7.16.

er profess that he is "blessed in the name of the Lord," and yet they will shout out blasphemy with the words, "Crucify [him]."[29] But these present events point to a prefiguration of the future. Even if there are conflicting interpretations and differences in the account about how we should treat these matters, the process of heavenly realities gives assurance even to those who are unwilling [to see them]. Jerusalem, then, is stirred,[30] as the strange events brought confusion to the amazed crowd.

4. He entered the Temple;[31] that is, he entered the assembly where his preaching was presented.[32] This is where he first expelled all the abuses of the priestly office by the right of his authority,[33] since he handed over those things which were graciously offered by all the people.[34] The freedom of giving should not entail a corrupt priest in the buying or selling of anything. The Lord overturned the chairs[35] of the sellers of doves in particular.[36] What dignity is there in the selling of doves? What benefits are reserved for the commerce of those who traffic in these birds such that the sellers appropriate for themselves the honored seats?[37]

But in every text we remember that there are expressions made in such a way that we must consider the force of the words more deeply. By the dove, we understand the Holy Spirit in keeping with the example of prophecy.[38] By the chair, the priestly seat is indicated. The Lord overturns the chairs of those who are selling the gift of the Holy Spirit through whom God's ministry is performed.[39] We recall his weighty admonition contained in the words of the prophet: *It is written, "My house will be called a house of prayer," but you have made it a "den of thieves."*[40] There is no need to think that the Jews in the synagogue were able to buy the Holy Spirit's coming. For they did

---

29. Lk 23.21; Jn 19.6.

31. Mt 21.12.

33. *iure potestatis.*

35. *cathedras.*

37. Behind Hilary's question is his notion of the *cathedra*, where the bishop sat in the sanctuary before the congregation (who remained standing for the service).

38. Acts 2.4–20.

40. Mt 21.13 (Is 56.7; Jer 7.11).

30. Mt 21.10.

32. *traditae.*

34. Cf. Mt 10.8.

36. Mt 21.12.

39. Cf. Acts 8.18–24.

not have the Spirit such that they were able to sell it,[41] nor was it anything that someone could buy. Rather, the present words are a prefiguration of abuses within the Church that are to be purified at the time when the Lord comes in glory.

5. The Lord also healed the infirmities of the blind and the lame in the Temple[42] while the people favorably followed his public acts of healing. But the chief priests were envious of the children shouting.[43] They censured the Lord by asking why he listened to these things,[44] which declared that redemption had come to the house of David. He responded to them that they had not read: *"Out of the mouths of children and infants, you have perfected praise."*[45] Although the judgments of wise men may fail, this glorious confession of him was expressed by young children and infants, to whom belongs the Kingdom of heaven. Because wise men and rulers of the world have perverted the wisdom of God, small children and nursing babes will proclaim the new birth of Christ. With these words, he left the city and the chief priests and stayed in Bethany.[46] By abandoning the unbelieving synagogue, he tarries in the church of the pagans.

6. *In the morning as he was passing into the city, he was hungry, and seeing a single fig tree along the way, he came up to it,*[47] and the rest. The very same pattern of heavenly realities is anticipated here. A figure of the synagogue is presented by the fig tree. Once the opportunity for repentance is given—during the time between his Passion and his glorious return—he is hungry for the salvation of his people, though he will find them barren, covered only with leaves.[48] In other words, they are like one who vainly boasts but is devoid of fruit. Indeed, they are sterile of good works, destitute of an expected outcome. Because the time for repentance has passed, the sentence of heav-

---

41. Using the variant reading *vendere;* see *Sur Matt.* II.128. Cf. PL 9:1037D.
42. Mt 21.14.           43. Mt 21.15.
44. Mt 21.16a.         45. Mt 21.16 (Ps 8.3 LXX).
46. Mt 21.17.
47. Mt 21.18–19. Hilary joins two parts of these verses together.
48. That is, no figs.

enly judgment will "wither" them for all time.[49] Even in this we will find a proof of the Lord's goodness. When he wanted to produce an example of healing which he himself administered, he exercised the authority of his power[50] on human bodies,[51] entrusting future hope and the salvation of the soul to the curing of sicknesses. But when he wanted to establish an example[52] of his severity toward those who are defiant, he indicated the harm done to the tree as an image of the future. He did this in order to teach us the danger of unbelief though without losing those whom he had come to redeem.

7. The disciples were amazed that the tree had withered at the instant of his word.[53] Of course the efficacy of the present deed offered a figure of the future. When he comes in the heavenly Kingdom, at that same time as his advent, the barrenness[54] of the Jews' unbelief will follow a sentence of eternal condemnation. The Lord positively asserts that those, if they have faith, will be able to do not only these things, but even greater things.[55] To be sure, they are going to judge Israel according to the previous promises, but also have all power[56] over the devil,[57] who is called a "mountain." For the Lord says thus: *If you have faith, you will not only do what was done to the fig tree, but also if you say to this mountain, "Pick yourself up and throw yourself in the sea," it will happen.*[58] O great is the reward of faith, the merit on which the authority of the faithful is so highly exalted! They are going to judge all humanity with a sentence of the same severity so that they can cast down the loftiness and might of the devil into the world's condemnation.

8. We should consider how the synagogue is compared to the fig tree.[59] Obviously this tree flowers differently from oth-

---

49. I.e., as Jesus' judgment on the tree caused it to wither.
50. *virtutis suae potestatem.*          51. Mt 21.14.
52. *formam.*                            53. Mt 21.20.
54. Allusion to the fig tree.
55. Mt 21.21, with a gloss from Jn 14.12.
56. *ius.*                               57. Cf. Lk 9.1.
58. Mt 21.21.
59. See Doignon, *Hilaire de Poitiers,* 306, concerning the figure of fruit as metaphor.

er trees in both its nature and development.[60] Its first flower
is found in its fruit, but it is not here (once it emerges) that
one finds a mature fruit. These are first called unripe figs[61]
according to common usage and prophetic authority.[62] But afterwards there bursts open an abounding potency of internal
fecundity, a fruit of the same image and form. Upon bursting
open they put forth leaves and, once the roots by which they
were anchored have withered, the leaves fall off and those buds
which remain bring forth the fruit into maturity. If it happens
that these unripe fruits should emerge in the hollow of the
stalk which extends from the same branch, they always remain
as such, and, unlike the unripe figs, they fall off. Only ones
that remain attached precede the rest of the fruit in its maturity. And this tree will produce a most beautiful fruit, which,
emerging with the other unripe figs, comes forth from the
hard clump[63] in between both of the stalks. For this reason,
the likeness proposed of the development of the fig tree to the
synagogue[64] is appropriate and useful.[65]

9. By the example of the unripe figs, [we understand that]
the [Jewish] people's first fruit was lost which had bloomed in
the beginning. Because of this loss, God's infertile people were
pushed aside by the people of the pagans who remain faithful
and steadfast unto the consummation of the ages.[66] As the first
believers from Israel, the apostles, are fixed between the Law
and the Gospel like the unripe figs, they will precede the rest
in the glory and the timing of their resurrection. Already in the
beginning of Genesis, we find a figure of this fact when Adam
and Eve covered their shame[67] with the foliage of this tree, hiding themselves from the coming of the Lord, who called out
to them. Because the unbelieving synagogue transgressed the

---

60. *condicione.*                          61. Na 3.12.

62. *grossa*, or "first ripe."

63. *claviculus*, a neologism (Kinnavey, 5).

64. The Gospel text mentions the Temple, not a synagogue, in the present
context.

65. Tertullian, *De resurr.* 33.5, compares the fig tree to "Jewish sterility."

66. Perhaps a reference to the Church.

67. Gn 3.7.

commandment of the Law, it hides its foul shamefulness and disgraceful confusion under a pointless covering of words, like the foliage of the fig tree. These details on the nature of this tree have been interjected in order that the suitability of the comparison can be understood. Now we need to consider the remaining order of events.

10. The Pharisees had seen many things more worthy to call great miracles, but they were now especially worried, and asked the Lord by what authority he did these things.[68] Again, the presentation of these facts encloses a profound mystery[69] of the future. The Pharisees found it especially necessary to question him about events in which a foreshadowing[70] of general danger was expressed. The Lord responded that he would explain by what power he was doing these things,[71] if they would tell him whether they thought that John's baptism was of heaven or of men.[72] But they hesitated at the danger of giving a response. If they acknowledged that it was from heaven, they would be found guilty for not believing in the authority of heavenly testimony; if they said it was from men, they feared the crowd since many regarded John as a prophet.[73] So they responded by saying that they did not know[74] (they certainly knew it was from heaven), because they were afraid that an admission of truth would prove them wrong. Plainly they had spoken with the intention of deceiving him about themselves. Because of their unbelief they did not know John's baptism was from heaven. Even if John's baptism had been of human [origin], they could not know it, because he was not.

11. *A certain man had two sons,*[75] and the rest. There are many important facts that can confound our understanding unless we observe an order of what comes first and that which follows.

---

68. Mt 21.23.
69. *ingens ... arcanum.*
70. *praeformatio.* Cf. *supra,* 4.24; 16.3; *infra,* 24.7.
71. Mt 21.24.                    72. Mt 21.25.
73. Mt 21.26.                    74. Mt 21.27.
75. Mt 21.28.

For who can comprehend why the older son[76] refused to go to work but later changed his mind in repentance and went forth into the vineyard?[77] And still Israel did not repent, but brought its hands against the Lord and with unholy words altogether[78] crucified its God.

What shall we think of the younger son who promised to go but did not?[79] And yet, the people of the pagans and sinners brought to fulfillment what was promised. For they went out and went to the work to which they were called. How should we think about those who did not go?

12. Next it is necessary to ask what the importance of the Pharisees' response was. They said that the younger son had complied with the will [of his father].[80] The reason for their response is not clarified such that a feigned agreement could be regarded as a profession of the whole truth. It would be better to betray a promise made rather than to fulfill all [the terms] without a promise. For who does not prefer to deny himself of what he asks for, especially if he is going to receive it? It is better than when what was promised is not given. We are grateful when a deed is realized in desperation, whereas we are sorrowful when hope has been lost, unless perhaps the purpose of the one asking is satisfied by the flattery of those who make the promise.

13. It is important to remember that the theme[81] of this comparison originated from remarks first made about John.[82] As a

76. Calling the first son "older" (senior) or the second son "younger" (iunior) is not in the Latin biblical text.

77. Mt 21.29.

78. Lit., "in its entirety" (universitas).

79. Mt 21.30.

80. Mt 21.31. The text implies that they said it was the first son or the "older" one. Hilary's confusion and forced interpretation is perhaps due to the ambiguity of working in the Latin MSS for this verse. Whereas some versions identify the primus ("first" son), the more common reading is novissimus (along with the Vulgate), which is variously understood as "the most recent" (i.e., the former) or "the latest" (i.e., the latter). Hilary seems to have adopted the second interpretation.

81. propositionem.

82. Supra, 21.10.

result, the Lord's example rebuked their [the Pharisees'] hesi-
tation of unbelief and their resulting need to be silent. But just
as we have indicated elsewhere,[83] it is appropriate to remember here also that although an underlying principle for present events is sometimes lacking in the context, an image of the
future may be explained without losing any of the clarity[84] of
what is prefigured. The first son is the people who come from
the Pharisees,[85] who have been admonished to the present day
by God through the prophecy of John so that they might obey
his commandments. This people, arrogant and disobedient,
were rebellious according to the present text. Possessing assurance in the Law, they rejected the need for the repentance of
their sins because they gloried in the noble prerogative from
Abraham. After the Resurrection of the Lord, which followed
his miraculous works, they[86] repented and believed in the time
of the apostles. They stopped relying on their deeds for a com-
mitment[87] to the Gospel's mission. In repentance, they confessed the sin of their former arrogance.

14. The younger son is [represented by] the crowd of publicans and sinners,[88] those who remain in the previous condition of sin. Through John, they are commanded to wait for
the salvation of Christ and to believe after being baptized by
John.[89] When the Lord says that they[90] had promised to go and
did not do so,[91] he shows that the crowd had not believed in
John. In other words, the Lord indicates that they did not go
because they were not able to accept the teaching of the Gospel
through the apostles until after the Passion (the mysteries[92] of
human salvation had to be accomplished). To be sure, the Lord
does not say that they did not want to go, but that they did not
go. The issue goes beyond the fault of unbelief because the dif-

83. *Supra*, 12.1; 19.4.
84. *efficientiae*.
85. Cf. the scheme of the two callings of people from Israel (*supra*, 20.11).
86. Like the first son (Mt 21.29).        87. *ad voluntatem*.
88. Mt 21.31.                             89. Mt 21.32.
90. In the person of the first son (Mt 21.29).
91. Because of their unbelief (v.39).
92. *sacramento*.

ficulty did not lie in their actions. It is not that the [younger] son did not want to go straightaway to the work to which he was ordered, but because he was not able to go. In this situation,[93] we see how a necessary delay is shown without incriminating one's will.[94]

15. In the response of the Pharisees there is a certain prophetic mandate. They admitted, against their own will, that the son complied with his father's will.[95] In other words, the younger son professed obedience, although he did not then bring it to realization because faith alone justifies.[96] For this reason publicans and prostitutes will be first in the Kingdom of heaven.[97] Because they believed John,[98] they were baptized for the remission of sins: they confessed Christ's Advent, they offered praise for his healing works, they received the sacrament of his Passion, and they acknowledged the power of his Resurrection.[99] Nonetheless the chief priests and Pharisees, seeing these things, despised them; they were not justified by faith, nor did they return through repentance to salvation. This is why their fruit will always be withered under the curse prefigured in the fig tree.

93. In the case of the second son.
94. Hilary's concern is to explain literally how the son who refused to go at first could be exonerated and thus identified with those (vv.31–32) who were sinners but believed.
95. Mt 21.29.
96. *fides sola iustificat,* a phrase that will later be utilized by some of the sixteenth-century reformers. For this history, see D. H. Williams, "Justification by Faith: A Patristic Doctrine," *Journal of Ecclesiastical History* 56 (2006): 649–67.
97. Mt 21.31.
98. Mt 21.32.
99. Cf. Phil 3.10.

# CHAPTER TWENTY-TWO

ISTEN TO ANOTHER *parable.*[1] *There was a landowner*[2] *who planted a vineyard and surrounded it with a wall,*[3] *and dug a winepress in it, and built a tower,*[4] etc. The whole issue[5] is clear. Even the chief priests and Pharisees understood that this was spoken of them,[6] which made them angry. But the significance of the persons mentioned and the comparisons made should be explained.[7] Here we understand that God the Father is the landowner who has planted his people Israel in anticipation of an excellent harvest.[8] He enclosed them within his wall,[9] sanctified by the name of the fathers, that is, by the nobility of Abraham, Isaac, and Jacob—just as someone being surrounded with a special protection.[10] He also equipped the prophets, like a kind of winepress into which he pours the fruitfulness of the Holy Spirit, who creates fermentation of a new wine, so to speak.[11] With the tower he has built the eminence of the Law,[12] which takes us from the bottom to the height of heaven and enables us to fathom[13] Christ's advent. In the tenants[14] is an image of the chief priests and Pharisees to whom the authority of teaching has been granted.

---

1. Hilary's commentary at this point no longer follows the usual chapter divisions of this Gospel. Moreover, Hilary's chapters become, on the whole, shorter than those of the earlier ones.

2. *homo ... paterfamilias.*

3. *sepem.* All Old Latin versions read *saepe* or *saepem.*

4. Mt 21.33.                     5. *quaestio.*

6. Mt 21.45.

7. Lit., "brought forward" (*proferendae*).

8. Jer 2.21.                     9. Cf. Is 5.1–5; 56.5.

10. Cf. Jb 1.10.                11. Cf. Acts 2.13–17.

12. Cf. 2 Cor 3.10.            13. *speculari.*

14. Mt 21.33.

2. In the servants, who were sent to gather the fruit,[15] we see the advance of the prophets who had often and in various ways tried to recall [the people]. Later on, more were sent than the first time, when, after the preaching of a few individuals, a very great number of prophets together were sent out. These were at various times beaten, stoned, and killed,[16] because they sought the fruit of the people by shaping and instructing them. In the sending of the son last of all, we understand the Advent and Passion of our Lord, who was thrown out[17] of Jerusalem as out of the vineyard[18] according to a sentence of condemnation. The plan of the tenants and their claim on the inheritance, once they had killed the heir,[19] was the vain hope that the glory of the Law could be preserved after Christ had been slain. In the return of the landowners,[20] we see the glory of the Father's majesty appearing in the Son at the time of judgment.[21] And in the response to the chief priests and Pharisees,[22] the inheritance of the Law is more worthily handed over to the apostles.[23] Finally the Son is himself the stone which has been rejected by the builders but erected as the cornerstone and is marvelous in the eyes of all.[24] Between the Law and the pagans, he is the conjunction of both buildings.

3. *The Kingdom of heaven is like a king who prepared a wedding for his son and sent his servants to call those invited to the wedding,*[25] etc. We must distinguish in this parable different times and discern[26] different persons. Concerning the person of the king and his son, there is a clear understanding. But there is an unusual[27] reason that the Father had prepared the wedding for his son and had issued invitations in this way. For the wedding preparation is specific to both the provider and the timing of the wedding.[28] Here the wedding is the sacrament of heavenly

---

15. Mt 21.34.

16. Mt 21.35.

17. I.e., rejected.

18. Mt 21.39.

19. Mt 21.38–39.

20. Mt 21.40.

21. Mt 16.27.

22. Mt 21.43.

23. See *supra*, 20.9; 21.1.

24. Mt 21.42; cf. 1 Pt 2.6–7.

25. Mt 22.2–3.

26. *dignoscenda*.

27. *nova*.

28. ... *et auctoris et temporis est nuptiarum*.

life and eternal glory imparted in the resurrection.[29] It is very appropriate that the wedding has been prepared by the Father, seeing that an eternal fellowship and its betrothal to a new body is a union already perfected in Christ.[30] And here, as at a previous point when we treated the issue of divorce,[31] we suggest carefully considering how the reason for the resurrection has been signified.[32] We should not ignore carelessly what was said in the person of Adam to Eve because it is a great sacrament.[33]

4. Those who were urged to come to the wedding banquet, already being invited, are the people of Israel: they are called to the glory of eternity through the Law. The servants sent to call those invited are the apostles. It was their special role to recall those whom the prophets had invited. Those who are sent a second time[34] with the prescribed stipulations are the apostolic men,[35] are the successors of the apostles.[36] The fattened calves are a glorious image of the martyrs, who were sacrificed as chosen victims for their confession of God.[37] But these fattened [calves] are spiritual men who, just as birds which are fed by heavenly bread for flight, received a rich food for the feed-

---

29. Cf. Tertullian, *De resurr.* 53: "Has not the flesh even now (in this life) the spirit by faith? ... [The flesh] has the name of *animate* (or natural) body, expressly because of the higher substance of the soul (or *anima*) in which it is sown, destined hereafter to become ... the spiritual body, in which it is raised again" (ANF 3.587).

30. 1 Cor 15.53–57.

31. *Supra,* 19.2.

32. The "wedding" of the resurrection marks the union of the flesh and the spirit. Cf. Tertullian, *De anima* 41.4 (*Sur Matt.* II.146, n.12).

33. Cf. Eph 5.31 (Gn 2.24: "the two will become one in flesh"). The compaction of arguments in this section is admittedly dense.

34. Mt 22.4.

35. *apostolici.* Tertullian, *Adv. Marcionem* 4.2.2, makes the distinction between *apostoli* (pertaining to apostles, such as John and Matthew) and *apostolici* (pertaining to writers such as Luke and Mark).

36. E.g., the concept that Polycarp was appointed bishop by the Apostle John at Smyrna, or that Clement was ordained by Peter at Rome; see Tertullian, *De praescr. haer.* 32.2; Irenaeus, *Adv. haer.* 3.3.4.

37. The glory of the confession of the martyrs is well celebrated. See Tertullian, *Ad. mart.* 2; Cyprian, *Ep.* 22.1; *Acta* of Perpetua and Felicitas (conclusion).

ing of others. Once all these have been prepared and gathered into a multitude, whose number is pleasing to God, the glory of the heavenly Kingdom is announced, just as is the calling of a wedding banquet.[38]

5. There were also those who neglected the summons;[39] some were occupied with worldly ambition, illustrated by the "field,"[40] and many others were detained by business because of their love of money. Others inflicted injuries and killed the servants sent to them,[41] which we see fulfilled in the lives of the apostles. But the depth of such wickedness is followed by an appropriate vengeance. Heavenly armies will be sent to destroy their entire company by the judgment of God and will burn them with eternal fire,[42] because they violated the state[43] of humanity through their hatred and homicide.

6. Seeing how the Lord speaks in this parable concerning the time of judgment at the resurrection, he directed the same remarks to the company of the pagans. When those who were first invited were found unworthy,[44] he commands his servants to go out into the roads.[45] Indeed, crimes committed in the past are forgiven by the gift of grace[46] (for we have very often remarked that the "road" should be understood as the state of the world). For this reason the servants are commanded to go out into the roads because a reprieve[47] is granted to all. The king then orders that everyone without exception is to be invited to the wedding; the bad as well as the good are to come.[48] The invitation had been meant to make people good since it is holy and proceeded from the highest sentiment of the one who makes the invitation. And yet through a corrupt will that refused to be corrected,[49] we must have discernment for those who are called.

38. Cf. Rv 7.4; 19.9, which speaks of a fixed number of elect from the twelve tribes of Israel who are called to the wedding feast of the Lamb.

39. Mt 22.5.                          40. Ibid.
41. Mt 22.6.                          42. Mt 22.7.
43. *adfectum.*                       44. Mt 22.8.
45. Mt 22.9.                          46. Eph 2.2–5.
47. *retroacta.*                      48. Mt 22.10.
49. *inemendatae.*

7. Although pretense is customarily employed in the well-known art of deceiving others,[50] whether we are deceived either covertly by another's plans or by the naïveté of our own judgment, it cannot be hidden from God. But when God entered into the company of [those who shared in] that happy resurrection, he saw a man at the table without wedding clothes,[51] and asked how he had gotten in.[52]

Had a specific dress been stipulated for those who were invited? Furthermore, if it was ordered that anyone should be invited, how could a specific[53] kind of dress be prescribed for everyone?[54] Or, if particular apparel was usually customary for wedding guests, could the hosts and their servants be exempt from it? Because the ability of discerning duplicity is not given to everyone and because human naïveté does not easily recognize the fraudulence of a deceitful mind, God alone discovers this evil man and his unworthiness in the wedding assembly. The wedding garments represent the glory of the Holy Spirit, the radiance of heavenly garments[55] worn by those whose confession to the good question,[56] is permanently reserved immaculate and whole in the assembly of the Kingdom of heaven.[57] This is why the man [without wedding garments] was taken up and thrown into outer darkness:[58] many are called and few are chosen.[59] It is not, therefore, that few are invited, but that a small number are chosen. There is a common good[60] in inviting humanity without exception, whereas those who are invited are justly elected from a determination of their goodness.[61]

50. A common criticism made of rhetors; Augustine, *Conf.* 5.6.10; *De doct. Chr.* 4.7.16–18.

51. Mt 22.11.                                  52. Mt 22.12.

53. *unus.*

54. Perhaps an echo of 1 Cor 15.40–44: "but the glory of the celestial is one, and the glory of the terrestrial is another" (v.40b, RSV).

55. Rv 19.8.

56. 1 Tm 6.12. Doignon (*Sur Matt.* II.151) sees here an allusion to the *interrogatio* at baptism, where the candidate answered by reciting the Church's creed. Cf. Tertullian, *De bapt.* 13.2; *De cast.* 20.7.

57. 1 Pt 1.4; Tertullian, *De bapt.* 10.7; 18.6.

58. Mt 22.13.                                  59. Mt 22.14.

60. *publicae bonitatis.*

61. *probitatis electio est.* This line suggests that Hilary understands God's election according to the divine foreknowledge of those who act righteously.

# CHAPTER TWENTY-THREE

HEN THE *Pharisees went out and made plans to trap him in his words,*[1] etc. Often the Pharisees were confounded and were not able to find an occasion for falsely accusing him on the basis of past deeds, for no one could impugn his deeds or words with any fault. Nonetheless, with a malicious intent, they attempted in every instance to find grounds for making an accusation. Surely the Lord has called all people away from their worldly sins and from the superstition of human religion[2] to the hope in the Kingdom of heaven.

The Pharisees tested him [to see] whether he would oppose secular authority on the basis of a prepared question, namely, whether it was necessary to render tribute to Caesar.[3] Since the Lord knew the inner secrets of their thoughts[4]—for there is nothing that God does not see which is hidden within men[5]—he ordered them to produce a denarius, and he asked what inscription and portrait was on it. They responded that it was of Caesar.[6] He said to them that one should render to Caesar what is Caesar's, and render to God what is God's.

2. O wholly miraculous response and perfect clarity of heavenly words! The entire matter has to do with negotiating between contempt for the world and the affront of opposing Caesar.[7] When the Lord declared which things should be rendered

---

1. Mt 22.15.
2. The term *superstitio* already had a long history in Christian apologetics. Both pagans and Christians used it to disparage one another. See R. L. Wilken's *The Christians as the Romans Saw Them,* 2d edition (New Haven, CT: Yale University Press, 2003).

3. Mt 22.17.  
5. Jn 2.25.  
4. Mt 22.18.  
6. Mt 22.21.

7. Cf. Tertullian, *De resurr.* 22; *De pat.* 7.2; *Apol.* 33.3, as it concerns the Christian's rejection of the world and responsibility within it.

to Caesar, he freed hearts[8] devoted to God from every worry and human need. If there is nothing left for us to render to Caesar, we will not be bound by the limitation of surrendering to him what is his. If we have a possessive attitude toward the things which are Caesar's and acknowledge his right of authority, and, if we behave like mercenaries who claim the right of another's inheritance,[9] then we can make no complaint about rendering to Caesar what is Caesar's and rendering to God what belongs to God: our body, soul, and will.[10] It is from God that we possess these [three], which grow and increase. As a result, we are completely justified in rendering to him everything, seeing that we owe to him our origin and development.

3. *On that day the Sadducees, who say there is no resurrection, came to him,*[11] and the rest. The Sadducees did not believe in the resurrection. Because the Lord preached about it, they put to him a trick question about how God's will was realized. How would he respond to the question: if seven brothers have the same wife, whose wife will she be at the resurrection?[12]

4. In general, public opinion accepted that nothing concerning the resurrected state was contained in the prophetic Scriptures.[13] But the Lord said, *You are in error, not knowing the Scriptures nor the power of God.*[14] It is written so that no ambiguity about the Lord's condemnation of such a view should remain.[15] Many are in the habit of posing these kinds of trick questions when it comes to the form of the resurrected feminine sex and whether it will be restored in a way consistent with its nature

8. *mentes.*
9. *alieni patrimonii procurationi.*
10. Cf. Tertullian, *De idol.* 15.3; *De corona* 12; for the threefold description of the person as body, soul, and will, see *supra,* 10.23.
11. Mt 22.23.
12. Mt 22.24–28.
13. Doignon claims that Hilary bases this view on Tertullian, *De resurr.* 19.2, who writes against those who reduce the doctrine of the resurrection from the dead to allegorical or figurative expressions concerning ignorance of God (*Sur Matt.* II.156, n.14). In terms of the Gospel accounts, it appears that most Jews did accept some kind of bodily resurrection. Lk 14.14; Jn 11.24.
14. Mt 22.19.
15. *auctoritas.*

and the functions of the body.[16] We lightly touch upon this point, usually neglected by so many, yet we are told that just such a question had been proposed to the Lord. When he was asked as whose wife of the seven brothers should she be regarded,[17] the Lord rebuked the Sadducees for their error because they did not know the Scriptures and the power of God, and because "people will neither marry nor be given in marriage."[18] It sufficed against the views of the Sadducees that their argument about the continuance of physical attraction was refuted as was their teaching that these joys of the body are worthless once their function ceases. But then the Lord adds: *They will be like the angels of God.*[19] Because the sacrament of the Scriptures and the authority of the divine power[20] show that women will be like the angels,[21] it is appropriate that just as scriptural authority deals with angels, so it does with our hope in the resurrection concerning women. Thus the Lord responded to the proposed question concerning the resurrected state.

5. About the resurrection itself, the Lord opposed their unbelief saying: *Have you not read what was said by God to you: "I am the God of Abraham, and the God of Isaac, and the God of Jacob"? He is not the God of the dead, but of the living.*[22] This statement was directed to Moses when these holy patriarchs had been at rest already for a long time. God was the God of those who [still] existed. They could not possess anything if they did not exist, because it is in the nature of things to subsist necessarily if something else belongs to it. And thus, to have God as God of the living (since God is eternal and not God of the dead) is to possess that which is eternal. How can we deny that they exist and will always exist, since they are acknowledged by the Eternal[23] one?

16. The exact reference of Hilary's remark is not clear, though he may have had in mind Tertullian, *De resurr.* 61, where scorn is poured upon those who deny the particulars of the bodily resurrection, especially when it comes to female reproductive organs. Such organs would, presumably, be superfluous in the resurrected state.

17. Mt 22.28.

18. Mt 22.30 (at the resurrection).

19. Ibid. The majority of Old Latin MSS read, "angels in heaven."

20. *divinae virtutis potestas.*　　　　21. 1 Cor 11.11.

22. Mt 22.31–32.　　　　23. Lit., "eternity" (*aeternitas*).

6. *The Pharisees, hearing that he had silenced the Sadducees, gathered together against him, and one of their number, an expert in the Law,*[24] *cross-examined him.*[25] Following the testing of the Sadducees, the Pharisees came. The Lord had consistently responded to the Sadducees concerning the resurrection so that the Pharisees might be convinced that the faith in the hope of the resurrection was contained in the Law from which they argued. But the Pharisees glorified themselves in having knowledge of the Law, which anticipated the future by comprising an image of the truth which would ensue.

The Pharisees asked him what the most important commandment in the Law was,[26] not realizing that the practice[27] of the Law had been perfected in Christ. He responded to their arrogant ignorance with the words from the Law itself, a response that included in itself all the teaching of the truth. For it is the very mission[28] of our Lord Jesus Christ to introduce the knowledge of God and to reveal an understanding of his name and authority. As the one who was sent, he has come, and as the one who proceeded from eternity,[29] he accomplished what was pleasing to God. And so he responded [to the Pharisees] that the first command is: *Love the Lord your God with all your heart, with all your soul, and with all your mind.*[30] There is nothing here other than what the Law contains, because the precepts of the Law represent a prefiguration[31] of those things which he will do. He reminded them that instead of glorifying themselves with their legal knowledge, they should love God Almighty with every affection of the mind, heart, and soul[32] so that they might confirm what he brought to mind by recalling the commandments of the Law.

---

24. Or, as some MSS read, "a doctor of the Law among them."

25. Mt 22.34–35. Most Old Latin versions are worded rather differently from Hilary's quotation, as well as being separated into two verses.

26. Mt 22.36.

27. *meditationem.*

28. *officium.*

29. *Ex aeternitate deductus.* Cf. Tertullian, *Adv. Prax.* 4.1.

30. Mt 22.37.                              31. *formam.*

32. The reminder is of Dt 6.5.

7. Then he added: *This is the great and first commandment. And the second is similar to this one: Love your neighbor as yourself.*[33] This [second] commandment follows and similarly indicates that it is the same as the first, in both function and value. For the love of God has no value without Christ, nor is the love of Christ of value without God.[34] The one without the other offers no benefit for our salvation. For that reason, he says, *On these two commandments hang all the Law and the prophets.*[35] All of the Law and the prophets pertains to Christ's advent. With their reinforcement,[36] the Lord's advent reveals knowledge of God.

As we have recently and frequently pointed out, we are discouraged from knowing anyone other than Christ,[37] and we are encouraged to put our love for God before father, mother, and children. How else does the commandment of loving one's neighbor bear a likeness to loving God (though one should forsake anything that acts as a rival for God's love),[38] unless the similarity of this commandment requires an equal love for the Father and the Son?

8. That the Pharisees could be accused by the words of the same Law and that a clearer understanding of one's neighbor may be presented, the Lord inquired of them what they thought of Christ: *Whose son is he? David,* they responded.[39] He said to them, how is it that David speaking in the Spirit calls him Lord who would be his son? And how is it that David said, *The Lord said to my Lord, "Sit at my right hand until I put your enemies as the footstool under your feet"?*[40] Truly Christ had to be engendered[41] from the seed of David, despite the similarity of name, according to which the Lord spoke to the Lord and placed him at his right hand *until he subdued all his enemies at his feet,*[42] which sig-

33. Mt 22.38–39.
34. Jn 14.23–24.
35. Mt 22.40. This is the epitome of the *regula fidei*, namely, the way in which the Father is wholly revealed in the Son. Cf. Tertullian, *De praescr. haer.* 14.4: "the faith."
36. *per supplementum.*                37. 1 Cor 2.2.
38. Jn 4.19.                          39. Mt 22.41.
40. Mt 22.44, quoting Ps 110.1 (Vg. 109.1).
41. *procreandum.*
42. Ps 110.1 (Vg. 109.1); Acts 2.34–35; Heb 1.13.

nifies the unity of substance in the fellowship of their name.[43] And thus he is given the right to be seated in judgment and authority in the subjection of all people. The Pharisees should have recalled that the substance of eternal power, authority, and origin resides in him who originated from David and that God was going to dwell in a man.

---

43. *consortio nominis substantiae unitatem.* Doignon sees here an amalgamation of the two formulas from Tertullian's *Adv. Prax.* 18.1 and 25.2. For the language of "unity of substance," see Tertullian, *Adv. Prax.* 2.

# CHAPTER TWENTY-FOUR

*HEN JESUS spoke to the crowd and to his disciples, saying, "On the seat of Moses sit the scribes and Pharisees,"*[1] etc. He showed that the glory of the Law bears witness to himself; the [same] Law revealed in him bore an image of truths to come. At every point, Christ's advent was intended.[2] Whatever is contained in the Law led to the advancement of the knowledge of Christ. This is the reason he commanded [his disciples] to submit to the Pharisees' teaching.[3] Because the latter sit in the seat of Moses, the Lord told the crowd and his disciples to obey all the commandments of the Law, while abstaining from the Pharisees' deeds and works lest their human customs and unbelief nullify the teaching of the Law. For the Pharisees impose the heaviest burdens of the Law on the people who are subject to them. And yet, the Pharisees do not move their finger when confronted with these burdens.[4] They prescribe that we should love the Lord with all of our heart and love our neighbor as ourselves,[5] while they themselves oppose the testimony of the Law, which is well known to them, attacking God in Christ because of his sufferings.[6]

They likewise inflate the glory of their words by wearing phylacteries,[7] though they do not understand that God, the author of eternal life, is in Christ. They magnify themselves as emissaries of the honor of the Law, with tassels hanging from their garments, though they are unfamiliar with the whole Law and its works. Nor do they recognize the power of the same Law, placing more value on sitting at the head of the table at banquets.[8]

---

1. Mt 23.1.    2. *meditabatur.*
3. Mt 23.3.    4. Mt 23.4.
5. Mt 19.19.
6. Another reference, albeit indirect, to those who deny divinity to the Son on account of his incarnate suffering; see *supra,* 23.7.
7. Mt 23.5.    8. Mt 23.6.

They are appointed for eternal fire rather than banquets (banquets are where the pagans sit with Abraham); they love the important seats in the synagogues, though they do not know their teacher according to the testimonies of the Law and the prophets; they love to be greeted in the marketplace,[9] though humility of heart and service is required for all to observe; they also desire to be called "teacher" by men,[10] though they are unfamiliar with the teaching of the Law and reject the Teacher of eternal salvation. Because all of these are profane and perverse things, the Pharisees are condemned for their imitation of them. Rather, listening to the Law and obeying its words—which speak of Christ—are demanded.

2. For those who know they are indeed his disciples, the Lord fulfills his teaching of complete humility so that they may remember that they are all brothers;[11] that is, they are the children of one Parent.[12] Through the generation of a new birth, they have put the origin of their earthly beginning behind them,[13] now having one teacher of heavenly teaching for everyone.[14] They must take up the glory of eternal honor by an awareness of their lowliness, since God will humble the proud and exalt the humble in glory.[15]

3. *Woe to you, scribes and Pharisees, you hypocrites, who close off the Kingdom of heaven.*[16] The Lord condemns their pretentiousness by referring to their punishment, seeing that "woe" is an expression of sorrow. He says that they close off the Kingdom of heaven because they hide the expression[17] of the truth within the Law, which is found in Christ. By the pretentiousness of their teaching they hide the fact of his bodily advent preached by the prophets. They do not enter the way of eternity in Christ, nor do they allow others to enter.

---

9. Mt 23.7.  10. Mt 23.8.
11. Ibid.  12. Mt 23.9.
13. For the terminology of conversion as a "second" or "new birth" that supersedes one's former life, see Cyprian, *Ad Donat.* 4; Tertullian, *De carne Chr.* 17.
14. Mt 23.10.  15. Mt 23.12.
16. Mt 23.13.  17. *meditationem.*

4. *Woe to you, scribes and Pharisees, you hypocrites, who devour widows' houses.*[18] With these people there is denial of the truth; with them is obstruction of others who seek salvation. They bar[19] the way to the Kingdom of heaven. Because of their ambition, they lay siege to widows' houses and plunder them by the dignity of their long prayers.[20] They seek knowledge of heaven through these prayers, as if they were drawing on a treasury of accumulated riches, so that the dignity of the Law would remain silent as it concerned grace. And thus they will receive the greater judgment since they will deserve the punishment for their own sins as well as the blame for the ignorance of others.

5. *Woe to you, scribes and Pharisees, you hypocrites, who traverse sea and land.*[21] By their wandering over sea and land, the Lord indicates that they represent those in all parts of the earth who will belittle the Gospel of Christ. Using the yoke of the Law, they compel others to oppose justification by faith[22] (for there were proselytes received into the synagogue from among the pagans). The paucity of those who will be converted [by the Pharisees] is indicated by the number *one.*[23] There was no faith left in their teaching when once Christ had been preached. But whomever they gained as one of their own became a child of Gehenna,[24] an offspring of punishment, a descendant of eternal judgment. Henceforth adoption into the family of Abraham will come from among the pagans.[25] But a new convert [of the Pharisees] will be a child of a twofold punishment because he has not obtained the remission of his sins following the [example] of the pagans, and because he has joined the company of those who had persecuted Christ.

18. Whereas the most reliable Greek editions and the Vulgate omit this verse (v.14), the Old Latin retains it.

19. *obseratio*—a neologism (Kinnavey, 3).

20. Mt 23.15.

21. Ibid.

22. Viz., *supra*, 5.7; 11.10; 12.22; 21.2 and 5.

23. Mt 23.15: "for you traverse sea and land to make a single proselyte" (RSV).

24. *filius fit gehennae*. For similar anti-Jewish polemic, see the brief sketch in Tertullian, *Apol.* 21.

25. Cf. Tertullian, *Adv. Iud.* 12.

6. *Woe to you, you blind guides, who say, "If anyone swears by the Temple, it is nothing."*[26] The Lord faults them for the reverence they paid to human observance while insulting prophetic tradition. They give honor to empty things and detract from those which should be honored. For the Lord himself gave the Law, and yet the Law does not contain its own fulfillment[27] but a preparation for fulfillment.[28] It is not on account of reverence that the ornamentation of the altar and the Temple derives its value; rather, it is from their beauty that an image[29] of the future is formed. Gold, silver, bronze, brass, pearl, crystal—each contains its significance according to nature.[30] The Lord accused the Pharisees of venerating the gold of the Temple and the gifts placed on the altar according to their religious ritual[31] since greater honor was given to the altar and the Temple.[32] The gold dedicated to the Temple, however, and the gifts on the altar were meant to be an image of the future. With the coming of Christ, reliance upon the Law was useless because Christ is not sanctified by the Law, but the Law by Christ. It is just as if he were placed on the Law as on a seat or a throne.[33] Whoever is regarded as devout, he accepts religion from him who is enthroned. A person is foolish and blind who venerates sacred things by neglecting the one who sanctifies them.[34]

7. *Woe to you, scribes and Pharisees, you hypocrites, who give a tenth of mint and anise,*[35] etc. The Lord denounced them for concealing their intentions and for hiding their sin. They do what the Law prescribes by tithing mint and anise so that they might be regarded by others as fulfilling the Law. They have, however, forsaken mercy, justice, faithfulness, and every sentiment of benevolence[36] that is their proper duty toward humanity. The

---

26. Mt 23.16.  
28. *meditabatur effectus.*  
30. *pro natura uniuscuiusque metalli.*  
32. Mt 23.17–19.  
27. *efficientiam.*  
29. *speciem.*  
31. *pro sacramentorum religione.*  
33. Mt 23.22.  

34. Mt 23.21–22. Compare Rom 1.25: "… because they exchanged the truth about God for a lie and worshiped and served the creature rather than the Creator, who is blessed forever! Amen" (RSV).  
35. Mt 23.23.  
36. Ibid.

tithing of herbs, which was useful for a prefiguring of the future, should not be omitted. It was appropriate for it to be practiced, in order to perform deeds of faithfulness, justice, and mercy, not in a contrived imitation, but in the truth of a tenacious will. Because there is less sacrilege in omitting the tithing of herbs than omitting the duty of benevolence, the Lord derides them[37] in their diligence for straining out gnats but swallowing a camel, given their lack of concern.[38] In other words, they avoid lesser sins but permit greater ones. The Lord also makes a similar threat of punishment to those who wash their cups and dishes on the outside while they themselves are not clean on the inside.[39] Although they make a useless display[40] of devotion, they forsake the wholly beneficial purpose [of the cups and dishes]. If, when we use the inside of a cup, it becomes dirty, what will be the benefit of having cleansed the outside of it? For this reason it is necessary that we seek the splendor of an inner conscience so that those things on the outside of the body may be clean.[41]

The Lord also compares the Pharisees to tombs that are beautifully made by human effort and acts of devotion, but are unclean on the inside with bones of the dead and remains of corpses.[42] They prefer the appearance of justice with empty words rather than possessing a corrupt conscience and mind.[43]

8. *Woe unto you, scribes and Pharisees, you hypocrites, who build tombs for the prophets,*[44] and the rest. The indictment of judgment is clear: the idea and concept of equity is instilled within each one of us by nature; the more fully equity becomes known, the less sinful deeds have any excuse.[45] For the people of the Law killed all the prophets, the former being incensed with hatred against a bitter prophetic rebuke, which publicly accused them of thefts, murders, adulteries, and sacrilege. Because the prophets denounced the people as unworthy of the heavenly Kingdom, given their works, while teaching that the pagans

---

37. I.e., the Pharisees.
39. Mt 23.25.
41. Mt 23.26.
43. Mt 23.28.
45. *veniae.* Cf. Rom 1.20.

38. Mt 23.24.
40. *iactantiam.*
42. Mt 23.27.
44. Mt 23.29.

were the future inheritors of God's covenant, these [same] prophets were subject to various kinds of punishment. The descendants, however, abhorred the deeds of their ancestors:[46] they cherished the books of the prophets, decorated gravesites, restored tombs,[47] demonstrating by such reverence that they had nothing to do with the guilt of their fathers' wickedness.

9. Seeing that they themselves acknowledged that the killing of the prophets was the worst sacrilege, what will excuse those who condemn Christ, who is the fulfillment of the prophets? Do they not abhor those deeds which they have committed multiple times? They are a generation of serpents and vipers[48] because they measure up to their fathers' willfulness.[49] How will they flee judgment, abhorring the murder of the prophets yet persecuting the Lord unto death on a cross? The blood of the just, from Abel to Zacharias, was shed by these men.[50]

Now the apostles are the prophets who have given their revelation of the future. They are wise because they have knowledge of Christ; they are the scribes because they have an understanding of the Law; they have been killed, stoned, crucified, and chased out from city to city.[51] If their persecutors had listened to them, they would have found pardon for their crimes. But for the sake of those who were killed, punishment was meted out against the apostles' killers just as it was for the crimes of their fathers.

10. *Jerusalem, Jerusalem, you who kill the prophets and stone those sent to you.*[52] Despite many forms of rebuke, the Lord always indicates the love of his mercy. This too is the basis of his sorrow,[53] given Jerusalem's refusal to return to the salvation he offered to her.[54] For Jerusalem had killed and stoned the prophets who

---

46. Mt 23.30.  47. Mt 23.29.
48. Mt 23.33.  49. Mt 23.32.
50. Mt 23.35. Cf. Lk 11.47–51.
51. Mt 23.34. Parallel of the opposites with the fate of Israel: faithful, Heb 11.32–38; Acts 7.51–53.
52. Mt 23.37. Hilary's wording of this passage is supported by only two of the Old Latin MSS.
53. *querela.*  54. Cf. *supra,* 18.10.

were sent to her. By identifying the name of the city, the Lord shows that the crime belongs to her inhabitants. And it shows, moreover, that the blood of Abel and Zechariah will come upon their descendants[55] because Christ has already lived, preached, and suffered among them.[56] If they had believed in him, not only would their faith escape the punishment for murdering the prophets, but they would obtain pardon according to the same judgment of the Lord's Passion. Since, however, they did not believe in him after his resurrection, they must now give satisfaction for the blood of Abel and Zechariah.

11. Even though he spoke these words in the flesh "found as a man,"[57] offering to every person his help,[58] he often wished to gather them according to the preaching of [his] prophets.[59] As it happened, he expended this affection in vain and to no purpose. Just as a hen gathers her young,[60] so he wished to cover them with his wings, as if he now had become an earthly and domesticated bird having wings as a bodily covering, granting to his young the warmth of eternal life, and teaching them to fly into the sky of a new birth.[61] Among birds there is one reason for being born, and another for living life. First, they are enclosed in the shell of the egg, which is like a barrier around the body. Then, after they have been kept warm by the care of the parent, they take flight. In the manner of this familiar and mostly earth-bound bird (viz., the hen), the Lord wished to gather them together under him so that after they had been

---

55. Mt 23.35.

56. Cf. Fortunatianus, *Comm. in evang.* 3.10–14, where the city of Jerusalem is identified as having rejected the warnings of the prophets and not receiving Christ, who came last of all.

57. Phil 2.7. The "words" refer to Mt 23.37–40.

58. An echo of Tertullian's *Apol.* 21.7: "He therefore appeared whose coming, preannounced by God, was to restore and illuminate humanity … namely, Christ, the Son of God, enlightener of the human race …" (for Latin text, see Dekkers ed., CCSL 1.123).

59. E.g., Is 54.7; Jer 23.3.

60. Mt 23.37.

61. Doignon suggests that Hilary is combining the traits of several themes here: the new generation at baptism is of the Spirit (*supra,* 10.24); every spirit has wings (Tertullian, *Apol.* 22.8); and those born again take flight (*supra,* 10.18). *Sur Matt.* II.178, n.24.

brought forth through physical birth, they would be reborn by the birth of another kind of generation. By his warmth they would be reborn in the heavenly Kingdom, just as if they were taking flight on wings.

Yet because they rejected this, their house is left deserted and desolate;[62] that is, they were unworthy for the Holy Spirit to dwell within them.[63] Since they began their "house" apart from God, remaining in the obstinacy of unbelief, they will not see him until the time when he returns in the name of the Lord,[64] even though they bless him through the confession of stubborn unbelief.

62. Mt 23.38.
63. Cf. Rom 8.9; 2 Tm 1.14; Fortunatianus, *Comm. in evang.* 3.19–22, likewise interprets (v.38) the deserted house as those who are desolate of the Holy Spirit within them.
64. Mt 23.39.

## CHAPTER TWENTY-FIVE

*ND AS HE was walking away from the Temple, his disciples approached and beckoned him to look at the structure of the Temple.*[1] After threatening that Jerusalem would be forsaken, he is shown the grandeur of the Temple's stature, as if it were necessary to stir him by its splendor. He said that it would be entirely destroyed and demolished since the stones of the entire structure would be knocked down.[2] But an eternal temple is one that is consecrated to be a habitation of the Holy Spirit, that is, the temple is a person who is worthy to become a dwelling for God by knowledge of the Son,[3] by confession of the Father, and by obedience to his commandments.[4]

2. Once the Lord had withdrawn to the mountain, his disciples came and asked him privately when this would happen [to the Temple] and by what sign they would recognize his coming, and about the end of the age. Here we have three questions in one [setting], separated by chronology and distinguished by the [degree of] significance in their meaning.

The Lord answers the first question concerning the destruction of the city [Jerusalem], an event confirmed by the truth of his teaching so that they should not be deceived by an imposter because of their ignorance. For there would come, even in the disciples' day, imposters who would claim they were the Christ.[5] He therefore warns them that the faith could be undermined by a pernicious lie. In fact, it happened that Simon the Samaritan, bolstered with diabolical works and words, led

---

1. Mt 24.1.　　　　　　　　2. Mt 24.2.

3. Cf. 1 Cor 6.19; 2 Cor 6.16.

4. The "trinity" of knowledge (*agnitio*), confession, and obedience, corresponding to Father, Son, and Holy Spirit.

5. Mt 24.4.

many astray by his miracles.[6] And because this happened during the time of the apostles, the Lord said, *the end is not yet.*[7] Still, the end is not yet until nations and kingdoms attack one another, and famines and earthquakes occur.[8] This is not dissolution of all things, but the beginning of sorrows[9] from which all evils would originate. He encouraged them to endure suffering: flight, scourging, death, and the pagans' public hatred towards them on account of his name.[10] On account of these troubles, many will be shaken, and will stumble in the face of increasing wickedness, and will be incited to hate one another.[11] There will be false prophets, as was Nicolaus, one of the seven deacons,[12] who will pervert many by falsifying the truth,[13] and because of mass wickedness, love will grow cold.[14] But for those who persevere to the end, salvation is assured.[15]

As the apostolic men[16] are scattered throughout all parts of the world, the truth of the Gospel will be preached.[17] Once the knowledge of the heavenly sacrament[18] has been disseminated to all humanity, the fall and end of Jerusalem is imminent. Punishment of unbelievers and fear of the city's destruction are the consequence when the faith is preached.[19] All this happened in Jerusalem, just as it had been foretold; the city was consumed—ruined by her stonings, by her expulsions, by her murder of the apostles, by her hunger, by war, and by her captivity.[20] For having rejected the preachers of Christ, she was shown to be unworthy of God's message and not worthy to exist.[21]

---

6. Acts 8.9–11. Simon becomes the archetypal heretic in Christian anti-heretical literature. See Justin, *I Apol.* 26; Irenaeus, *Adv. haer.* 1.27.4; Tertullian, *De idol.* 9; *De anima* 57; Origen, *Contra Celsum* 6.11.

7. Mt 24.6.                              8. Mt 24.7.

9. Mt 24.8.                              10. Mt 24.9.

11. Mt 24.10.

12. Acts 6.5; Rv 2.6, 15. Irenaeus, *Adv. haer.* 3.11.1.

13. Mt 24.11.                            14. Mt 24.12.

15. Mt 24.13.

16. See *supra*, 22.4, for use of "apostolic men" (*viri apostolici*).

17. Mt 24.14.

18. Which is salvation through Christ.

19. Just as the prophets before the apostles preached. God's judgment and salvation reveal continuity between OT and NT.

20. Jerusalem's destruction is characterized by these things that she did as well as by the things that happened to her as a result.

21. *Supra*, 10.10. Cf. Acts 7.51–53.

3. Then there follows a sign of his future advent. When they see the *abomination of desolation* standing in the holy place,[22] we should understand his glorious return. Concerning this matter, I think that our comment is superfluous[23] given the teaching of the most blessed Daniel[24] and Paul.[25] That which is spoken by each writer concerns the times of the Antichrist. He is an *abomination* because he rises up against God by claiming for himself the honor due to God.[26] As the *abomination of desolation,* he is going to render the earth desolate by war and bloodshed in keeping with its sacrilege.[27] Because the Antichrist was received by the Jews, he will stand in the holy place,[28] where God used to be invoked by the prayers of his saints and where the Antichrist is received by unbelievers with the same honor with which they venerated God.

4. The error of the Jews will be that, having rejected the truth, they adopted a lie. The Lord warns them to abandon Judaea and flee to the mountains,[29] lest the violence and contagion of those who will believe in the Antichrist be brought among them. But for all who remain faithful, they will be safer in the deserted places of the mountains than in the busy avenues of Judaea.

5. When he says, *And those who are on the rooftops should not come down to pick up anything in their houses,*[30] it is a statement which defies explanation in word or action that human beings can understand. The one on the rooftop who is supposed to depart Judaea cannot leave that place until he comes down. Moreover, what is the purpose of staying on the roof as opposed to remaining in the house? We have often taught, however, that the sig-

22. Mt 24.15.
23. Following Perrin's (p. 146) emended reading of Doignon's text.
24. Mt 24.15 (Dn 9.27).
25. 2 Thes 2.4.
26. "Abomination" is related to idolatry in prophetic literature; see, e.g., Ezek 8.10; Jer 13.27; Mal 2.1; Dn 11.31; 12.11.
27. On the prophetic theme of desolating the earth, see Is 34.10, 62.4; Jer 12.11; Ezek 6.14.
28. Mt 24.15; Dn 11.31–32.          29. Mt 24.16.
30. Mt 24.17.

nificance of words and places requires contemplative thought if we want to find the importance of its heavenly teaching.[31]

The roof is the summit of the house and the lofty perfection[32] of the whole dwelling. A house without a roof is not a house. The one who stands on the top of his house, that is, in the perfection of his heart[33]—renewed by regeneration, elevated in spirit, perfected by the divine gift of absolution—will not have to descend into the lower desires for the things of this age. Nor will he have to abandon the height of his rooftop because he was seduced by the passions of the body inside.[34]

*And that whoever is in the field should not go back to pick up his cloak.*[35] He who obediently follows the commandment should not return to former cares of life.[36] Nor should he desire any clothing of the body,[37] lest he return to the cloak of his former sin with which he once covered himself.[38]

6. *Woe to pregnant women and nursing mothers.*[39] This verse can be understood simply as pertaining to the delay of their flight. Hampered by the weight of the womb, it is difficult for them to flee from the imminent destruction of that time. But in what way did their gender[40] and capacity for procreation deserve this? Perhaps the phase of women's lives which occurred at this time is supposed to be especially cursed. May this not be so! But in no way can anything evil befall a person except by his own fault.[41] We should not believe that the Lord was speaking [literally] about the burden of the woman's womb when he says, *Woe to pregnant women.* Rather, he was directing us to souls burdened with the weight of sin.[42]

---

31. Cf. *supra,* 10.1.
32. *celsa perfectio* (i.e., "completion").
33. *corporis.*
34. *interioribus corporis illecebris.*
35. Mt 24.18. Other MSS read, "turn back to take up his clothing."
36. Cf. Eph 4.22: "Put off your old nature which belongs to your former manner of life and is corrupt through deceitful lusts" (RSV).
37. Cf. Col 3.8.                           38. Cf. ibid.
39. Mt 24.19.                              40. *condicio sexus.*
41. In the fourth century, human free will with responsibility for one's *conditio* was the position of most writers.
42. See 2 Tm 3.6.

By remaining on the rooftop or in the field, they cannot escape the storm of wrath that is reserved for them.[43] Indeed, suffering is a natural consequence of pregnancy, and the womb cannot give birth without distressing the whole body. Souls that are found in like manner will be confined to their own burden and suffering.

*Woe also to those who are nursing.*[44] It is no less difficult for the infant who is weaned to flee than it is for the one who is still breast-fed. But why is it unfortunate for the one who is breast-fed[45] when there is no difference in age or time between the one fed with milk and the one who is weaned?[46] Instead, this verse equally shows the weakness of souls who are brought to knowledge of God as by milk.[47] Lacking the power of perfect food, let them be instructed by utilizing their frail, weak appetite for knowledge of divine things.[48] It will be *Woe* for them because they will not have fled from their sins nor received the food of true bread;[49] they are too weighed down to flee from the Antichrist and too inexperienced to resist him.[50]

7. For this reason we are urged to pray that our flight be neither in the winter nor on the Sabbath.[51] That is, we should not be found in the coldness of our sins[52] or indifferent to good works. The heaviness and intolerable state of affliction weighs upon everyone.[53] For the sake of God's elect, those days will be shortened so that a shorter of passage of time[54] may lessen the impact of oppressing calamities.[55]

---

43. Cf. 1 Thes 1.10.

44. Hilary interprets the phrase *vae nutrientibus* (Mt 24.19) in the passive (reflexive) sense, resulting in the paraphrase *illis quoque vae erit quae nutrientur,* which Doignon sees as a reflection of Juvencus's *Evangelicae historiae* (4.127–28), which discusses the developing state of birthing and sucking of the young (*Sur Matt.* II.188, n.26).

45. *nutriatur.*              46. *decessisse de lacte.*

47. Cf. 1 Cor 3.2.           48. *perfecti cibi virtute.*

49. Jn 6.55.                 50. Mt 24.23–24.

51. Mt 24.20.

52. Cf. Lactantius, *Inst.* 2. 9, 10; coldness is the image of death, which comes by sin (Rom 5.12).

53. Mt 24.21.

54. *degrassandi tempus.* The verb *digrassor* is a neologism that means "to move about" or "continue" (Kinnavey, 10).

55. Mt 24.22.

8. Because there will be those cast into great tribulation, false prophets will make the promise that help in Christ is at hand. They will falsely allege that Christ is found in many and various places,[56] and will lead the oppressed and troubled into the service of Antichrist. In order to deceive others, false prophets will say at one time Christ is in some deserted place.[57] And, as a way of imprisoning them under the rule of the Dominator,[58] they will claim at another time that Christ is in some inner room.[59] The Lord, however, declares he has no need for hiding places or being recognized by a very few individuals.[60] Rather, he will be present everywhere and in the sight of everyone just as lightning, coming from the east, spreads its light toward the west.[61] As it flashes from any one place it is seen everywhere. Lest we remain ignorant of the place of his coming, he says, *Wherever there is the body, there the eagles will gather.*[62] He calls the saints "eagles" from the spiritual flight of their bodies,[63] and he shows that their gathering, brought together by the angels, will be at his Passion.[64] There we will rightly wait for the brightness of his advent, where he wrought for us eternal glory by the suffering of his bodily humiliation.[65]

56. Mt 24.23.

57. The desert is the habitation of evil and deceiving spirits. Cf. *supra,* 2.2.

58. I.e., Antichrist.

59. *penetralibus.* Mt 24.24.          60. That is, a select few.

61. Mt 24.27.          62. Mt 24.28.

63. I.e., the rapture.          64. Mt 24.31.

65. There is the suggestion in Hilary's remarks that he has absorbed the millennial vision of the future that characterizes second- and third-century writers. See Tertullian, *Adv. Marc.* 3.24; Victorinus of Poetovio, *In Apoc.* 20.6 and *De fabrica mundi* (frag.).

# CHAPTER TWENTY-SIX

*MMEDIATELY AFTER the tribulation of those days, the sun will be darkened,*[1] and the rest. He indicates his glorious advent and majestic return by *the darkening of the sun, the eclipse of the moon, the falling of stars,* the shaking of the heavenly bodies,[2] the display of portentous signs, the lamentation of the pagans when they recognize the Son of Man in the glory of God,[3] and the appointing of the angels with trumpets for the gathering of the saints[4]—the opening of freedom for all. It so happens that a huge tree comes from a mustard seed;[5] it so happens that a statue taken from the stone of a mountain covers the whole earth;[6] it so happens that the city will be made visible to all;[7] it so happens that there will be a light from the wood which illuminates the universe;[8] and it so happens that from the humility of death comes the glory of God. Through the revelation of all these events,[9] the Lord wants us to know about the time of our redemption when we will be transferred from the corruption of the body to the honor of the spiritual substance.[10]

2. The sign of the times, which we are supposed to know, the Lord compared to the fig tree. When its branches become

1. Mt 24.29.
2. Lit., "heavenly powers" (*virtutum caelestium*).
3. Mt 24.29 (quoting from Is 13.10).
4. Mt 24.30–31.                              5. Cf. Lk 13.19; Dn 4.10–11.
6. Dn 2.35. This sudden move to Daniel is due to the apocalyptic context of Mt 24.
7. Mt 5.14–15; Rv 21.2–4.
8. The cross; cf. Jn 3.19–21. The Son's redemption frees all those in darkness so that they may come to the true light. (See Jn 9.5.) Or, Hilary may be drawing on the imagery in Tertullian's *Adv. Iud.* 10. Based on the Septuagintal reading of Ps 96.10 (LXX 95.10), "God has reigned from a tree," which is the basis of Tertullian's claim that, when on the cross, Christ defeated the darkness of death.
9. Mt 24.26–31.                              10. 1 Cor 15.44.

tender and blossom, we are made to understand that summer is near.[11] But the sequence[12] of the summer season and that of a tree [which blossoms] are completely different. For there is a sizeable interval between the beginning of spring, when the branches of the tree swell with buds, and the summer, when the branches become green in foliage. By this we should recognize that the verse is not speaking about this tree. In fact, we already dealt with the property of the fig tree at an early point.[13] We read that Adam clothed himself with the foliage of this tree,[14] covering his shameful conscience;[15] that is to say, he clothed himself under the Law as if with a garment of his sin.

The branch of the fig tree should be understood as the Antichrist, the son of the devil, the doorway[16] to sin, an advocate of the Law. When the branch begins to green and blossom, then summer is close at hand—the day of judgment will be realized. The blossoming of the branch is recognized as a kind of overflow[17] of sins for those who rejoice in them.[18] Indeed, there will be then a flowering of evildoers, an honoring of the wicked, and delight in sacrilege. For then, it is obvious that the scorching heat[19] of summer, that is, the heat of eternal fire, is near at hand.[20]

3. In order that there would be complete assurance about these future events, and by saying *Amen* in declaring the truth,[21] the Lord adds that our generation will not pass away until every one of these things has happened.[22] Those things which are thought to be firmly in place, namely, heaven and earth, will be no more, whereas his *words cannot pass away*.[23] That which is

---

11. Mt 24.32.

12. *natura*.

13. *Supra*, 21.8–9.

14. Gn 3.7.

15. *Supra*, 21.9.

16. *portio*.

17. *viriditate*.

18. See Prv 2.14; Sir 11.16.

19. *aestus* (Rv 7.16).

20. Mt 24.33.

21. This presentation of "Amen" may stem from its use in the liturgy as in Tertullian, *De spect.* 25.5, or perhaps in Ambrose, *De myst.* 9.54. See *Sur Matt.* II.196, n.7. But the reason for "Amen" is that it is the Latin word of v.34, meaning "truly" or "surely."

22. Mt 24.34. Hilary has personalized this verse for his hearers by rewording *haec generatio* to *generationem nostram*.

23. Mt 24.35.

created, that is, made whole from nothing,[24] possesses within itself the necessity of non-being[25] and is brought into being from
eternity, containing within itself the power to endure.

4. Concerning the end of that time, the Lord removed the
weight of our anxiety by saying that no one knows that day.
Not only are the angels ignorant of it, but he himself [does not
know].[26] O inestimable mercy of the divine goodness! Has God
the Father denied the Son knowledge of that day by hiding his
intentions, even though the Son said, *All things have been committed to me by my Father?*[27] How could everything be committed to
him if there is something denied to him? But he delivered to us
everything which he received from the Father.[28] The Word[29] possesses in himself the certainty, not so much of future events that
will happen, as of the events that have happened.[30] For this reason the day has been set but without further qualification.[31] Even
though God permits a generous amount of time for our repentance, he recognizes our anxiety, always a fear of the unknown.
By telling no one about his will when it comes to setting this day,
he prevents any further qualification of his words.[32] As it was at
the time of the flood, that great day will burst into the course of
our lives, into the midst of all our business and misery.[33]

24. *de nihilo.* That God made creation out of nothing had become a doctrinal fixture of catholic orthodoxy by Hilary's time.

25. *ut non sint.*                          26. Mt 24.36.
27. Mt 11.27.                              28. Jn 15.15.
29. *Verbum.*

30. Hilary has to be careful with the discrepancy between Mt 11.27 and
24.36. He has studiously avoided attributing any weakness to the incarnate
Son. Hilary's allowance that Christ does not know the future is an admission
he never would have made if he had knowledge of the "Arian" reliance on this
passage for their denial of the Son's divine equality with the Father.

31. *extra definitionem.*

32. Hilary contradicts this explanation when he later becomes familiar
with anti-Nicene arguments related to the Son's professed ignorance (Mt
24.36). In *De trin.* 9.58–75, he presents a series of scriptural texts to show that
the Son was not ignorant of the day in actuality, but feigned ignorance for the
disciples' sake (so that they would continue to hope in perseverance), and because his seeming ignorance was part of the "divine plan" to be revealed. The
length and repetitiveness of the arguments used in *De trin.* suggest that Hilary
was aware that he was altering his position and that the former position in his
commentary was vulnerable to "Arian" exegesis that stressed the difference
between the natures of the Father and Son.

33. Mt 24.37–39.

5. In fact, the Lord shows there will be a distinction in the taking of believers: although two men are located in a field, one is taken and the other is left behind,[34] and of the two women who are grinding, one is rejected and the other is chosen,[35] and of the two who are in bed, one stays in it and the other leaves.[36] He teaches here about the distinction between unbelievers and believers: some are left behind while some are taken. When God's wrath is kindled, the saints will be gathered into his storehouses, as the prophet declares,[37] but the faithless will be left as fuel for the fire from heaven.[38]

The two men in the field are two peoples in the world, believers and unbelievers, whom the day of the Lord surprises in the midst of their life's activities.[39] Two shall be separated: one left behind and the other taken. The same logic is at work concerning the women who are grinding: the millstone is the work of the Law. Because some of the Jews believed through the apostles, as they believed through Elijah,[40] they will be justified through faith. It is this one group which will be taken on account of this same faith that produces good works. The other group will be left behind in the fruitless works of the Law, grinding in vain, never to produce the bread of heavenly food. The two in bed are those who preach the same message about the Lord's Passion, about which there is one and the same confession on the part of the heretics[41] and of catholics.[42] But the catholic truth will preach the unity of the Father and the

34. Mt 24.40.                              35. Mt 24.41.
36. Hilary is following the Old Latin version, which adds to v.41 *duo in lecto* (or, *duo erunt in lecto iacentes*), *unus adsumetur et unus relinquetur.*
37. Is 26.20.                              38. Mt 3.12.
39. Cf. 1 Thes 5.2; 2 Pt 3.10.            40. On Elijah, see *supra,* 17.4.
41. Tertullian had already observed that heretical and orthodox Christians used the same confessional language while holding conflicting doctrinal positions (*Adv. Prax.* 29). The precise *confessio* Hilary has in mind here is probably the baptismal creed of Poitiers. See *supra,* 1.2. As Augustine would observe decades later, it was not enough simply to repeat the local church's creed in order to ensure orthodoxy. "Under color of the few words drawn up in the Creed many heretics have endeavored to conceal their poison" (*De fide et de symbolo* 1.1, trans. John H. S. Burleigh, *Augustine: Earlier Writings,* ed. John H. S. Burleigh [Philadelphia: Westminster Press, 1953], 353). The issue of rightly interpreting the familiar lines of the creed was at stake.
42. The term "catholics" is commonly used in conciliar documents of the fourth and fifth centuries to denote one who is doctrinally orthodox.

Son, and their common *theotēs*,[43] which we call *deity,* whereas the falsehood of the heretics will impugn that same truth with many outrageous arguments.[44] Thus, one of the two in bed will be left behind and the other taken because the judgment of God's will shall decide between the faith of them both.

6. And so that we should realize that his ignorance of the day[45] is kept secret for us all, not without a reason for [understanding] the usefulness of silence, he warned us to be watchful for the coming of the thief, [46] and to adhere assiduously to prayer as those who are occupied with all the works of his teaching. For he shows that the devil is a watchful thief who seeks to take away spoils from us[47] and who attacks the houses, [that is], of our bodies, in order to break into them with the arrows of enticement and of his purposes, while we are negligent and given to sleep. It is appropriate that we be prepared therefore because ignorance of the day exacerbates the stressful anxiety of anticipation held in suspense.

43. The accusative form appears here: *theotēta.* See *supra,* 16.4.
44. Hilary never names the "heretics" who recite the same creed and accept the unity of deity as he does. Nevertheless, this group "impugns that same truth" in order to support their arguments. A kind of Spirit-Christology best fits Hilary's description of his opponents here and elsewhere. *Supra,* 12.18.
45. Cf. Mt 24.36, 42.                    46. Cf. Mt 24.43.
47. Cf. Mt 12.29.

# CHAPTER TWENTY-SEVEN

**W**HO THEN *is the faithful and wise servant whom the Lord places in charge over his household?*[1] and the rest. Although the Lord exhorts us generally toward tireless and focused vigilance,[2] he issues a special charge to the rulers of the people, that is, the bishops, about their watching for his coming. The Lord identifies the faithful and wise servant as the one given charge[3] over the household, to care for the needs and the interests of the people entrusted to him.[4] If the servant hears what the Lord says and obeys his instructions, that is, if the servant has the advantage and truth of the Lord's teaching, he will nourish the household[5] by strengthening the weak, by repairing what is broken, by correcting what is perverse, and by dispensing the Word of Life[6] as eternal food. If the servant does these things with perseverance, he will obtain glory from his Lord,[7] just as a faithful distributor and practical manager would receive, and will be placed over all the Lord's possessions.[8] In other words, the servant will be placed in God's glory since there is no better reward than this.[9]

2. Counting on the long patience of God[10]—which is prolonged for the advancing of human salvation[11]—the servant, however, becomes insolent toward his fellow servants[12] and gives himself over to worldly evils and vices. While he is absorbed

---

1. Mt 24.45.
2. Lit., "preoccupation with vigilance" (*vigilantiae curam*).
3. *praepositum.*
4. Cf. Cyprian, *Ep.* 63.1, referring to the bishops who are given charge (*praepositos*) over the Lord's churches.
5. *familiae.* Cf. Cyprian, *Ep.* 74.9.1.  6. *verbum vitae.* Phil 2.16.
7. Mt 24.46.  8. Mt 24.47.
9. Cf. 1 Pt 5.2–4.  10. Mt 24.48.
11. 2 Pt 3.9.  12. Mt 24.49.

with meticulous care for satisfying[13] his present appetites, the Lord will come on a day which he thought would never come.[14] Instead of the servant receiving the promised possessions, his allotment is shared with the hypocrites in eternal punishment,[15] because he had not counted on the Lord's advent; and because he did not obey the commandments, and because he became engrossed in the present life, and because he lived the life of the pagans, and because he was oblivious to judgment, he subjected the household in his care to hunger, thirst, and slaughter.

3. *Then will the Kingdom of heaven be compared to ten virgins,*[16] and the rest. From what was said earlier, we can understand the reason for this passage. The whole has to do with the great day of the Lord, in which the secrets of human thought will be revealed by the knowledge of God's judgment.[17] Moreover, the true faith of the God for whom we wait will gain the certain benefit of hope. Clearly there is in the five wise virgins and in the five foolish ones[18] a division established between believers and unbelievers.[19] This is according to the example of Moses, who had received the Ten Commandments[20] written on two tablets.[21] It was necessary that everything be written on each. On these double-slabs[22] there is signified the proper division between the right and the left,[23] and between the good and bad, even though these [two sides] are joined in one testament.

4. The bridegroom and the bride is our Lord God in the body. For as the Spirit is wedded to the flesh, so the flesh is to

---

13. *exercens.*                          14. Mt 24.50.
15. Mt 24.51.
16. Mt 25.1. Hilary is rightly following the wording of this verse in the Old Latin.
17. Cf. 1 Cor 3.13.
18. Mt 25.2.
19. This interpretation may stem from Hilary's familiarity with *De decem virginibus,* attributed to Victorinus of Poetovio (*Sur Matt.* II.204, n.4).
20. *decem verba.*                       21. Ex 32.15.
22. *duplex pagina.*
23. A metaphor used for distinguishing the good (right) from evil (left), since the right hand was the one of blessing. See Mt 25.32–34.

the Spirit.[24] When the trumpet finally sounds the alert,[25] we go out to meet only one spouse: the two have become one now that the humility of the flesh has passed over to spiritual glory.[26]

In this first encounter, we are prepared by fulfilling the obligations of this life for the resurrection from the dead.[27] The lamps[28] are the light of shining souls radiant from the sacrament of baptism. The oil[29] is the fruit of good works.[30] The jars[31] are human bodies, in whose inward parts the treasure of a good conscience should be stored.[32] But the sellers (of the oil),[33] who need the mercy of believers, are the ones providing the goods which are sought from them. For the satiety of their own need, they are selling to us a conscience of good works. This is the abundant fuel of an inextinguishable light which we should buy and store up for the benefit[34] of mercy.

The marriage[35] is the reception of immortality, the joining of corruption and incorruption into a new alliance.[36] The delay of the bridegroom[37] is the time of repentance. The falling asleep of those waiting is the rest of the believers and temporary[38] death of everyone who comes to the time of their penitence.[39] The shout in the middle of the night[40] for all who are unaware is the sound of the trumpet that precedes the coming of the Lord[41] and that arouses everyone to go out to meet the Bridegroom. The taking up of the lamps[42] is the return of the souls to their bodies, and the light is the shining conscience of good works, within the confines of their bodies.

---

24. Modeled on Tertullian's *De resurr.* 63.1: "Both natures (spirit and flesh) he has already joined together in his own self. He has fitted them together as bride and bridegroom in the reciprocal bond of wedded life" (ANF 3.539). The "Spirit" here refers to the divine nature, not the Holy Spirit. Cf. Tertullian, *De carne Chr.* 14: Christ is called "the spirit of God," as an expression of the Son's divine nature.

25. Mt 25.6.

26. Cf. *supra*, 10.24.

27. Cf. Tertullian, *De resurr.* 34.11.

28. Mt 25.1.

29. Mt 25.3.

30. *Supra*, 5.2.

31. Mt 25.4.

32. 1 Tm 1.5, 19.

33. Mt 25.9.

34. *fructibus*.

35. Mt 25.10.

36. Cf. 1 Cor 15.53–54.

37. Mt 25.5.

38. *temporaria*.

39. See Tertullian, *De anima* 55.4–5; 58.8.

40. Mt 25.6.

41. 1 Thes 4.16.

42. Mt 25.7.

5. The wise virgins are those who, having taken an opportune moment for action while in the body, initially prepared themselves[43] to meet the Lord. But the foolish virgins, who were careless and negligent, had concern only for the circumstances of the moment. Forgetful of God's promises, they carry no hope of the resurrection in themselves. Because these foolish virgins could not go out to meet the bridegroom with lamps unlit, they implored the ones who were wise to share some of their oil.[44] The latter responded that they could not give them any because perhaps there would not be enough for everyone.[45] In other words, no one should be supported by another's works and merits. It is necessary for each of us to purchase oil for his own lamp. The wise virgins urged the foolish to go back in order to buy oil, even if the latter would be late in obeying the commandments of God. They intended to make themselves worthy by having lamps lit for their meeting with the bridegroom. While they were waiting, the bridegroom made his entrance. Together with him the wise virgins, now ready with their lighted lamps and veiled,[46] entered the wedding feast.[47] In other words, the wise virgins entered into heavenly glory at the very moment of the coming of the Lord in his splendor. And because there is now no longer an opportunity for repentance, the foolish run, pleading that the door be opened to them.[48] But the bridegroom answered them, "I do not know you."[49] For the foolish did not come to render service to the one arriving,[50] nor did they present themselves at the sound of the blowing trumpet,[51] nor did they remain with the wedding party as it entered. Rather, they procrastinated, and they lost the opportunity for entering the wedding feast.

43. Mt 25.4.
44. Mt 25.8. Lit., "borrow oil" (*oleum mutuentur*).
45. Mt 25.9.
46. *operiebantur*. Doignon points to Tertullian's parallel use of the term *operiri* in *De vel. virg.* 7.2, in reference to 1 Cor 11.6. *Sur Matt.* II.209, n.18.
47. Mt 25.10.                              48. Mt 25.11.
49. Mt 25.12.                              50. Viz., the bridegroom.
51. Though the passage here says nothing about a trumpet, but only the shout of a voice, this could be an eschatological allusion to Rv 1.10; 4.1, "The great voice as of a trumpet."

6. *For it is as if a man about to go out on a journey called his servants and handed over to them his possessions,*[52] and the rest. The dividing of the money is unequal,[53] although the difference should not be attributed to the one doing the dividing since the Lord says that each one had received according to his ability.[54] Each servant received as much as he was capable, so it was his decision to oversee the handling of affairs seeing that he was the one making the purchases.[55]

The Lord indicates that he himself is the master of the house.[56] The duration of his journey is the time[57] given for repentance. He who sits at the right hand of God[58] in heaven has provided the whole human race an opportunity[59] for [responding in] faith and the works of the Gospel. Each servant accepted a talent according to his measure of faith;[60] that is, each one accepted the preaching of the Gospel from the one preaching it. This [message] is the incorruptible possession of the Master, the patrimony of Christ, reserved for those who will inherit eternity.

7. That servant who received five talents is the faithful people under the Law. With this beginning he doubled his merit by rightly and appropriately fulfilling the task of the evangelical faith.[61] In the settling of accounts, a careful check of procedures[62] is made in order to insure the profit of the heavenly words and for distributing the talent as deserved. To the one who had been assigned five talents, ten in total were gained at the return of the master.[63] In other words, this servant was found in the faith just as he was in the Law; he was obedient according to the ten precepts of the five books of Moses because

---

52. Mt 25.14.  53. Mt 25.15.
54. *virtutem.*
55. Earning five more talents or two or none.
56. *paterfamilias.*  57. Lit., "space" (*spatium*).
58. Cf. Mk 14.62; Lk 22.69; Heb 1.3.  59. *potestatem.*
60. Cf. Rom 12.3.
61. *evangelicae fidei.* Cf. Mt 25.16. See *supra,* 4.18, regarding the Gospel's message, not abrogating, but surpassing the Law, also given by God.
62. *iudicii.*
63. Mt 25.20.

of grace that comes through the Gospel's justification.[64] He is therefore told to enter the joy of the Lord, where he is received with the honor of Christ's glory.

8. That servant who was assigned two talents represents the people of the pagans who have been justified by faith; by their profession of the Son and the Father, they have confessed our Lord Jesus Christ as God and man, both by the Spirit and by the flesh.[65] For faith is from the heart, and confession from the mouth.[66]

These are the two servants who were assigned the talents. In the first case the whole mystery[67] is realized in the five talents. In other words, what was known in the Law was doubled by the faith of the Gospel, so that the second one gained an increase of two talents by his effort.[68] Even though there was a difference in the amount entrusted and returned, the reward given to both servants by the master was the same.[69] By this we may know that the faith of the pagans has been put on the same level as those who believe according to the Law that they know.[70] With the same praise, the second servant is also told to enter into the joy of the Lord. By doubling of the money we find that works were added to faith. What one believes in his mind,[71] he accomplishes through deeds and actions.

9. The servant who received one talent and hid it in the ground[72] is the people who abide by the Law, completely carnal and foolish, possessing no spiritual understanding nor entering the power of the Gospel's preaching.[73] Rather, it is on account of their jealousy of the pagans' salvation that they hid the received talent in the ground. Neither did they use the talent nor offer it to others for their use. Instead, they thought that the Law was sufficient for salvation. When an explanation was demanded from the servant, he said, "I was afraid of you,"[74]

64. Mt 25.21.
65. Cf. Tertullian, *Adv. Prax.* 26–27.
66. Rom 10.9.                          67. *omne sacramentum.*
68. Mt 25.17.                          69. Mt 25.23.
70. Rom 3.29–30.                       71. *opinione.*
72. Mt 25.18.                          73. Cf. Rom 1.16–17.
74. Mt 25.25.

as though reverence and fear of the ancient commandments prevented the use of the Gospel's liberty. And so he said, "Here is what belongs to you,"[75] as if he had come to a halt in those things which the Lord commanded.

10. To hide that talent in the ground is to conceal the glory of the new preaching[76] under the encumbrances of the bodily passion.[77] He who denies that Christ the Lord—whose coming and Passion are derived from the Law—was sent for the salvation of the pagans, will not want to obey the Gospels. For he says, "I know that you are a hard man; you harvest where you have not sown, and gather where you have not seeded."[78] The present state of nature does not yield a harvest without seed, and there is no gathering without seeding. But this manner of speaking is wholly spiritual. We have said that this people, derived as they are from the Law, are ignorant neither of the Lord's coming nor of the salvation of the pagans. But they are unfaithful because they knew the fruit of righteousness had to be harvested in the places where the Law was not sown and it had to be gathered among the pagans who were not scattered from the seed[79] of Abraham.[80] It is for this reason that this man is "hard," specifically, one who would justify without the Law; who would gather without scattering, and who would harvest without seeding.

11. They will be entirely without pardon for hiding the preaching [of the Gospel] and for burying the talent assigned to them. They knew they were going to harvest without seed and gather what they had not sown. It would have been better to give the talent to the bankers,[81] that is to say, to the en-

75. Ibid.

76. Cf. *Ep. ad Diog.* 2.1: "You must become like a new man from the beginning, since, as you yourself admit, you are going to listen to a really new message"; trans. Eugene R. Fairweather, *Early Christian Fathers,* ed. Cyril C. Richardson (Philadelphia: Westminster Press, 1953; repr. New York: Macmillan, 1970), 313–14.

77. Both a polemical *topos* (e.g., Tertullian, *Apol.* 21.17) and an important polemic of Hilary's christological defense.

78. Mt 25.24b.                          79. *stirpe.*

80. Cf. Rom 4.13.                        81. Mt 25.27.

tire human race, preoccupied with worldly affairs. At least the talent entrusted would be put to use for the master who demanded a profit from each investment. On account of this misuse, the talent that had been buried was taken away from the servant.[82] Not only was the Gospel removed, but also the Law, and given to the one who had doubled his five talents. Thus the Lord declared, *To everyone who has it will be given, and he will have an abundance; but he who has not, even what he has will be taken away from him.*[83] The one who has, is able to have more because it is easy to grow rich in the increase of wealth, whether by generosity or through work. But how will one do it who does not sustain a loss? To those who have the use of the Gospels, the honor of the Law is also conferred, but the one who has not faith in Christ, even what honor he seems to have from the Law, is taken away from him.

82. Ibid.
83. Mt 25.29.

# CHAPTER TWENTY-EIGHT

*HEN THE Son of Man comes in his majesty and all the angels with him,*[1] and the rest. The Lord himself clarified the complete meaning of this statement. He is mindful of the time of judgment and the moment[2] when he will separate the faithful from the unfaithful,[3] and distinguish between the fruitful and the unfruitful, removing the goats from the sheep, placing each on his right and on his left.[4] He will establish those on his throne who are worthy according to their goodness or wickedness. He shows that he is with the least of his children: those who serve him with the attitude[5] of his humility, who feed him with those who hunger, who give him a drink with those who thirst, who invite him among the strangers,[6] and who clothe him with those who are naked, and who visit him with those who are sick, and who comfort him with those who are distressed.[7] He is transfused[8] into the bodies and minds of believers everywhere such that these devoted services to humanity may deserve grace, whereas their refusal provokes rejection.[9]

2. After this instruction, when he revealed the coming of a glorious return, he now told his disciples that he was going to suffer[10] so that they might learn of the close connection between the sacrament of his cross and the glory of his eternity. Integral to this occasion, the Jews took counsel on how to kill him. Once the chief priests assembled together, they waited for an opportunity to commit such a crime.[11]

1. Mt 25.31.      2. *adventu.*
3. Mt 25.32.      4. Mt 25.33.
5. *exspectatione.*      6. Mt 25.35.
7. Mt 25.36.
8. *transfunditur.* Cf. *supra,* 10.27; 12.15; *infra,* 33.6; Tertullian, *De carne Chr.* 17.3.
9. Mt 25.41–46.      10. Mt 26.1–2.
11. Mt 26.3–4.

# CHAPTER TWENTY-NINE

*HILE JESUS was in Bethany at the house of Simon the leper, a woman came to him, holding an alabaster jar of costly perfume,*[1] and the rest. At the time of his Passion, it is not for nothing that a woman poured costly perfume on the Lord's head as he was reclining at the table.[2] The disciples became indignant at this act, saying the perfume ought rather to be sold for the needs of the poor.[3] Nonetheless, the Lord approved of the woman's deed and promised there would be an eternal memorial of this deed when the Gospel is preached.[4] In the end, Judas hurried off to sell his salvation.[5]

2. This woman is a symbol of the pagan peoples who offered glory to God in the Passion of Christ. She anointed his head—for the head of Christ is God.[6] The perfume is the fruit of good works.[7] For the purpose of caring for the body, it is especially pleasing to the feminine sex.[8] In honor and praise of God, she lavished meticulous care upon his body and the full affection of a devoted heart.[9] But the disciples, as often is the case, are concerned for the salvation of Israel; this perfume should have been sold and used[10] for the poor. Yet this woman was not going to sell this perfume, whereas the poor, according to prophetic inspiration, are presented as those in need of faith.[11]

---

1. Mt 26.6.
2. Mt 26.7.
3. Mt 26.8–9.
4. Mt 26.13.
5. Mt 26.14–15.

6. 1 Cor 11.3. Yet another remark that Hilary would not have said (or cited) had he known about Homoianism, which subordinates the Son to the Father. As far as I know, he never mentions 1 Cor 11.3 again.

7. Cf. *supra*, 5.2.

8. See Mt 26.13 and 27.1–7. The first eyewitnesses of the resurrected Christ were two women.

9. *pretiosae mentis.*

10. Following Perrin's correction of the text from *suum* to *usum* (p. 146).

11. See Ps 68.6; 109.22 (cf. Rv 3.17).

The faith of the pagans had to be purchased for the salvation of this needy people.[12]

The Lord said to the disciples that there are many opportunities when they may care for the poor, but that salvation can be extended to the pagans only by his command; they have been buried together with him[13] through the pouring out of this woman's perfume.[14] Regeneration is not accorded until we die together with him in the profession of faith at baptism.[15] It is for this reason that whenever this Gospel is preached, her deed will be told. As Israel draws back from the glory of the Gospel, it is preached by the faith of the pagans. In emulation of the person of Judas, Israel has been impiously inflamed by all his hatred, and incited to destroy the name of the Lord.[16]

12. Speaking ironically.

13. Cf. Rom 6.5.

14. Mt 26.12.

15. Rom 6.4; Col 2.12.

16. Mt 26.3–4; 14–16.

# CHAPTER THIRTY

N THE FIRST DAY of Azymes,[1] *the disciples came to Jesus saying, "Where do you want us to make preparations for you to eat the Passover?"*[2] and the rest. The disciples were told to go to a certain man and say to him that the Lord, along with his disciples, wished to celebrate[3] the Passover with him.[4] They did as they were told and prepared the Passover.[5] But it was necessary that they should know how to proceed as well as learn the name of the man. Otherwise, they would be uncertain where to go or how to execute the orders for which they were sent.[6]

Even so, the prophetic utterance[7] [of the Lord] is connected with the task of accomplishing the present activity. The Lord did not name the man with whom he was going to celebrate the Passover (for the Christian name was not yet held in honor by believers[8] who recognized God truly with eyes of the heart[9] and faith). We are supposed to know that the apostles prepared the Passover of the Lord with the man who received a new name[10] at the time of the Lord.

1. I.e., Feast of Unleavened Bread.
2. Mt 26.17.
3. Lit., "make the Pasch" (*pascha ... facere*).
4. Mt 26.18.
5. Mt 26.19.
6. The apostles, as the name indicates, were those "sent" by the Lord (Tertullian, *De prescr. haer.* 20.4).
7. *sermo prophetiae.*
8. Despite the anachronism, Hilary seems to be thinking of the time when the name Christian was the object of a profession of faith. Tertullian, *Apol.* 2.3; 2.10.
9. Cf. Eph 1.18, "the eyes of your hearts" (RSV).
10. The expression "new name" is found in the second- and third-century polemical literature, e.g., Cyprian, *Test.* 1.22 (citing Is 65.13–15); Tertullian, *Ad nat.* 3; *Adv. Iud.* 13.

2. After these things, Judas is indicated as the traitor,[11] after whose departure the Passover is completed with the receiving of the cup and the breaking of the bread.[12] He was not worthy to partake in the communion of the eternal sacraments. Indeed, we understand that Judas had immediately left from the meal because he returned with the crowd.[13] He clearly could not have drunk with the Lord since he was not going to drink from the cup in the Kingdom. The Lord promised that all who were drinking from the fruit of the vine at that time would drink with him thereafter.[14]

*When they had sung a hymn, they returned to the mountain.*[15] In other words, once everything was fulfilled by the power of the divine mysteries,[16] they went out joyfully, rejoicing together in heavenly glory.[17]

3. The Lord also told the disciples about their coming weakness.[18] On that same night [as his betrayal] they all would be confounded by fear and a loss of faith. The certainty of this fact is also confirmed by the authority of ancient prophecy: "Once the shepherd is struck down, the sheep will be scattered."[19] Nevertheless, he said that he was going to precede them into Galilee as the risen one,[20] so that the promise of his return might console them in their weakness.

---

11. Mt 26.15–16, 21, 24–25.

12. Matthew's Gospel does not specify the moment when Judas left the group, but Lk 22.21–23 (contrary to Matthew) implies that Judas was present for the entire Passover meal as well as for Jesus' institution of the bread and cup.

13. Mt 26.47.

14. Mt 26.29.

15. Mt 26.30; Hilary cuts off from the verse the qualifier *oliveti* ("of Olives").

16. *divinorum mysteriorum virtutibus* (cf. 1 Cor 15.46).

17. Oddly, this is all Hilary has to say about the Last Supper. His haste to move through the passages of 26.20–30 was probably related to his preoccupation with explaining the seeming contradiction of the Divine Son confessing that his soul was troubled and sorrowful (26.37–38). This passage will become a *locus classicus* for those who wish to stress the stark reality of Jesus' Incarnation and that he must be subject to all human emotions.

18. *infirmitatis.*                          19. Mt 26.31; Zec 13.7.

20. Mt 26.32.

But Peter responded impetuously in defense of his faith: even if the others should fall away, he would never be one to fall.[21] For he was carried away by the degree of his affection and love for Christ so that he did not perceive the feebleness of his flesh and the certainty of the Lord's words. Indeed, his words were not going to be realized. The Lord said to him, "Before the cock crows, you will deny me three times."[22] Like Peter, the others likewise avowed that they would never abandon the profession of his name for fear of death.[23] With full determination for their ministry, the disciples bolstered themselves by the resolute will of faith.[24]

21. Mt 26.33.

22. Mt 26.34.

23. Mt 26.35. Confession of the name (of Christ) was central to the early apologetic and martyrdom literature. See Acts 2.38; 3.6; 4.12; *Mart. Poly.* 12.1; Justin, *Apol.* 4; Tertullian, *Apol.* 2–3; *Ad nation.* 3.

24. Given the context, this last remark of Hilary's should probably be taken as ironic.

# CHAPTER THIRTY-ONE

HEN JESUS *went with his disciples into a field*[1] *which is called Gethsemane, and said to his disciples, "Sit here while I go over there to pray,"*[2] and the rest. He welcomed the disciples' trust[3] and the steadfastness of their will devoted to him, but he also knew that they would be thrown into confusion and despair.

He told them to wait together in that place, while he went forth to pray, taking with him Peter and the sons of Zebedee, James and John.[4] Once he had taken them aside, he began to be sorrowful and troubled, saying that *his soul was sorrowful unto death.*

2. There is the opinion of some[5] that on account of his condition, sorrow had occurred in God, and the fear of his coming Passion weakened him, because he said, *My soul is sorrowful unto death,*[6] and, *Father, if it is possible, let this cup be removed from me,*[7] and again, *The spirit is willing, but the flesh is weak,*[8] and finally,

---

1. The Old Latin versions identify several different settings where Jesus and disciples entered: a field, an estate, or a villa (as does the Vulgate).

2. Mt 26.36.  3. *fidem.*

4. Mt 26.37.

5. This party is never named in the Commentary, but we cannot assume Hilary is referring to "Arians." See D. H. Williams, "Defining Orthodoxy in Hilary of Poitiers' *Commentarium in Matthaeum*," *JECS* 9 (2001): 151–71. The concern here, as it has been throughout the commentary, is not the subordination of the Son to the Father (see Hilary's closing remarks in *infra*, 33.3, n.17), but how the Son's divinity should be reckoned with his Incarnation. This christological issue is repeatedly raised in different guises: *supra*, 3.5; 5.15; 8.6; 12.8. Compare 31.2, n.5; Hilary, *De trin.* 1.31–32, which returns to the debate over Christ's words in Gethsemane. Hilary again opposes any who would twist the circumstances and words of the Passion into contradicting the divine nature in Christ. But in this case the purpose of Hilary's argument is to refute the assertion that the Son's Passion must make him a creature and subordinate to God.

6. Mt 26.38.  7. Mt 26.39.

8. Mt 26.41b.

for the second time he says, *Father, if this cup cannot be removed unless I drink from it, may your will be done.*[9] Some want to attach the neediness to his spirit[10] because of the body's weakness, as if the taking of flesh in its feeble condition corrupted the power of his incorruptible substance, or as if eternity received a fragile nature. If he is sad to the point of fear, if weak to the point of pain, if anxious to the point of death, eternity will be subjected to corruption, and thus it will fall into corruption as an effect of its many weaknesses.[11] Eternity will become what it was not: sad because of anguish, anxious because of fear, shocked because of grief, and so eternity is changed into fear. If it could in fact become something which it was not, it would not continue in the same way in which it once was.[12]

God, however, is always without measurable time, and, such as he is, he is eternal. Eternity remains in infinity,[13] extended

9. Mt 26.42.

10. *Spiritui* is in reference here to the Latin way of expressing generally the divine substance (cf. Tertullian, *Adv. Prax.* 29).

11. This line represents a kind of finale for the point Hilary has been making all along; the Incarnation does not rule out the reality of an infinite nature—both natures can subsist with each other without violating the other—which is Tertullian's argument in *Adv. Prax.* 27.11: "Because God as man was born in her, he hath builded her by the will of the Father: certainly <we find him set forth> as in every respect Son of God and Son of Man, since we find him as both God and Man, without doubt according to each substance as it is distinct in what itself is, because neither is the Word anything else but God nor the flesh anything else but man. Thus also the apostle teaches of both his substances: Who was made, he says, of the seed of David—here he will be man, and Son of Man: Who was defined as Son of God according to the Spirit—here he will be God, and the Word, the Son of God: we observe a double quality, not confused but combined, Jesus in one Person God and Man. I postpone <the consideration> of 'Christ.' And to such a degree did there remain unimpaired the proper being of each substance, that in him the Spirit carried out its own acts, that is, powers and works and signs, while the flesh accomplished its own passions, hungering in company of the devil, thirsting in company of the Samaritan woman, weeping for Lazarus, sore troubled unto death—and at length it also died"; Latin version and trans., E. Evans, *Tertullian's Treatise Against Praxeas* (London: SPCK, 1948), 173. Cf. *De carne Chr.* 18.6–7.

12. Tertullian, *Adv. Hermog.* 12.4: "The eternal (*aeternitas*) cannot be changed because, if it were changed, the eternal would not exist" (see Kroymann ed., CCSL 1.407). Novatian, *De trin.* 4.24: "Whatever is that which is God must always exist, because it is necessary that he always exist, preserving himself by his own powers" (see PL 3:920A).

13. *aeternitas autem in infinito manens.* Tertullian (*Apol.* 48.11) defines God, whose proper substance is eternity; Novatian, *De trin.* 2.11, *semper aeternus.*

as it were in these things which have been and in those things which will follow; it will be always complete, incorruptible, perfect. Apart from [eternity] nothing remains if it exists apart from him. Eternity is not bound to a particular place, but everything within it is capable of conferring upon us that which is his own, lacking nothing in itself which it has given.

3. But their entire idea is as follows: they think that the fear of death occurred in the Son of God, and assert that he proceeded,[14] not from eternity nor was he brought forth from the Father's infinite substance,[15] but was produced out of nothing[16] through him who created all things.[17] He was derived *ex nihilo*, and had a beginning from things that are made, and was established within time. Because of the anxiety produced in him by sorrow, because the suffering of the Spirit with the suffering of the body, because of the fear of death—such that he could fear death and was capable of dying, it was possible for him to die. Although he will be present in the future, he is nevertheless not, from him who begot him, eternal in the past. If these men

14. *prolatum.*

15. The Son was in the Father before he "proceeded" as an independent entity (Hanson, *The Search*, 468). See *supra*, 16, n.22. It has been rightly noted that Hilary is making a distinction of time in the career of the Word, "before he was born," that which he was in the Father, and that which he possessed by means of his birth once he proceeded from the Father. Such a position negates the eternal generation of the Son, since he is eternal, not because his birth is eternal, but because by his birth he comes into full possession of the eternal divinity. This undermines the idea that Hilary had been exposed to the terminology and emphases that governed pro-Nicene theology.

16. *ex nullo.* Hilary would have already been hardened to the feasibility of this argument through Tertullian's *Adv. Prax.* 7.6–8: "But I affirm that from God nothing void and empty can have come forth, for he is not void and empty from whom it has been brought forth: and that that cannot lack substance which has proceeded from so great a substance ... from what is empty and void nothing can be made. [Can you describe as] an empty and void object that Word of God whom Scripture calls the Son, who also is designated God—'And the Word was with God, and the Word was God' [Jn 1.1]?" E. Evans, ed. and trans., *Tertullian's Treatise Against Praxeas,* 138. Cf. Tertullian's *Apol.* 21.11 for key terms relative to the generation of the Son.

17. Some MSS read *per eum qui eum creavit effectum* (instead of *per eum qui omnia creavit ...*) (PL 9:100D). Doignon (*Sur Matt.* II.228 n.8) suspects that some copyists corrected the *eum* to *omnia* in order to protect Hilary from any suspicion of Arianism.

were capable of being receptive to the Gospels through their faith and a commendable life, they would know that the Word was in the beginning God and from this beginning with God.[18] They would know that he was born from what he was, and that he possesses that into which he is born because he is himself in possession of what he was before he was born.[19] In other words, the one who generated[20] and the one who is begotten have the same eternity.[21] Nothing in God can die nor is there any fear in God within himself. For in Christ, God was reconciling the world to himself.[22]

4. We must examine this whole passage[23] so that when we read that the Lord was sorrowful we may find the reasons for his troubled state. Earlier, he warned that [the disciples] would all fall away. Peter responded, full of confidence that even if others should be shaken, he would not be moved,[24] to whom the Lord likewise responded that he was going to deny him three times.[25] Nonetheless, Peter and all the rest of the disciples swore that they would not deny him even if it meant their deaths.[26]

Proceeding on, he told his disciples to wait together while he prayed.[27] Having taken Peter, James, and John with him, he began to grieve.[28] He did not grieve before he took them, nor did

---

18. Using the prologue of John was exceedingly common in Latin christology to show unity of substance of the Father and the Son. See Tertullian, *Adv. Prax.* 7.8; 8.4; 12.6; 13.3; 16.1; especially 21.1; though in 19.6 he uses Jn 1.1 to show that, unlike the Father, the Spirit had a beginning.

19. *natum esse ex eo qui erat et hoc in eo esse qui natus est quod is ipse est penes quem erat ante quam nasceretur.* Cf. Tertullian, *Adv. Prax.* 5.3: "... because the Word itself, having its ground in reason, shows reason to be prior as being its substance" (Evans, *Against Praxeas,* 135, slightly modified); *Adv. Hermog.* 5.3: *Si a deo accepit quod est dei, ordinem dico aeternitatis* (ed. Kroymann, CCSL 1.401); Novatian, *De trin.* 31.4, PL 3:978.

20. *gignentis.*

21. Tertullian, *Adv. Prax.* 7.4: "[E]vidently under the name of Wisdom and of Reason and of the whole divine mind and spirit [we are to understand] the Word, who became Son of God when by proceeding from him he was begotten" (Evans, *Against Praxeas,* 137).

22. 2 Cor 5.19.
23. Mt 26.33–37.
24. Mt 26.33.
25. Mt 26.34.
26. Mt 26.35.
27. Mt 26.36.
28. Mt 26.37.

his fear begin until they were with him. His agony did not take place for his own sake, but for the sake of those who were with him. We should remember that he had taken no others with him than those disciples. To these same men it was also shown that the Son of Man was going to come into his Kingdom when, standing on the mountain with Moses and Elijah, he was enveloped in the full splendor of his eternal glory.[29] So the reason for having taken the disciples was the same now as it was then.

5. Then the Lord said, *My soul is sorrowful unto death.*[30] Did he say, "My soul is sorrowful because of death"? Certainly not. Had he been afraid of death, he should have referred to it for what it was. But it is one thing to fear something until it happens and another to be afraid because of the thing itself.[31] Something may not produce a [certain] cause because things turn out differently from the way in which they start.

The Lord had said earlier, *You will fall away this very night on account of me.*[32] He knew that his disciples were going to be terrified and put to flight, and would deny him. Because blasphemy against the Spirit is not forgiven either in this world or in the one to come,[33] the Lord was afraid that they would deny God when they observed his being killed, spat upon, and crucified. This is the reason that preserved Peter when he denied him: *I do not know the man,*[34] since any word against the Son of Man will be forgiven. The Lord is, therefore, *sorrowful unto death.* It is not the fear of death, but the process of death.[35] Later on, the faith of believers will be established by the power of resurrection.

6. Following this, *Stay here and keep watch with me. And going forward he fell with his face to the ground in prayer.*[36] He told the disciples to remain with him and stay alert. For he knew that, under pressure from the devil,[37] their faith would be put to sleep.

---

29. *Supra,* 17.2–3.
30. Mt 26.38.
31. *Supra,* 31.1–2.
32. Mt 26.31.
33. *in aeternum.* Cf. Mt 12.31.
34. Mt 26.72.
35. That is, the timing of the disciples' weakness.
36. Mt 26.38–39.
37. *ingravante diabolo.*

So he told them to keep watch with him since the same passion would fall on them.

7. Then he prayed, *My Father, if it is possible, let this cup pass from me, yet not as I will but as you will.*[38] He asked that the cup pass from him. He certainly did not say, "Let this cup pass by me." This would be a prayer of one who feared for himself. But it is one thing to pray that it pass by him and another that it pass from him.[39] In the matter of what passes by him, he himself is removed from the trouble of what is passing by.[40] By asking that it may pass from him, he is not seeking that he should be passed over, but that when it has passed from him, it may withdraw into another.[41] Was it possible for Christ not to suffer?[42] And yet, even from the foundation of the world this sacrament was revealed in him for our salvation.[43] Did he not want to suffer himself? Did he not commit the blood of his body earlier to be poured out for the forgiveness of sins?[44] How is it he said, *Father, if it is possible,* and, *Not as I will, but as you will?* His whole fear, accordingly, is for those who were going to suffer. Because it is not possible that he did not suffer,[45] he asks for those who were going to suffer after him, by saying, *Let this cup pass from me.*[46] In other words, just as I drink the cup [the Lord says], so

38. Mt 26.39.

39. Now that Hilary has attributed all the Son's weakness to other causes rather than himself, he is committed to this kind of forced logic from the biblical passages.

40. *a molestia transeuntis.*

41. I.e., the disciples.

42. This suggests that the notion that Hilary wholly rejected the suffering of the incarnate Son needs significant qualification. R. P. C. Hanson, *The Search for the Doctrine of God* (Edinburgh: T & T Clark, 1988), 497–502. But see Carl Beckwith, *In the Shadow of the Incarnation* (Notre Dame: University of Notre Dame Press, 2008), 71–96.

43. Cf. Eph 1.9; 3.9.

44. Mt 26.28.

45. This was a difficult issue for Hilary to explain adequately, given the reality of Christ's temptation in Mt 4. See J. Doignon, "L'*argumentatio* d'Hilaire de Poitiers dans l'*exemplum* de la Tentation de Jésus (*In Matthaeum* 3, 1–5)," *Vig. Chr.* 29 (1975): 296–308. Hilary's concept of the Son's suffering is best revealed in *De trin.* 10.23–35. While Christ was truly tempted and subjected to suffering, his divine *virtus* (power) prevented him from feeling pain as we do because of his sinless state.

46. Mt 26.39.

let them drink it in hope without discouragement, without a sense of sorrow, and without the fear of death.

8. He says, *if it is possible,* because flesh and blood shrink in terror from these things, and it is hard for human bodies not to sink beneath their affliction. That which he says, *Not as I will, but as you will,* means that he would rather they not suffer, lest perhaps they should despair in suffering, but that they win the glory of his co-inheritance[47] without the hardship of suffering. He did not ask that they should not suffer; as he said, *Not as I will,* but what the Father wills, so that the strength of drinking the cup may pass from him to them. It was the will of the Father that the devil must be conquered, not only by Christ but also by his disciples.

9. After this, he returned to the disciples and found them sleeping,[48] and he reproached Peter for not keeping watch with him for at least one hour.[49] He spoke to Peter among the three because he had been the one to boast that he would not fall away with the others.

Earlier Jesus indicated the reason[50] for his fear when he said, *Pray that you not enter into temptation.*[51] This he wanted (and the reason for having given us the prayer: *Lead us not into temptation*),[52] lest the weakness of the flesh have power over us. The reason why he told them to pray is that they would not come into temptation, which he shows by saying, *The spirit is willing, but the flesh is weak.*[53] This statement was certainly not in reference to him, but for their sakes.[54] How can the passage *the spirit is willing* pertain to him, if he said previously that his soul was sorrowful unto death?[55] He instructs them to keep watch and

47. *cohereditas,* a neologism (Kinnavey, 3).
48. Mt 26.40.
49. Ibid.
50. Reading *causas* instead of *causae* (Perrin, 146).
51. Mt 26.41.                          52. Mt 6.13.
53. Mt 26.41.
54. Hilary will continue to use this exegetical explanation in *De trin.* for scriptural passages that attribute weakness to the Son.
55. I.e., the contradiction between the two phrases demonstrates that the passage is not describing the Lord.

to pray lest they fall into temptation, and lest they succumb to the weakness of the body. For this reason, he prays that the cup may pass from him if possible, because of the utter weakness of the flesh in drinking it.

10. Again he went away and prayed, *Father, is this cup not able to pass unless I drink it? May your will be done.*[56] Since his disciples were going to suffer on account of the justification of faith,[57] the Lord assumed all our bodily weakness in himself, and he fixed to the cross, along with himself, everything which renders us vulnerable to sin.[58] He bore our sins and endured our sorrows for us,[59] since we must fight against the devil in the combat of suffering[60] with the fervent zeal of our faith. All the weaknesses[61] of our sorrows were put to death by his body and his suffering. And so the cup could not pass from him except he drink it because we are not able to suffer except by his Passion.[62]

11. That upon his return he found them sleeping yet again,[63] shows that many of us are possessed by a kind of sleepy faith during the time of the Lord's absence. Again he prayed, repeating the same words,[64] and when he returned, he told them to keep watch, having already reproached them for sleeping, with the words, *Are you still sleeping and taking your rest?*[65]

56. Mt 26.42. Hilary's text omits the "if." The Old Latin and Vulgate read, *si non potest hoc transire* ...

57. The disciples' (or apostles') suffering for the Gospel is a common theme for Hilary; *supra*, 10.10; 14; 20.20; 22.5.

58. *universa ea quibus infirmabamur*, which for Hilary carries not merely the idea of weakness, but of concupiscence or tendency to sin. *Supra*, 7.7; 31.2; *De trin.* 6.37.

59. Cf. Is 53.4.

60. This may be an abridged reference to the "combat of the martyrs" in parallel to Tertullian's *Ad mart.* 1 (*Sur Matt.* II.237, n.23); nonetheless, Christian martyrs were generally understood as fighting the devil: *Martyrdom of Polycarp* 2.4; *Passio Perpetuae* 10.14; Eusebius, *HE* 5.1, 23, 27.

61. *imbecillitatum.*

62. We suffer with Christ's sufferings, but only his sufferings are redemptive and usher in justification by faith.

63. Mt 26.43.                    64. Mt 26.44.

65. Mt 26.45.

After assiduous prayer and repeatedly coming and going from the disciples, the Lord removed the fear, restored confidence, made an invitation to rest, and now steadfastly awaits the Father's will for us saying, *Let your will be done*. By his drinking the cup that would pass to us, he received the weakness of our body, the anxiety of our fear, and the very pain of our death.

When the Lord returned to them and found them sleeping the first time, he rebuked them; he was silent during the second time; and on the third occasion he told them to take their rest. The interpretation of this is as follows. In the first instance, he finds them scattered, mistrustful, and fearful after his resurrection;[66] in the second, when their eyes were too heavy to perceive the liberty of the Gospel,[67] he visited them, sending the Spirit, the Paraclete.[68] Tied down for some time by an attachment to the Law, the disciples were possessed by a kind of sleepy faith. Yet, on the third occasion, that is, upon his glorious return, he will restore them to confidence and rest.

---

66. Cf. Lk 24.37, 41.
68. Cf. Jn 20.22.

67. Cf. Lk 24.30–35; Acts 1.6–11.

# CHAPTER THIRTY-TWO

HILE HE WAS *still speaking, behold Judas, one of the twelve, came and with him a large crowd.*[1] In all of these points we find the orderly arrangement[2] of the Passion. The kiss of Judas[3] has meaning that teaches us to love our enemies and those who we know will commit violence against us.[4] For the Lord did not reject his kiss. Because he said to Judas, *Do what you are going to do,*[5] he gives in this statement the power for his betrayal.[6] For he who had the prerogative to call upon twelve thousand legions of angels[7] against traitors was certainly able to take action easily against the schemes and plots of a single man. The Lord likewise said to Pilate, *You do not have power over me except what is given to you.*[8] Judas was given the power with the saying, *Do what you are going to do.* Just as criminal intent is measured according to the ill will of the action, Judas could accomplish what he already wanted to do.

2. *One of those who were with him drew his sword and cut off the ear of the servant of the high priest, and the Lord said to him, "Put your sword back in its place. For all who use the sword will die by the sword."*[9] This man was already judged since by using the sword he will die by the sword. Death by the sword is not usual for all who use it, since fever or some accident kills a great number of those who have used the sword out of necessity, whether in service of legal judgment[10] or in fighting off robbers. Nevertheless, the ear of the high priest's servant is cut off by the apostle. In

1. Mt 26.47.
2. *ratio.*
3. Mt 26.49.
4. Mt 5.44.
5. Jn 13.27.
6. *traditionis suae potestatem.*
7. Mt 26.53.
8. Jn 19.11.
9. Mt 26.51–52. Hilary's version of v.51 varies from the Old Latin at a number of points, though the meaning is not greatly affected.
10. *iudicii officio;* that is, the *ius gladii* or "justice of the sword."

other words, the hearing of a disobedient people subject to the priesthood was cut off by Christ's disciple, and that ear which did not hear in reception of the truth was now amputated.[11] In fact, the entire crowd advanced against the Lord armed with swords. He ordered that the sword be put away[12] because the Lord would one day destroy them not by human means, but by the sword of his mouth.[13] If, according to his statement, everyone who uses the sword will be killed by the sword, then the sword was rightly drawn for the death of those who were using it to commit a crime.

3. The rest of the events follow a pattern:[14] false witnesses were procured,[15] and the priest was ignorant of the very Law in which he boasted when he sought assurance with an oath whether [the Lord] was the Christ[16] as if the Law and the prophets did not covertly speak of him. In fact, the priest himself confessed Christ unwillingly when the Lord said to him, *You have said it.*[17] As soon as he heard of his majesty, the priest tore his own clothes;[18] that is, he tore the veil which covered the Law.[19] With fists and spitting,[20] every kind of insult was inflicted on Christ in order to consummate the debasement of his humanity.[21]

4. We must carefully consider in what context Peter made his denial, even though we treated this previously.[22] At first, he says that he did not understand what she [servant-girl] was saying.[23] Then he denied that he belonged to Jesus' followers.[24] And the third time, he declared he did not know the man.[25] It is true that Peter denied the Lord, though very nearly without sacri-

11. See Rom 10.17 for the implication.
12. *recondi* ("to be resheathed").         13. Rv 19.15. Cf. *supra,* 10.23.
14. *ordinem.*                                              15. Mt 26.59–60.
16. Mt 26.64.                                            17. Ibid.
18. Mt 26.65.
19. Cf. Mt 27.51. An allusion to the tearing of the veil in the Temple.
20. Mt 26.67.
21. A slight play on the words *homo* ("man") and *humi* ("in" or "on the ground").
22. *Supra,* 31.5.
23. Mt 26.70.
24. Fits with Mk 14.69–70, rather than Matthew's account.
25. Mt 26.72, 74.

lege because he had been the first to recognize him as the Son of God.[26] Nevertheless, because he was doubtful on account of the weakness of his flesh, he wept bitterly.[27] Peter could not evade the weight of his guilt knowing that he had already been warned.

5. Finally Christ was brought before Pilate, judge of the pagans. He who was without guile or sin could not be found guilty according to the Law. *Then when Judas, who betrayed him, saw that he was condemned.*[28] Driven by remorse, Judas returned the blood money to the priests, but because he was the author of selling out innocent blood,[29] his admission of selling likewise accused the faithlessness of those who bribed him. So they[30] responded, *What is that to us? See to it yourself.*[31] Their admission is shameless and blind. They understood that they had bought innocent blood and believed they were beyond the threat of judgment. By saying, *See to it yourself,* they established the guilt of their transaction. The testimony of the one who was bribed is set against the sin of those who made the bribe.

Judas then withdrew and hung himself[32] for having condemned Christ. The time of Judas's death took place during the Lord's Passion, when Hades[33] was shaken[34] and the heights of heavens[35] were torn apart to the amazement of all elements in their normal course,[36] even to the point of forgetting their [usual] functions.[37] In the case of Judas, he was neither visited

26. Hilary is not trying to minimize Peter's action. We must remember that Hilary's definition of blasphemy (against the Holy Spirit) is to deny that the incarnate Christ is anything less than God (*supra*, 5.15; 12.15–17). To deny Jesus the man, as Peter does, quite literally in the passage, *se hominem non posse,* is a denial though it does not qualify as blasphemy.

27. Mt 26.75.

28. Mt 27.3.

29. Lit., "blood of the just one" (*sanguinis iusti*).

30. The chief priests and elders.          31. Mt 27.4.

32. Mt 27.5.                                              33. Lit., "lower regions." (*infernis*)

34. Based on 1 Pt 3.19 and described before Hilary's era in a popular narrative about Christ's Passion, the *Acts of Pilate*. Cf. Tertullian, *De anima* 55.5.

35. Lit., "all of the upper regions" (*supernis omnibus*).

36. Cf. Tertullian, *Ad nat.* 2.5.14, that the heavenly elements or bodies forget not to fulfill their course in certain orbits.

37. Nature "forgets" its usual functions during Christ's crucifixion: Mt 27.45, 51b–53.

among the dead[38] nor had he an opportunity to repent among the living after the Lord's Resurrection.

6. Because the silver pieces that were returned were blood money and not Corban,[39] they were not permitted to be mixed in with the money offered [to the Temple treasury].[40] The priests purchased, after deliberation, a potter's field and designated it as a burial ground for strangers.[41] This is a tremendous prophetic sacrament,[42] because in these wicked deeds there are deep[43] and amazing presentiments.[44]

The work of the potter is to fashion vessels from clay; by whose hand a vessel or something more beautiful is fashioned from the very same material.[45] The field is said to be the world[46] as declared by our Lord's own words.[47] With the price paid for Christ, the world is purchased; that is, he attains everything that belongs to him[48] although he is assigned to a grave of strangers and paupers. None of this concerns Israel since everything of this world which is gained is used by others; the whole of this world is utilized by others, those who will be buried by the cost of Christ's blood, by which the whole world was purchased.[49] For he received from the Father all things which are in heaven and on earth.[50] This too applies to the potter's field since all things belong to God, by whose hand we are fashioned just as the potter wishes. Because we have died and have been buried together with Christ,[51] we will find in this field eternal rest from our pilgrimage. As an assurance of this fact, the prophecy from Jeremiah is added[52] so that the authority of

38. 1 Pt 3.19–20.
39. The term appears only once in the New Testament, namely, in Mk 7.11, and means literally, an offering in the Temple (presented to God).
40. Mt 27.6.
41. Mt 27.7.
42. Mt 27.9 (that is, the potter's field as a burial ground).
43. *plena.*                                    44. *miraculi.*
45. Cf. Rom 9.21.                               46. Mt 13.38.
47. Ibid.
48. As maker and sustainer of the world; cf. Col 1.20–22; Eph 1.10–11.
49. Hilary is combining several themes of redemption here: Acts 20.28; Eph 1.7; Col 2.12.
50. Mt 28.18.                                   51. Rom 6.4.
52. Mt 27.9–10.

the divine voice, uttered much earlier, may be elucidated in the fulfillment of these events.

7. When Pilate asked whether he was king of the Jews, he responded, *You say it.*[53] Yet how different is the statement which he had made to the priest! When the latter had questioned whether he was the Christ, he had said, *You have said it.*[54] This is because the entire Law proclaimed that Christ would come. He responded to the priest in the past tense[55] because the Law had always said that Christ would come. But to the one ignorant of the Law, asking whether he was king of the Jews, the Lord said, *You say it,* because salvation of the pagans is through the faith of a personal confession.[56] And although Pilate speaks about what was unknown to him, the chief priests denied those things which had been spoken before.[57]

53. Mt 27.11.
54. Mt 26.64.
55. Lit., "it was understood by the priest as a past event" (*respondetur . . . de praeteritis sacerdoti*).
56. *praesentis confessionis.* Reference to the new believers' confession at the time of baptism.
57. A hint at exculpation of Pilate is already found in early Christian literature, especially *Acts of Pilate* 9.2–5, "Letters" of Pilate to Claudius and to Tiberius, and the *Gospel of Peter* 11. See *infra,* 33.1.

# CHAPTER THIRTY-THREE

*HILE PILATE was sitting on the tribunal, his wife sent him a message saying, "There is nothing between you and this just man."*[1] An image of the pagans is in this woman, who, already believing,[2] summoned her husband and an unbelieving people to faith in Christ. Because she herself had suffered much for Christ,[3] she invited her husband to the same glory of a future hope. And so Pilate washed his hands and bore witness to the Jews that he was innocent of the Lord's blood.[4] While the Jews have accepted upon themselves and their children the crime of shedding the Lord's blood, the pagans, by washing themselves,[5] are daily passing over to a confession of faith.[6]

2. Then Pilate, in light of the custom observed during Feast days[7] in which he was supposed to release one prisoner whom the crowd demanded, offered to free Jesus. At the instigation of the priests, the people instead chose Barabbas,[8] whose name means "son of the father." Already is the mystery[9] of their future unbelief shown here: instead of Christ they preferred the "son of the father," namely, the Antichrist, who is the man of sin and the son of the devil.[10] Incited by their leaders, the Jews chose the one who is reserved for damnation rather than the Author of their salvation.

---

1. Mt 27.19.
2. *fidelis.*
3. Mt 27.19 (in a dream).
4. Mt 27.24.
5. I.e., in baptism.
6. Cf. Tertullian, *De bapt.* 5.6.
7. Lit., "of the festal day" (*solemnis diei*).
8. Mt 27.21.
9. *arcanum.*
10. 2 Thes 2.3–4; Jn 8.44; Acts 13.10. Hilary's definition of the Antichrist as "son of the father" shares the later fourth-century meaning as exhibited in Ambrose, *In Lucam* 10.102, and Jerome, *De nominibus hebraicis* 97.

3. After the Lord was beaten, a scarlet robe and a purple cloak[11] were put on him and a crown of thorns. With a reed in his right hand he was mocked as they knelt and worshiped him.[12] It is clear that by assuming all the weaknesses of our body, the Lord was being steeped in the scarlet-colored blood of all the martyrs who will follow and to whom belongs the Kingdom with him.[13] With honor worthy of the prophets and the patriarchs, the Lord is clothed in purple. He also is crowned with thorns, that is, the sins of the pagans who pierced him. In this way glory could be derived from pernicious and worthless things that encircled the head of God. For the points of the thorns are the sins from which the crown of Christ's victory is woven.[14] By the reed held in his hand we understand the strengthening of the weakness and frailty of the same pagans. Furthermore, his head is struck, though a wound inflicted by the reed is not, I think, a serious injury to the head. Rather, a typological reason[15] is served by this: specifically, the weakness of the pagans,[16] which was previously held in Christ's hand, rests in God the Father, who is his head.[17] Amid all these particulars, while Christ is being mocked, he is worshiped.

4. As they were going out, they placed the wood[18] of his Passion on a certain man from Cyrene.[19] The Jews were unworthy to carry the cross of Christ, so it was left to the faith of the pagans, both to take the cross and to suffer together with him. The location of the cross is such that, placed in the cen-

11. Mt 27.28 (scarlet robe); Mk 15.17 (purple cloak). Hilary conflates the two accounts.

12. Mt 27.29. These were the soldiers of the governor.

13. Cf. Rv 6.9; 7.13–17; 18.24. A reflection of the third century's view that those Christians who were martyred for the faith were immediately translated to heaven; Tertullian, *De anima* 55; Cyprian, *De exhort. mart.* 13.

14. Cf. 1 Cor 15.54–55: "When the perishable puts on the imperishable, and the mortal puts on immortality, then shall come to pass the saying that is written: 'Death is swallowed up in victory. O death, where is thy victory? O death, where is thy sting?'" (RSV).

15. *typica in eo ratio.*

16. Lit., "of the pagan bodies" (*gentilium corporum*).

17. Cf. 1 Cor 11.3: "God is the head of Christ."

18. I.e., the cross.

19. Mt 27.32.

ter of the earth,[20] it stands, as it were, above this world, offering equally to all pagan peoples the means of embracing the knowledge of God.[21]

He refused to drink a mixture of wine and gall which was offered to him,[22] because the bitterness of sin is not mixed with the incorruption of eternal glory.[23] And his garments, which, rather than being torn, were divided up by casting lots,[24] signified that his body remained incorruptible.

5. And so it was that the salvation and life of all was hung on the tree of life.[25] To his left and right, two thieves were crucified,[26] showing that the whole human race everywhere is called to the sacrament of the Lord's Passion. But because there is a difference between believers and unbelievers, there is an overall division between those on the right and those on the left.[27] The thief placed to the right was saved by the justification of faith.[28]

Its disgrace is compounded when Israel accused itself of unbelief with the words: *Here is the one who would destroy the Temple of God and in three days rebuild it,*[29] and the rest. This is presented as the greatest and the most difficult issue of all. What pardon will there be for these when, after three days, they see the rebuilding of the Temple of God in his bodily resurrection?[30] No less do the two thieves heap insult on him for his sufferings,[31]

---

20. *positus in medio terrae.* The idea that the cross was at the center of the earth stems from longstanding description of the place of crucifixion as at the middle of the world. See Pseudo-Cyprian's *De ligno crucis:* "there is a place at the center of the world called Golgotha." Cf. Tertullian, *Adv. Marc.* 3.18.4–5.

21. Cf. Is 2.2–4, also utilized by Cyprian, *Test.* 2.18.

22. Mt 27.34.

23. Scriptural backdrop for the antithesis of bitterness with the divine life; see Rom 3.14 and Eph 4.31.

24. Mt 27.35; Jn 19.24.

25. There is an implicit reference to the two trees of life: one is in Paradise, and the other is the cross, as portrayed in Commodian, *Instructiones* 1.35.11–14.

26. Lit., "adfixed" (*adfiguntur*); Mt 27.38.

27. Cf. Mt 25.32–33. See *supra,* 28.1.

28. This was the thief on the right, who sought to enter Christ's Kingdom.

29. Mt 27.40. Hilary changes the beginning of the verse from second to third person singular.

30. The destroying and rebuilding of the Temple is a metaphor for Jesus' body in Ps.-Cyprian, *De montibus Sina et Sion* 4.

31. Mt 27.44.

which shows how the scandal of the cross will be for all believers.[32]

6. As there is a dividing between the hours of night and the day, so too the number of three days and nights is fulfilled,[33] while the veiled mystery of divine action is realized in the confusion of all creation.[34] Then there is the cry unto God which is the voice of the Lord's body[35] attesting to the separation of the Word of God as it withdrew from him. Why did he cry out about being abandoned, *My God, my God, why have you forsaken me?*[36] He is abandoned because it was necessary for him to be subject to his humanity until the finality of death.[37] Moreover, we must consider carefully why he drank sour wine given to him from a sponge on a stick[38] and then rendered up his spirit with a cry.[39] The wine is the honor and power of immortality, which turned sour on account of our sin and negligence. Although the wine had soured in Adam,[40] Christ accepted it from pagan hands and drank it. It was offered that he might drink from a sponge on a stick; that is, he received the corporeal sins of pagans, sins that corrupt eternally. He transferred these sins of ours to himself and to the communion of his immortality. After he had finished drinking, as it reads in John, he said, *It is completed,*[41] since he had drained the cup of all the sin of human corruption. And because there was nothing else that needed to be done, he breathed out his spirit[42] with a loud shout, saddened that he bore not all of humanity's sins.[43]

32. Cf. Gal 5.11.

33. As in the sign of Jonah, Mt 12.40.

34. I.e., darkness during the day, Mt 27.45; earthquakes, 27.51.

35. *corporis vox est.* For Hilary's view of the relation between Christ's divinity and his body, see Introduction, 29–30.

36. Mt 27.46. Cf. Tertullian, *Adv. Prax.* 30.1–2.

37. Mt 27.46.                              38. Mt 27.48.

39. Mt 27.50.

40. 1 Cor 15.22: "For as in Adam all die, so also in Christ shall all be made alive" (RSV). Cf. Irenaeus's discussion of how Christ, another Adam, conquered the conquered state of the fallen Adam. *Adv. haer.* 3.23.6–8; 5.1.3.

41. Jn 19.30.

42. Lit., "he emitted his spirit to the outside [of his body]" (*extrinsecus spiritum ... emittit*). Cf. Tertullian, *De resurr.* 18.8.

43. *dolens non omnium se peccata portare.* That is, the sin of Judas. See *Sur*

7. Then the veil of the Temple was torn,[44] and from that moment the people were divided into factions while the honor of the veil[45] was removed along with the protection of its guardian angel.[46] The earth quaked,[47] for it had not the capacity to receive the Lord among the dead. *Rocks were split apart,*[48] for the Word of God and might of his eternal power pierced all that is fortified and strong as he entered them. *And the tombs were broken open,*[49] for the bonds of death were loosed. *And many bodies of the saints who slept were resurrected.*[50] By illuminating the darkness of death and shedding light upon the gloom of Hades,[51] he took the spoils from death itself[52] at the resurrection of the saints[53] who saw him immediately. But Israel's crime of unbelief was compounded when the centurion and guards, upon seeing these contradictions of all nature, confessed him as the Son of God.[54]

8. There are the facts that Joseph (of Arimathea) asked Pilate to turn the body over to him,[55] and wrapped it in a linen sheet,[56] and placed it in a new tomb which had been cut out of rock, and a huge stone was rolled in front of the entrance to the tomb.[57] Provided that this is the right order of events and that it was necessary to bury him who would soon be resurrected from the dead, still, every one of the acts would not have been described unless there was some importance to them.

Joseph presents a figure[58] of the apostles, which is the rea-

---

*Matt.* II.257, n.20. Cf. *supra,* 32.5 (Jn 13.11). It seems an odd remark to make at this point since Hilary has just proclaimed the totality of Christ's redemptive action (*omne vitium humanae corruptionis*). Moreover, it is incongruent for Hilary to attribute the personal experience of *dolens* to the Son, whereas he has made a painstaking case in 31.3 against the Son's experiencing genuine sorrow or suffering as we understand it.

44. Mt 27.51.
45. Cf. Ex 40.3; Lv 16.2.
46. 2 Bar 6.7 describes how God sent an angel into the Holy of Holies in order to guard the veil and mercy seat, etc., until the end of times.

47. Mt 27.51.                          48. Ibid.
49. Ibid.                              50. Mt 27.52.
51. *infernorum.*                      52. Col 2.14.
53. Mt 27.52–53.                       54. Mt 27.54.
55. Mt 27.58.                          56. Mt 27.59.
57. Mt 27.60.                          58. *speciem.*

son (though he was not numbered among the twelve apostles) why he is declared as the Lord's disciple.[59] It was Joseph who wrapped the body in a clean linen sheet, the same linen sheet[60] on which every kind of animal was let down from heaven to Peter.[61] From this, it is perhaps not superfluous to understand from the representation of this linen sheet that the Church is buried together with Christ[62] because in this sheet, just as in the Church's confession, the diversity of clean and unclean creatures[63] has been assembled.[64] Thus, the Lord's body is laid to rest in an empty and new chamber, hewn out of stone, just as through the apostolic teaching Christ is conveyed into the hard heart of the pagans hewn out by the labor of teaching, making a rough and new chamber where fear of God had never entered before. Since nothing except Christ ought to enter our hearts,[65] a stone was rolled in front of the entrance. Just as no author before him had conveyed to us divine knowledge, so nothing would be conveyed after him.

Then there was their[66] fear that the body should be stolen,[67] and the guarding and sealing of the tomb, which bear witness to their folly and unbelief. They wanted to seal the tomb of the one who had awakened a dead man from his tomb, as they had seen.[68]

9. The earthquake on the morning of the Lord's Day[69] is the power of the resurrection as the sting of death is destroyed[70] and the darkness of death is illuminated. Hades is shaken with alarm at the resurrection of the Lord—the Lord of the heavenly powers. The angel of the Lord descending from heaven, rolling the stone back [away from the entrance], and sitting on the tomb,[71] is a token of the mercy of God the Father sending to

59. Mt 27.57.

60. Perhaps an echo of Cyprian's *De unit. eccles.* 7, wherein an untorn garment is the symbol of the Church's unity. The point of the vision was to show the unity of Jews and Gentiles.

61. Acts 10.11–12.

62. Cf. Rom 6.4; Col 2.12.

63. *animalium.*

64. Cf. Cyprian, *De unit. eccles.* 5.

65. See *supra,* 11.1.

66. Mt. 27.63–64.

67. Mt 27.64.

68. E.g., Lazarus (Jn 11).

69. Mt 28.1 says, "toward the dawn of the first day of the week" (RSV).

70. 1 Cor 15.55–56.

71. Mt 28.2.

the Son, who arose from Hades, the assistance of the heavenly powers. And so he is himself the first sign[72] of the resurrection[73] so that it may be proclaimed as a particular means of serving[74] the Father's will.

The Lord immediately greeted and presented himself to the women, who had been encouraged by the angel.[75] This was done so that when the women announced his resurrection to the waiting disciples, they would declare it from Christ's own mouth rather than the angel's. Because the women were the first to see the Lord, it is they who greet him, it is they who fall prostrate before him, and he tells them to declare him to the apostles.[76] Now the customary pattern,[77] which had been from the beginning, is reversed. Whereas death had its beginning from the female sex, the same sex was the first to bring the tidings of the glory, the sighting, the benefit, and the news of the resurrection.[78] The guards, who had seen all these things, were paid to keep silent about the resurrection and to lie about a theft [of the body].[79] In other words, [God's] glory is denied by the honor and desire of the world whose honor is found in money.[80]

[Remaining text missing.]

72. *index.*　　　　　　　　　　73. Mt 28.6–8.
74. *quodam famulatu.*　　　　　75. Mt 28.5–9.
76. Mt 28.10.
77. *ordo;* i.e., of creation and the fall.
78. A not uncommon exegesis with an implicit precedence in parallels drawn between Eve and Mary. See Irenaeus, *Adv. haer.* 5.19.1: the former obeyed the serpent, the latter the angel; the former disobeyed God, the latter was obedient to God; "just as the human race was subjected to death by means of a virgin, so it is freed by a virgin"; *Irenaeus of Lyons,* ed. Robert Grant (Routledge, 1997), 171. See also Tertullian, *De carn. Chr.* 17.
79. Mt 28.11–15.
80. The text ends suddenly here. Manuscripts present several different endings: "Here ends the Book of the Blessed Hilary on Matthew"; "Here ends the Book of the Holy Hilary, Bishop of Poitiers"; "Here ends the Commentary of the Blessed Hilary, Bishop of Poitiers, on the Gospel according to Matthew."

*APPENDICES & INDICES*

# APPENDIX I. AN ECHO FROM
# THE LOST ENDING

Hilary, *De trinitate* 2.1 (SC 443.274–76)

For believers it was enough that the utterance of God entered into our ears through the witness of the Gospel by the power of its truth, when the Lord said: *Go now and teach all nations, baptizing them in the name of the Father, and the Son and the Holy Spirit, teaching them to observe all things whatsoever I command you. And lo, I am with you for all days unto the end of the age.*[1]

What is not included in that utterance concerning the sacrament of human salvation? Or is there anything that remains, or is hard to understand? It is entirely complete as from completeness, and has proceeded from perfection.[2] For the utterance compromises the words' significance, the realization of the issues involved, the proper ordering[3] of sequences, and an understanding of the [divine] nature. It orders [us] to baptize in the name of the Father, the Son, and the Holy Spirit,[4] that is, with a confession of the Author, of the Only-begotten, and the Gift. There is one Author of all things, for there is one God the Father, from whom all things come; and one Only-begotten, our Lord Jesus Christ, through whom are all things; and one Spirit, the Gift in all things.

Everything, therefore, has been arranged according to its powers and benefits: one Authority from whom is all; one Offspring[5] through whom is all; one Gift who is the perfect hope. Nothing is found to be lacking in such fulfillment: within which the eternal infinite is in the Father, Son, and Holy Spirit, resemblance in the image, the benefit in the gift.[6]

1. Mt 28.19–20.
2. An alternative reading: "perfect from the perfect."
3. *ordinem.*                      4. Mt 28.19.
5. *progenies.*
6. M. Milhau, "Hilaire de Poitiers, *De Trinitate* 2, 1: Formule baptismale et foi trinitaire," *Studia Patristica* 38 (2001): 435–48, which briefly surveys twentieth-century scholarship on what is manifestly part of a baptismal confession theologically glossed by Hilary.

# APPENDIX II

## The *Capitula* of Hilary's *In Matthaeum*[1]

Unlike Coustant's edition (1693) in PL 9, which presents the chapter headings in the text, Doignon has separated them based on the likely conclusion that the headings were added by a later hand since one of the oldest groups of manuscripts does not include them. It is also apparent that the descriptions of most of the *capitula* do not match the content in Hilary's chapter.

I. Concerning the Nativity of Christ; concerning the Magi with their gifts; concerning the killing of the infants.

II. Concerning the return of Jesus from Egypt; concerning the preaching of John and his baptism and baptism of the Lord.

III. Concerning the temptation of the devil; concerning the fasting of Jesus for forty days; concerning Peter and Andrew who were fishermen.

IV. Concerning the beatitudes and precepts; concerning the reconciliation of a brother; concerning adultery; concerning the cutting-out of one's eye or hand; concerning oaths and almsgiving.

V. Concerning prayer and fasting; concerning treasure in heaven; concerning the light of the body; concerning two masters; concerning food and clothing; concerning birds; concerning lilies of the field and the grass; concerning anxiety about the day; concerning the twig and the plank in one's eye.

VI. Concerning pearls before swine; concerning false prophets; concerning building one's house on a rock.

VII. Concerning the leper whom the Lord cured; concerning the paralytic boy of the tribune; concerning Peter's mother-in-law; concerning many and diverse matters.

VIII. Concerning the disciples' awakening of Jesus in the boat; concerning the two demoniacs in the land of the Gerasenes.

IX. Concerning the paralytic who was cured and carried away his

---

1. For problems with these *capitula*, see Introduction, 35. Coustant points out several inconsistencies between the topics announced in *cap.* XIII, XIV, and XV (PL 10:913A–B) and the content of the corresponding chapters, as well as the fact that Hilary (or a later hand) provides headings for thirty-four chapters although our extant text goes only as far as thirty-three.

bed; concerning Matthew the publican; concerning the fasting of the Pharisees and of John's disciples; concerning the patch put on the garment; concerning the blood flow of the woman; concerning the raising of the official's daughter from the dead; concerning the two blind men; concerning the deaf and mute man.

x. When he sends the twelve apostles with his teaching.

xi. John sends a message to Jesus from prison, and Jesus speaks to the crowd about John. Also, Jesus' confession to the Father.

xii. The disciples wish to eat grain; and on the Sabbath Jesus cured the man's withered hand; he cured the blind man and the demoniac; concerning the blasphemy of the Spirit; concerning the fruit of good and bad trees; concerning every careless word; concerning the Ninevites and the queen of the South; concerning the seven spirits with the eighth; concerning his mother and brothers.

xiii. Sitting in the boat, Jesus spoke to the crowd in parables; concerning the sower of good seed; concerning the tares and wheat;[2] concerning the mustard seed; concerning the yeast hidden in the flour, and the explanation of the tares;[3] concerning the treasure in the field; concerning the fine pearl; concerning the net let down into the sea.

xiv. Concerning the scribe in the Kingdom of heaven; concerning the brothers and sisters of the Lord;[4] concerning John's head on a plate; concerning the five loaves and the two fish; when the Lord walked upon the sea and he lifted up Peter, who was overwhelmed.

xv. Concerning the washing of hands and how those things that defile do not enter the mouth but come from it;[5] concerning the daughter of the Canaanite woman; concerning the seven loaves and few fish; concerning the sign of the prophet Jonah.[6]

xvi. Concerning the yeast of the Pharisees; concerning Peter's confession and the Lord's blessing.

xvii. When the Lord is seen on the mountain with Moses and Elijah and the voice is heard from heaven; when the Lord heals the boy with lunacy; concerning the faith of believers; concerning the two drachmas that were demanded and the coin in the fish's mouth.

xviii. Concerning the prohibiting of the small children and concerning their humility, which ought to be emulated; concerning the cutting-off of the hand, foot, or eye; concerning the lost sheep; concerning the brothers who needed correction first in private, [then] with two witnesses, later on in the presence of the church; about always offering forgiveness.

2. The Commentary does not treat the parable of the tares (Mt 13.24–30).

3. The Commentary does not treat Christ's explanation of the tares (Mt 13.36–43).

4. There is no mention of sisters in this chapter (*supra,* 14.2; cf. Mt 13.56).

5. The Commentary does not treat this subject in Chapter 15 or elsewhere.

6. This topic is treated in 16.2, and many MSS put this part of the heading in *capitulum* XVI. See PL 10:917A, 1007B.

XIX. The one who put a stranglehold[7] on his fellow servant after the master had forgiven him of his debt; and one should not divorce[8] his wife; concerning eunuchs; the difficulty of a rich man entering the Kingdom of heaven.

XX. Concerning the hope of the apostles;[9] concerning those last ones to be made first when the workers were brought to the vineyard; concerning the sons of Zebedee; concerning the one who reclines at the head table; concerning the two blind men who sat along the road.

XXI. Concerning the ass and its colt; concerning the money changers who were ejected from the Temple; concerning the cursing of the fig tree; concerning the two sons sent into the vineyard; concerning the publicans and prostitutes.

XXII. Concerning the vinedressers who kill those sent to them for the purpose of gathering fruit; concerning those who were indiscriminately invited and the wedding garment.

XXIII. Concerning tribute and the image of Caesar; concerning seven brothers with the same wife; concerning the greatest commandments; concerning the Son of David.

XXIV. Concerning the seat of Moses on which sat the scribes and Pharisees;[10] concerning the closure of the Kingdom of heaven by the same men and their devouring of widows' houses, and those traveling over sea and dry land, saying, "Whoever swears by the Temple, it is nothing";[11] and those who tithed mint and dill, and built the tombs of the prophets; concerning Jerusalem, which kills the prophets and stones those who were sent to her.

XXV. Concerning the disciples asking about the construction of the Temple; how "those who are on the roof should not come down to take anything out of the house, and those who are in the field should not return for their coat";[12] concerning pregnant and nursing mothers.

XXVI. Concerning the obscuring of the sun, moon, and stars.

XXVII. Concerning the faithful servant whom the Lord placed over his household.[13]

XXVIII. Concerning the ten virgins; concerning the man preparing to go abroad who delivered his substance over to his servants.[14]

---

7. *suffocat.*

8. Lit., "dismiss" (*dimittere*).

9. It is not clear to what this refers since the "hope" (*spes*) pertains to those workers in the parable who were hired first and expected to receive more wages.

10. A near quotation from Mt 23.2.

11. Mt 23.16.

12. A quotation from Mt 24.17–18.

13. Some MSS add: "Concerning the ten virgins; concerning the man who was preparing to go abroad, who delivered his substance over to his servants" (cf. *cap.* XXVIII).

14. The content of this entire *capitulum* applies to Chapter 27.

XXIX. Concerning the advent of the Son of Man coming in his majesty.[15]

XXX. Concerning the woman who approached Jesus in Simon the leper's house, holding an alabaster jar of precious perfume.[16]

XXXI. Concerning the first day of Azymes [Feast of Unleavened Bread], in which the disciples came to Jesus, saying, "Where do you want us to prepare for you to eat the Passover?"[17]

XXXII. When Jesus came into the garden called Gethsemane, he said to his disciples, "Sit here, while I pray over there"; concerning the sorrow of his soul unto death; concerning the cup, if possible to pass from him; concerning the willingness of the spirit and the weakness of the flesh, and again, "Father, it is not possible for this cup to pass unless I drink of it; may your will be done."[18]

XXXIII. Concerning Judas, who was one of the twelve disciples, coming to Jesus with a large crowd in order to betray him; concerning the sword which he ordered Peter to return to its place.[19]

XXXIV. Concerning Pilate, while sitting as tribunal, whose wife sent him a message, saying, "Have nothing to do with that just man"; concerning those who walked up to the cross and wagged their heads, saying, "Here is the one who was going to destroy the Temple and rebuild it in three days."[20]

Here end the *capitula*.

15. The content of this entire *capitulum* applies to Chapter 28. A simple quotation of the first line of 28.

16. The content of this entire *capitulum* applies to Chapter 29.

17. The content of this entire *capitulum* applies to Chapter 30. In this case, the *capitulum* has merely copied the opening Scripture verse of Mt 26.17.

18. The content of this entire *capitulum* applies to Chapter 31.

19. The content of this entire *capitulum* applies to Chapter 32.

20. The content of this entire *capitulum* applies to Chapter 33.

# GENERAL INDEX

Abelard, 33

Abraham, 42, 50, 51, 92, 119, 133, 196–97, 205, 211, 227, 229, 236, 241, 242, 265

Acts of the Apostles, 16

Adam, 54, 57, 100–101, 112, 124–25, 196, 200, 224, 231, 255, 290

adoption (of believers), 53, 61, 242

allegory. *See* exegesis

Ambrose of Milan, 10, 37, 175n54, 255n21, 287n10

Ammianus Marcellinus, 7n24

angels, 58, 80–81, 100, 150, 195, 196, 236, 253, 256, 282, 293

*Apocalypse of Paul,* 196n34

Apostle, the. *See* Paul

apostles, 50, 51, 58, 62, 64–66, 94, 104, 106, 108, 111–12, 116, 119, 121, 127, 133, 140–42, 144–45, 154, 163–65, 169, 175, 182–83, 188, 194, 208–10, 213–16, 218–19, 224, 227, 230–32, 245, 249, 270, 291–93

*Apostolic Tradition,* 43n30

Aquitania, 36

"Arians," 5n19, 9, 21–23, 30, 37, 100n39, 147n83, 256n30, 273n5

Ariminum, council of, 6, 8

Arius, 203n40

Arles, council of, 4n12, 5, 22, 23

Arnobius of Sicca, 3

Asia Minor, 5

Athanasius, 131n21

*auctoritas,* 102, 112, 124, 130, 133, 143, 173, 180, 195, 135

Augustine, 4n10, 9, 11n46, 31–33, 74n6, 175n54, 181n31, 233n50, 257n41

authority. *See potestas*

Auxentius, 8

baptism, 51–55, 73, 86, 125, 150, 174, 198–99, 209–10, 225, 227–28, 261, 268, 286–87, 297. *See also* Christ

Barnes, T. D., 5n14

Beckwith, Carl, 278n42

Béziers (Baeterrae), 5, 22, 26

birth. *See* Christ, Nativity of

body (physical human), 76, 78, 80, 82, 90–91, 102–3, 105–8, 112, 116, 121–22, 124–26, 131–32, 173, 176, 181, 183–84, 186, 190, 192–93, 220, 235–36, 251–53, 258, 261, 265, 267, 274, 275, 279–81, 289, 291. *See also* Christ, Church

Borchardt, C. F. A., 23n91

Briggman, Anthony, 26n98

Brisson, J. P., 10n40

Buffer, Thomas, 27n103, 172n31

Burns, Paul, 4n10, 5n19, 21n81, 34n125, 147n83

Burton, Philip, 36n129

Casamassa, A., 35

Cassiodorus, 3

Christ, advent of, 228–30, 240, 260, 265; as an example, 59, 280, 288; baptism of, 14, 52, 53; body of, 93, 106, 107, 147, 169, 177–78, 181, 183, 186, 192, 211, 241, 253, 260, 280, 289–90, 292–93; divinity of, 13, 15, 24–26, 29, 43, 44n32, 46, 52, 54–56, 65, 92, 98, 100–102, 118, 137, 141, 146, 147, 156, 180, 183, 217, 240, 258, 261, 264, 268, 273–75; humanity of, 27, 29, 52–55, 63, 178, 183, 196, 256, 264, 273–75, 280–81, 283, 290; Incarnation of, 24–25, 27–30, 43, 65, 73, 84–85, 93, 151, 156, 167, 181, 183; Nativity of, 135, 143,

302

# INDEX OF HOLY SCRIPTURE